D0404344

BEYOND BODY
BEYOND MIND

Overcome Uncertainty,
Transcend Challenge and Hardships
& Fulfill Your Dreams

DR SUKHI MUKER

Beyond Body Beyond Mind

© 2012 by Dr Sukhi Muker

Printed in the United States of America

All rights reserved. No part of this publication may be reproduced or transmitted in any form or by any means, electronic or mechanical, including photocopying, recording, or by any information storage and retrieval system, without the prior written permission from the publisher or the authors, except by reviewers who may quote brief excerpts in connection with a review in a newspaper, magazine or electronic publication. Contact the publisher for information on foreign rights.

ISBN-13:978-1479285891

ISBN-10:1479285897

⊚ The paper used in this publication meets the minimum requirements of the American National Standard for Information sciences—Permanence of Paper for Printed Library Materials, ANSI Z39.48-1992.

I dedicate this book to the true gifts of life that are
disguised as challenge and hardships.
You are the catalyst that drives us to live beyond
the veils of domestication and discover that
special something that lives within all of us.

CONTENTS

PROLOGUE 1

INTRODUCTION 5

PART I

CHAPTER 1: Your Past is Not Your Future 11

CHAPTER 2: The New Science of Living 37

PART II

CHAPTER 3: Strategy 1 — Shift Your Paradigms 63

CHAPTER 4: Strategy 2 — Life is an Inside-Out Journey 83

CHAPTER 5: Strategy 3 — Take Inspired and Progressive Action 107

CHAPTER 6: Strategy 4 — Use Your Whole Mind 133

CHAPTER 7: Strategy 5 — Manage Your Life 163

PART III

CHAPTER 8: Strategy 6 — Live Symbiotically 197

CHAPTER 9: Strategy 7 — Be Abundant 227

CHAPTER 10: Strategy 8 — Pour Your Heart into It 261

CHAPTER 11: Strategy 9 — Life Integration 283

CHAPTER 12: Conclusion: The Four Motivating Levels of Life . 315

ACKNOWLEDGEMENTS 331

FOREWORD

I first met Dr. Sukhi and his wife, Kate, when they showed up at my door in New York City. I'd agreed to meet them without much information about who they were. Normally, I don't invite strangers over—but for some reason I intuitively knew this connection was important. The moment they walked in the door I felt a tremendous presence of power surrounding Dr. Sukhi. I sensed that this man was tapped into a power much greater than himself: the power of spirit. After a little conversation I came to realize that his openness and willingness to be of service to the world are what allowed him to tap into this high level of consciousness. He entered my home as a stranger and left as a dear friend.

In my time spent getting to know Dr. Sukhi he's proven to be exactly as I'd expected. He's a true force of nature. Dr. Sukhi walks his talk. He has overcome great trauma, healed immense wounds and defied the expectations of the body and the mind. I perceive him as a modern-day superman. Who runs 100-mile marathons and Ironman—*multiple* times? Dr. Sukhi does. His desire to live a life beyond his wildest dreams has led him to achieve this type of accomplishment. And he's done it once again with this incredible book, *Beyond Body Beyond Mind*.

In this amazing book, Dr. Sukhi shares his truth with you, the reader, to help you know you're not alone. He fearlessly offers up his personal dark night of the soul, and in sharing how he transformed his pain into purpose, he's created an authentic guide for transformational healing.

Beyond Body Beyond Mind taps into the obstacles we all face and helps us recognize how we hold ourselves back from true happiness and life flow. He provides not only eye-opening research but empowering guidance: when you follow the exercises in this book, you'll be able to create powerful, positive change—physically, mentally, emotionally and spiritually.

Dr. Sukhi's mission as a doctor, writer, husband and friend is to help others fully experience their ideal state of health and abundance. This beautiful messenger has achieved a beautiful mission. Allow Dr. Sukhi to be your guide to awaken your own capacity to live a miraculous life.

Gabrielle Bernstein
Author of Spirit Junkie

"Only as high as I reach can I grow,
only as far as I seek can I go,
only as deep as I look can I see,
only as much as I dream can I be."

—*Karen Ravn*

PROLOGUE

Three a.m. Focus. Focus. Focus. You're letting things slip away. You're a mess. You're a screw-up. What have you done . . . what have you done?

I was naked, bathed in a cold sweat, and pacing around my room literally pulling the hair out of my head. I had been up for three days, in complete isolation on a binge.

Too many pills. Too much blow. Too much booze. My heart is racing. I can't handle this anymore. I can't live this life. You're an idiot. You messed up. You've gone too far.

The internal chatter was so loud I thought my head would explode. I was screaming silently in rage.

You're ugly. You're not good enough. You're not strong enough. You're weak. You're a disgrace.

It hurts too much.

The tears poured down my face. I collapsed into a ball and contracted into a fetal position. My hands wrapped around my belly.

I can't handle the pain. Make it go away. Somebody help, please help me. God, if you exist, I've never asked for your help before. I'm asking now. Help me, help me please. I'm losing it, I can't think straight. I can't handle it anymore I just need it to go away. Nobody's around. I'm alone. Nobody cares. Nobody loves me. I'm dirt. Somebody please help, anybody, please help me!

I was screaming at the top of my lungs. But it didn't matter. I was totally alone.

I should just end it all. All the pain will be gone. I can make it go away.

I had been suicidal for months, strategizing on the best way to end my life. "Yes, I can make it go away! I can end it all here, right now!" I screamed in a rage. "I'm going to blow my fucking brains out. That'll save me. All the pain will be gone." I crawled on all fours to my dresser and fumbled through the folded clothes in a desperate search for my Glock. When I couldn't find it, I dragged myself to my closet and grabbed my sawed-off shotgun instead. I lay back down on my side. My breaths were heavy and tears poured down my face. I pumped the sawed-off shotgun, loading the cartridge into the chamber.

This was it.

It's all going to be okay now. See, God: I don't need your help. I have it all under control.

I placed the tip of the muzzle in my mouth and wrapped my lips around the cold metal. I bit down as hard as I could, cracking my teeth.

This is the end.

Lying on my side, I gripped the shotgun in my mouth with both my hands. I placed my toe on the trigger. I looked down the top of the barrel and the world fell silent. Everything became extremely silent. I paused for several moments and thought about nothing. Then with one swift motion I thrust my foot down on the trigger.

INTRODUCTION

"It is never too late to be what you might have been."
—George Eliot

Awesome! Now that you've made the decision to explore the process of accessing your inner power and fulfilling your dreams, you're probably wondering what the plan is. I was inspired to write this book to help you overcome the obstacles and challenges that are preventing you from fully experiencing your ideal state of health, happiness, abundance and peak performance in every area of your life. Quite simply, this book will empower you to rock your most extraordinary life in a fun and inspired way. You will move beyond your finite body and mind, where limitations live, and access your infinite self, where your wildest dreams materialize. It presents a simple and accessible science that explores and reveals the universal laws that underlie our existence, a true, powerful and enlightened way of being.

Most significantly, this book is for you. It is a story, guide and practical manual to help you better understand why you make certain choices, why you live the way you do, and how you get specific results that can be changed at any time. It will give you the inspiration, motivation and practical tools to transform your life fully. When this journey is complete you will be able to create unwavering certainty and live with your greatest ideals and visions. This book will empower you to move beyond your perceived limitations of mind and body to create your best and most awesome life!

What you are about to read is a synthesis of my life experiences, including everything I learned as a troubled youth and the personal transformations I've made over the past 20 years as a student of life, doctor of chiropractic, healer, athlete, professional speaker, peak performance strategist, family man, teacher and human being. I have blended science and universal laws with my personal history, stories of ordinary people having extraordinary experiences, my innovative teachings, and wisdom from some of the greatest minds and texts in history.

You will learn an original nine-strategy approach to tapping into your source of personal power so you can live from that place every day. I developed this approach using 10 years of postsecondary education and reading and referencing more than 1,000 books and articles. This work, combined with my unique life experiences, has led to the creation of this text that is beyond any facts, information and wisdom I have learned elsewhere.

Please know that this book is about you creating and living a life that you'll love. It's available to everyone—regardless of your age, class, education, health or color. It's about getting real results in the real world. It's about fulfilling your dreams. Not only do I teach people how to master their lives, I am living proof that this formula actually works— because I live it every day. I am a participant as well as a teacher. You don't have to hit rock bottom like me to finally wake up and realize that things need to change. I am going to take you through the 10 areas of your life that require mastery: health, emotions, intellect, spirit, family, social life, finances, career, inner character and quality of life. Every chapter will build on the ones before it, and the steps for each strategy to personal power will ensure your growth and evolution. You will break through obstacles to create a more purposeful and compelling life. You will have more energy and creativity, and you will feel more peaceful with your thoughts and feelings. Finally, you will know how to create and manifest all the things you desire in every area of your life. You are going to love this adventure. In no time you'll be accessing your inner power and fulfilling your dreams.

What You Can Expect

As you embark on this journey to create an extraordinary life, you will begin to shine light on the dark areas of your life. This process has touched the lives of countless people and has consistently produced results empowering people just like you to fulfill their dreams. You will experience transformations in your health, wealth and happiness. Once you close the last chapter you will be able to access your inner power on demand and create unwavering certainty physically, mentally, emotionally and spiritually. I am going to guide you through powerful and efficient strategies that I use in both my personal and professional lives to help get you where you must be to fulfill your dreams.

When I studied in school, the process was highly systematic. General biology came before cell biology and microbiology. Physics came before quantum mechanics. Algebra came before calculus. The same holds true for accessing your inner power, creating unwavering certainty and fulfilling your dreams. This book was designed systematically to maximize your growth and mastery of life. You will move beyond your finite body and mind to access your infinite power and potential.

In the first chapter I share my personal story of how I was raised in a life of crime, violence and drugs, and how I eventually hit rock bottom.

Being plagued with a diseased mind and failing body has been one of my greatest challenges, yet it has also served as my greatest gift and catalyst for transforming my life and becoming a teacher.

In Chapter 2, I begin to share the new science of life that will lay a solid foundation for the rest of this journey. In Chapter 3 the first of nine innovative strategies to personal power begin, and this is when your personal transformations will start. At the end of these chapters there are very specific exercises that will ensure you don't just understand these ideas intellectually, but that you begin to fully experience them to your core. These exercises will take you to that place of deep inner power and certainty.

The first five strategies will focus on you at the individual level. They are going to help you become more aware of your present life and the beliefs, choices and actions that have produced your current results, state of being and quality of life. As you become more self-aware you will see that life can never rock or break your spirit. By the end of the fifth strategy you will begin to experience a state of self-autonomy.

Self-mastery and autonomy is the foundation from which all other dynamics of your life will grow. You must have complete dominion over yourself in order to create bigger, better results in your inner and outer worlds. You can't start building the roof of a house before the foundation is poured. Similarly, independence, self-autonomy and self-mastery are your foundation, and they'll come naturally from con-sistently applying the first five strategies. Your words and actions will come from your powerful core.

The final four strategies will continue to build a more purposeful, pow-erful and compassionate you. Specifically, they will empower you to more effectively create and influence the world around you. You will begin to move beyond yourself and build strong connections with the people, places and things around you. You will release negative thought patterns and replace them with more positive and productive ways of thinking. You will open up to deeper, more meaningful relationships and collaborations. New opportunities for learning, productivity, growth, abundance and service will arise. You will get over feeling lost, stuck, mired in challenging relationships and harboring fear of failure (and success). You will begin to produce extraordinary results in every area of your life.

Strategies 6, 7 and 8 will enable you to fully experience a state of interdependence, and strategy 9 will open up the doorway to your greatest state: self-actualization. This is the culmination of and reward for all your life experiences, choices and efforts. It is the highest state within a level of consciousness any person may experience. This is the engagement of your greatest potential. It is when you have moved beyond the limitations of your finite body and mind and are attuned to the extraordinary and infinite you. This is where you can access your inner power on demand and create unwavering certainty to fulfill your most extraordinary dreams.

Are you ready? Buckle your seat belt!

Thanks for playing big,

Dr. Sukhi

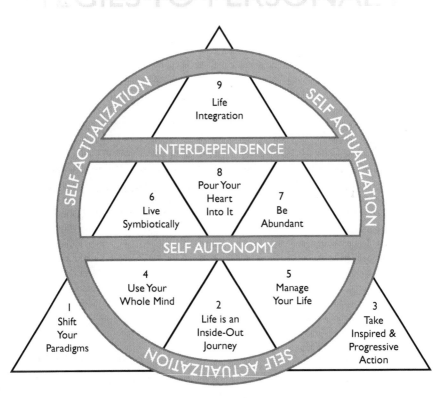

PART I

CHAPTER 1

YOUR PAST IS NOT YOUR FUTURE

"We fail to realize that mastery is not about perfection. It's about a process, a journey. The master is the one who stays on the path day after day, year after year. The master is the one who is willing to try, and fail, and try again, for as long as he or she lives."
—George Leonard

In the Beginning

It was a cool and wet evening in Glasgow, Scotland, and on this special November day in 1973 I was brought into the world. I spent most of my first few weeks of life in an incubator—I had a serious viral infection and doctors were concerned that my immune system would not be able to handle the touch of my loving parents. They visited me frequently, and after several weeks they were relieved to finally take me home to be with them and my brother, Raj, who was three.

I've been told that as a baby I was adorable yet extremely loud and challenging. Raj would often ask my parents, "Could we return him back to the hospital and get another one?" In retrospect, this foreshadowed what my family would endure over the next 19 years.

My earliest childhood memory goes back to when I was three years old. My family was living in Edinburgh, Scotland. Raj was in grade one and was an especially kind and gentle young boy. I remember him coming home on several occasions in tears because some boys at school were making fun of him and beating him up. I remember the anger and guilt that I felt because I was unable to help him. These feelings continued to build over the next few weeks—until this one special day. My brother ran into the house in a crying rage. I looked out the window and saw the bullies on the road laughing and pointing. I sprinted to the kitchen, grabbed a knife, and ran out the front door. I heaved my intimidating three-year-old physique at them and screamed with butter knife in hand: "Who hit my brother?" My mother ran out, scooped me up, and calmed me down from my rage.

At the young age of three I began to adopt this distorted perspective of the world, seeing people as angry, violent and just plain bad. I didn't trust anybody and didn't feel safe, including in my own home. As a young child this paradigm was further solidified. I truly believed that the world was a hostile place and in order to survive I had to be as tough as nails.

Where I Came From

"If you bring forth what is within you, what you bring forth
will save you. If you do not bring forth what is within you,
what you do not bring forth will destroy you."
—Jesus Christ

My parents were both raised in villages in Punjab, India, though my father was born in Pakistan. Several months after his birth, national independence was declared and all Indians had to return to Indian soil while all Pakistanis had to return to their land. My grandmother carried him in her arms during a violent and gruesome journey through Pakistan, Kashmir, Himachal Pradesh and Punjab.

My grandfather has shared many stories with me of how he and his two brothers led a group of more than 100 families back into India. He lost all his farmland and many of his friends, and he took the lives of many men during this war. He cautioned me to be mindful throughout life, as the essence and vibration of a warrior ran strongly through our family. He always warned me that it could be expressed as amazing light or terrifying darkness.

My father's family, which had grown to four children, was living in an Indian village when my grandfather decided he wanted better opportunities for his children. With this intention held clearly in his mind, he saw an opportunity arise. He had a connection to somebody in Scotland who was willing to sponsor my father. At the time, my dad was only a teenager. Although he did not want to leave his family, his father ordered him to go to Scotland so he'd have the chance at a better life— and be able to earn money to help his brothers and sister have better lives with more choices.

At 16, my father left India and his family for a foreign culture and land. Over several years he got settled and found good work. One day, he made an important call home. He was ready to get married, so he called his father and said, "Byjee, find me a bride." Several months later, my parents met at their wedding ceremony in Glasgow, Scotland.

My mother was raised in a village several hours from my father's town. She was one of eight children and as a result was actually raised by her grandparents because her immediate family did not have enough space in their home. When she was 18, all four of my grandparents had arranged the marriage between my mother and my father. She was terrified to leave her land and her culture for some unknown country to be with an unknown man. I am in a deep place of gratitude for everything my parents sacrificed, as everything I have experienced may never have been possible.

I have visited India many times throughout my life. The last two visits have been very special to me, as I was able to bring my wife, Kate, to visit my family and this extraordinary land. When I observe India's extreme duality, I think about how easily I could have been one of the multitudes of children playing on dirt roads in northern Indian villages. My ideas, values and culture would have been radically different in that environment. The power of my grandfather's vision, backed up by his actions, and the challenges my parents have overcome completely changed their destinies and ultimately mine.

A Change of Plans

"Vision without action is a dream. Action without vision is simply passing the time. Action with vision is making a positive difference."
—J. Barker

In the late 70's my father decided to throw a twist in things again. People were talking about all the opportunities in a foreign land called Canada. My father was enticed, so he booked a flight to see it for himself. He left my mother, Raj, and me in Glasgow. I can still remember this day as if it were yesterday. I was a highly perceptive child and I could sense change in the air. My father was saying good-bye. I was hysterical and wouldn't let him go. I clung to his shirt desperately, crying, screaming and begging him not to go. My mother eventually peeled me off and Dad was gone. My mother did not handle change well, and I remember the next few months without my dad as very challenging for the three of us. My response was simply to grow thicker skin and "man up."

A few months later, my parents had put in place all the arrangements for us to leave Scotland and move to our new home in Vancouver, British Columbia, Canada. My father did not return to Glasgow. The three of us simply boarded a plane and headed west. My father was embarking on a new adventure, taking another risk. A new chapter of our lives had begun.

A New Beginning

*"Do not fear risk. All exploration, all growth is calculated. Without
challenge people cannot reach their higher selves. Only if we are willing to walk over the edge can we become winners."*
—Unknown

I hadn't seen my father in three months, and I believe that the feeling
of abandonment so deeply wounded me that I completely disconnected
from remembering that I even had a father. We were greeted at the air-
port with a typical Indian welcoming. I recall walking next to Raj and
saying, "There are a lot of brown people in this Canada." He replied,
"I think they're here for us." It seemed like a hundred Indians were
standing at the arrival terminal with ear-to-ear smiles. They smothered
us with hugs and kisses, and I kept thinking, "Weirdos, get your paws
off me." Who were these people? I was lost in a sea of anonymous
Indians—no Raj, no Mom in sight.

I fought my way through the forest of legs, found my brother, and clung
to his arm. In the distance I saw my mother hugging a man I didn't
recognize. I immediately became defensive and mad: "Who's that man
touching Mom?" I yelled to Raj. He replied, "I don't know, but I think
it's Dad!" My father's appearance hadn't changed much. Clearly I had
already become proficient at disconnecting and repressing anything
that caused me stress, pain or sadness. Our family was together again.

Reuniting with my dad among these strange people, in a new city and
foreign country, was a lot to process as an inquisitive four-year-old.
My defenses were on red alert. My family did not have an exorbitant
amount of money, and although my dad was ready to bring us over we
spent the next year living in the tiny attic of a house. I can remember
feeling that people in Canada did not know how to build homes prop-

erly because my parents could not stand up fully, as their heads would hit the roof. The attic measured 175 square feet with a four-foot ceiling. Canada struck me as a strange place. My parents' choice to move us there was not instilling a great deal of confidence in me. I was becoming angrier and questioned everything.

Shortly after our arrival, Raj was ready to return to school. This day was pivotal in terms of creating my paradigms of the world. My parents dressed my brother in the typical school uniform he'd wear in Scotland: dark grey dress pants, white shirt, navy tie and navy jacket. I can remember looking at my older brother, whom I looked up to immensely, and sensing his nervousness. We arrived at the public school in East Vancouver and the first thing I noticed was that the other students were not wearing uniforms. In fact they dressed, looked, acted and spoke very different from the people in Scotland.

As the four of us walked down the hallway I experienced something that I still have not forgotten. Many of the children were pointing and laughing at my brother. When he spoke they would make fun of his Scottish accent. I remember looking up at my parents and thinking, "My parents love me, my parents will do their best for Raj and me— but they do not have a clue about this Canada and the people in it." My brother was in tears as other children ridiculed him from a distance. My parents didn't protect him. They didn't even say a word.

On this monumental day as a four-year-old, I decided that I was going to have to figure things out for myself. The only person who could take care of and protect me was *me*. My wounds formed at a young age and the protective armor had already begun to harden.

My parents spent most of their days working long, hard hours at a factory to make ends meet. My companion was Raj, my gentle and loving brother. After school we would cook our meals together (beans and toast, my favorite!) and play in the streets until my parents came home. I was five years old and Raj was eight. From this age we would take care of each other during the long summer days and late evenings while our parents were at work. We could not afford a baby-sitter, and East Vancouver in the late 70s and early 80s was not the most forgiving environment. Crime, drugs, and violence surrounded us daily.

As a young child I had an incredible ability to sense and perceive the states of other people—a gift I have developed fully as an adult. I quickly learned this was a unique trait that not many others possessed. I found it difficult to share what I could see and feel, as others just did not understand. I felt even more isolated as a result, and out of fear of being judged and ridiculed by others I decided to repress my true nature and gifts. I adopted the common herd mentality and looked outside myself for answers. I lived and figured things out through the wonderful educational institute of "the streets."

Embracing My Environment

> *"Talents are best nurtured in solitude, but character is*
> *best formed in the stormy billows of the world."*
> —J. W. von Goethe

Life in East Vancouver was always eventful, and there were always other kids around. As a child I didn't really fit in. I was unpopular and bullied. I felt my parents didn't understand me and couldn't help me, so I learned from my peers instead. I began to embrace my hostile environment and delved deeper and deeper into the vibe of fear and hostility.

In elementary school I got good grades, but I was quite overweight and a minority in a predominantly Caucasian culture (this was before the major immigration boom of the 80s). At home my parents raised me with ideas that I thought simply were not applicable in Western culture or at least the tough streets of East Van. It was as if I was living two lives. At home I would speak another language, eat different food, celebrate different festivals and holidays, be filled with Indian ideals and ideas—and of course watch Bollywood movies. At school I would try to integrate with the Western world, doing my best to figure it all out for myself. My early years were stressful. I didn't fit in, I didn't understand the connection between Eastern and Western cultures, and I chose not to trust anyone.

Before the age of 10 I was what most would call a geek. I was teased regularly for the way I looked, acted and dressed. My parents could not afford to dress me with the latest styles. I can remember looking at a pair of Nike runners in the store and dreaming of one day having them on my feet and retiring my low-budget knock-offs.

The message was clear and simple to me: we were poor, I was a geek, I felt miserable, and life just sucked. I thought that perhaps if I was tough, cool and rich everything would be perfect. I certainly felt life couldn't get any worse.

At the time, I had a strong affinity for the ringleaders of the different neighborhood cliques. These were tough, strong alpha males whom others respected and feared. I wanted to become one of them. I did not want to be a benchwarmer—I wanted to be a first-string player in the East Vancouver game of life.

I thought that maybe the source of happiness was strength, popularity, material wealth and money. After exhausting my tolerance for bullying—and after getting severely beaten up when I was 10—I decided my life was going to change. I was not going to get pushed around anymore. Nobody was going to make me feel this way. So I embarked on a journey to become an alpha male: cool, tough, and living life my way.

Disconnecting

> *"If you limit your choices only to what seems possible*
> *or reasonable, you disconnect yourself from what*
> *you truly want, and all that is left is compromise."*
> —Robert Fritz

Over the next year I transformed myself. I woke up early to do an intense Navy SEAL boot-camp training routine that I found in a beat-up muscle magazine on the side of the road while walking home from school. I did it before school every day, and I lost all my baby fat and gained muscle. Despite being the brightest student in my class, my interest in school diminished, my priorities shifted and I did just enough to be a solid "C" student.

As I continued down this path, the chasm between my parents and teachers and me grew wider. My peers were now raising me. In high school I continued to build my armor and lived behind the tough-guy facade. I began lifting weights and immersed myself fully in martial arts. I spent more time skipping school than I did in the classroom. I got into drugs and alcohol, crime and violence. I became a gangbanger. My relationship with my parents withered.

I thought I was an invincible, streetwise teenager with all the answers. After getting arrested for assault, breaking and entering and theft, my life began to spiral out of control. The tension between my parents and me was unbearable. Not knowing what to do with this out-of-control teenager, my father threatened not to bail me out if I got arrested again. The next time I landed in jail, he kept his word. Juveniles can only be released to a legal parent or guardian. My father hung up the phone when the police called, and I was officially all alone. I was 14 years old, and I didn't speak to my parents again for years.

Once I got out of jail I spent the next few months crashing at my friends' families' homes. After exhausting all of them I had nowhere to go and had too much pride to return home. With no money and just the clothes on my back, I ended up wandering the streets and sleeping on park benches. It was a long, cold January of living homeless and scared—and having no idea what to do next. It's amazing how strong of a motivator fear can become. I decided school was a complete waste of time, so I officially dropped out and over the next four years opted for a Ph.D. in crime, violence and drugs. I was living my warped dream.

By 18 I had made connections in the deeply rooted criminal underworld of the West Coast, all the way from South America to Canada. I was driving a Porsche 911 Turbo and had more money than I could ever imagine. I could buy virtually anything I desired. I would spend my days sleeping and my nights partying and making money. This was it: I had found the source of happiness. I had material wealth, respect on the streets, and hot women.

Life's Challenges are Blessings in Disguise

"Be extremely careful for what you wish for in life,
because you may just get it."
—Dr. Sukhi

The disconnection between how I was living my life and expressing my true authentic nature was immense. I was completely disconnected, living life like a firecracker. I had no regard for human life; I did not care whether I lived or died. As this life I created kept growing, it inevitably got too big to control and I began to feel held hostage by it. I couldn't leave the house unarmed. I lived in a mind and body that were plagued by fear. My health was deteriorating. I began to use drugs heavily just to cope. I was beginning to develop anxiety and getting paranoid about other people. All the appeal of money, wealth and perceived power had vanished. I thought this lifestyle would bring me happiness. I could not have been more wrong. I needed to escape; I needed to leave this life.

I had delved deeply into the life of crime and violence, and with my ultra driven A-type personality I was moving up the ladder far too quickly. I was focused and determined, working more than 60 hours a week. Prominent people had taken notice of my ambition and success and figured that if I was no longer around, my connections and business could be added to their empires. It was an interesting world in that simply knocking off somebody was considered a legitimate way to reduce competition. When I was in my mid-teens, these people put a contract on my head—if someone murdered me they would be paid a lump sum of $25,000. My life had now been relegated to a shallow number. It was a massive blow to my even more massive ego. When I learned about it, my first reaction was: "I'm only worth *that*?"

Once a targeted person is dead, all the business they created moves to the open market for other people to acquire. Every time I left my house I carried a loaded gun and looked over my shoulder every minute. I was gripped with paranoia. Every sound alarmed me and made my heart race. I only had a handful of friends I could trust, as I knew that the people closest to me could take my life at any time. I would nod in and out of sleep every night and lay with a gun underneath my pillow. Most evenings I would have nightmares about being tortured and murdered. My head felt as if somebody was driving an axe through the center of it; the pain became unbearable. I thought about contacting my parents, but I didn't even know where I would begin. I felt overwhelmed and completely isolated, and I was running out of options.

One life-saving skill I developed was the ability to walk into any setting and scan the scene, so that within seconds I had assessed everyone and figured out their story. I knew who was a cop, who was a criminal, who was safe, who was checking me out, who was a threat. I would never sit with my back to an open space for fear of being attacked or shot. In fact, even today when my wife, Kate, and I go for dinner, she knows that I still prefer to sit with my back to the wall so I can see everyone and not get taken by surprise.

Today I still scan every person I meet, and whenever I walk into a room I can read everyone in literally seconds. I developed this intuition as a child and have now mastered it as an adult. Yet today I use it for a much different purpose. I'm not trying to figure out whether someone is out to get me; instead I use it in service of others as a healing doctor, speaker and seminar leader.

I always tell people today that life never gives us anything we cannot handle. Often we encounter people, events and situations that seem overwhelming, intimidating or irreparably terrible or tragic. However, I have learned firsthand that there is a blessing in everything we experience. Times of extreme stress, challenge or strife are the moments that contain the greatest gifts and blessings. Although having a contract on my life was one of my most frightening experiences, it also turned out to be one of my greatest blessings. It gave me the opportunity to see life through a different lens, as it was the catalyst that sent me back to my roots in a distant land.

A Glimpse of a Different Way

"When you are in a state of allowance the universe
will give you the gift of a glimpse. It is a sneak preview
of your life's coming attractions."
−Dr. Sukhi

Through a series of synchronous near-death experiences I decided I had to leave Vancouver. I had been involved in a high-speed car chase in which my car was shot up. One of my close friends was murdered moments before I was supposed to meet him at a restaurant. The only way I could cope with that life was by taking ridiculous amounts of heavy narcotics. I hadn't slept in weeks and experienced my first drug overdose. I was 15 years old, my life was out of control, and I knew the heat in the city was too great to overcome. I was either going to kill myself or somebody was going to do it for me. If I was going to survive I had to leave the city.

The only safe place I could think of was a land that was an eternity away. As a child my parents would take me to their motherland, India. I had deep connections to my paternal family in India and innately knew that they would accept me unconditionally. I had an exorbitant amount of money in my safe to fund the trip, so I contacted my family and let my parents know that I was leaving. Although I didn't communicate with them directly, my brother kept them updated on my whereabouts. Two days later I left. When I stepped on to the plane I felt like a 10-ton weight had been lifted off my shoulders.

India is a unique place. It's very dense, packed with people living in extreme poverty, lavish wealth and everything in-between. I stayed with relatives in a village and began to experience a completely different way of living and being. At first I was living in a small house with very little privacy. I slept on a cot in a hallway. There were no modern toilets, I bathed outside with a cup and bucket, and the kitchen consisted of a small outdoor room with a fire for a stove and single hot plate. In Vancouver I'd been a serious meat and pizza eater, but in India I became a vegetarian. The weather was warm and I was surrounded by people who lived with the mere basics of life. India was an entirely different world to me, and I began to look at life through new lenses.

I eventually started traveling to different parts of the country and experiencing its diversity. I truly began to wake up and see life for what it is. Specifically, I began to awaken spiritually. My parents were religious, but I didn't believe in God—I would say God was for weak people. In India people had a notion of spirituality and connection that was foreign to me. People with nothing, and I mean absolutely nothing, were actually *happy*. This rocked my world as a teenager. I spent time in temples and monasteries. I connected with elders, began to meditate and practiced yoga. I learned about the Sikh, Hindu and Buddhist religions. I began to learn ancient Yogic teachings about health, life and prosperity. I had experiences that allowed my true nature to step forward. I began to actually hug people, something I was afraid to do, and feel an authentic connection with others. I would give away hundreds of dollars every day to underprivileged families and homeless people on the streets so they could feed themselves. I think for the first time in my life I was able to fully experience joy and compassion through the gift of giving. It had taken me 15 years of living to get a taste of what inner peace and happiness may feel like. The life I had created in East Vancouver felt light years away. Although I did not cognitively understand my experience, I would be forever changed as a result of my year in India.

In fact, my experience was so profound that I did not want to leave. I did not want to return to Vancouver, and I was afraid of who I had become. My pure self within me wanted to stay in India and live in a monastery, to become a monk. When I was in a small village in northern India I lived off the land and tended to the earth each day. I would spend all my days in nature and isolation. This was the longest period of time in years that I had been drug-free, and I found that I was able to think and see clearer. Why on earth would I want to leave this blissful state within myself?

However, in life we must do what we fear most. An elder assured me that this was not my journey, and that if I stayed in India I would be avoiding my fears, not facing them. The fears would resurface if I didn't face them, and processing them was an integral part of my journey. He also told me that all my experiences were a part of my education and training, as one day I would become a teacher of life. I was 15 years old and could not comprehend that at the time. I simply looked at him with confused appreciation. Leaving India was hard—I knew what I was returning to. Yet the seeds of a completely different way of living and being were planted deep within me.

When I returned home to Vancouver I didn't know what I was going to do. I didn't know what I was going to say to friends. Afraid to speak my truth, I said nothing. I simply buried everything I had learned and experienced. The armor was back on and I went back to my old ways. It's astounding how many faces we all have, and how by changing our environment we seemingly can morph into completely different people.

Living with this internal polarity was killing me. My actions had no integrity. I was contributing to all the negative elements in the world and helping to make it a horrible place rather than a better place. I had become the lowest common denominator and I knew it. Everything I had achieved had come at the expense of others. But still I did not stop. I kept living in the gutter, and I coped with it by disconnecting from the feelings and experiences I'd had in India. There is no easier way to disconnect than by using drugs. I did drugs every day and dug even deeper into my life of crime and violence. At the age of 17 I had been in more than a hundred street fights. I had hurt others and others had hurt me. I had been jumped and severely beaten on several occasions. I was in chain fights and knife fights. My mind and body had been through the spin cycle of a washing machine dozens of times. I had broken my clavicle, knuckles and several ribs. I'd fractured my jaw and gotten my teeth knocked out. My nose had been broken six times. I'd even been stabbed in the arm and shot—the bullet missed my heart by only a few inches. My world was crazy and unforgiving in a way I'd never experienced before and haven't seen since. I was constantly entering hostile environments with unpredictable people and behaviors. When I think back on my life I truly feel that it is a miracle that I survived it.

At the time I thought I was losing my mind. The divide between the way I was living and my true nature was becoming impossible to bridge. It was manifesting mentally, emotionally and physically. My body began to fail me and I would seize up and lay on the ground in agony. It felt as if I'd been drinking acid and was rotting from the inside out. It was absolutely impossible to be alone with my thoughts, and my emotions were a roller coaster of torment and turmoil. Drugs were the only thing that could numb the pain. That's what Western domestication taught me through media and television. If you have a problem and can't handle the effects, mask it with drugs so you get into a delusional state of drug-induced comfort, thinking the source of the problems are gone—when in fact you've just buried them even deeper. Pushed or prescribed drugs are not the solution to your life's problems or challenges. Yes, copious amounts of drugs numbed the pain temporarily, but the highs wore off and I needed more and more just to get the same feeling. The pain and angst I felt within myself were inconceivable. I never knew I could be so utterly miserable.

At age 18 I reached a tipping point. On the outside I appeared to have everything—but on the inside I had nothing. I had lost friends to drug overdoses, jail and murder. I had been shot, I had been stabbed, and I hated myself. My life was a disaster. I was depressed, I was afraid, and I was lost beyond all comprehension. I was losing the game of life. I didn't want to play anymore.

These feelings escalated over the next few months as the idea of suicide became increasingly appealing. I had turned to strong prescription drugs and copious amounts of recreational drugs taking doses as high as 10 times the legal limit. I was losing myself and losing touch with reality. I didn't leave my house for weeks; I didn't even talk to anyone. I had completely isolated myself and was living in a barricaded, dark, drug-fueled, suicidal state.

Finally, after a severe three-day drug binge, I made my first and last attempt at suicide. I went through all the right motions, but I missed one small step in my overdosed state: I forgot to turn off the safety clip. That procedural mistake saved me and gave me another chance at life.

Life is Always Unfolding Perfectly

"At various points in our lives, or on a quest, and for reasons
that often remain obscure, we are driven to make decisions
which prove with hindsight to be loaded with meaning."
— Sri S. Satchidananda

Four days later I woke up from my binge. I was at the lowest point in my life. My mind and body were screaming at me to mask the pain I felt within myself. *More drugs. I need more drugs!*

Snapshots of my life flashed through my mind. Childhood. My friends. India. My family. Something deep within me told me I needed help. Who could I trust? The only people in my world that loved me unconditionally: Dad, Mom and Raj. I mustered up every last bit of energy I had and partially clothed myself. *I've got to get home! Get me home.*

So I went back home. I went to my parents' house and stood fumbling on the doorstep, finally working up the nerve to knock. My mother greeted me with open arms. I hadn't spoken to her in almost four years.

My mother looked at me and said, "*Mit*, what's wrong?" (*Mitta* is short for "sweetie" in Punjabi.) She could see right away that I wasn't my usual confident, ego-filled self. I hugged her, broke into tears and said in a shaky voice, "Mom, I'm really tired, I'm so tired, I just need to go to my room and rest." I walked up the stairs to my old room. Not a lot had changed, from the old heavy metal posters to the freshly-made bed to the tough and rebellious preteen vibe.

I spent the next three months in my parents' home in a nearly catatonic state. In fact, the entire time I was there, I was lying in my bed, sleeping, thinking, and processing. Without the drugs to numb my feel-

29

ings and pain, these months were the darkest of my life. I was going through extreme drug withdrawal. I thought about killing myself every day. Every dark thought and emotion I knew was coursing through me. I was angry, sad, anxious, depressed, afraid and lost. I had lost my thirst for life. I couldn't eat, I couldn't talk. I could hardly summon the energy to go to the bathroom. I was completely immobile and helpless.

My family never asked me a single question. My mother would try to feed and clean me. Raj would visit me in my room daily and just be with me. He would talk and I would listen unresponsively. My dad would crawl into my bed each morning, wrap his arms around me and tell me how much he loved me. I did not love myself, but my family loved me unconditionally. I experienced firsthand the ability of love to heal. Unconditional love is the most powerful force in the universe. My mother, father and brother are the heroes of my life. They saved me.

Months passed and I began to eat and move my body again. I began to speak again. I began to become Sukhi again. Although the process was slow, I was healing myself from the inside out and it was necessary and perfect. With no drugs or surgery I eventually began to smile again. The seeds that were planted within me from India were beginning to grow and blossom. The layers were peeling away and I felt my essence begin to express itself, the essence that I had buried so deep within me. My life was unfolding in pure synchronous fashion.

We Must Do what We Fear Most

*"As far as we can discern, the sole purpose of human
existence is to kindle a light in the darkness of mere being."*
—Carl Jung

I was now a 19-year-old high-school dropout faced with a huge challenge. The only friends I knew were deeply involved in a way of life that I just did not want anymore. Some of them I had known since I was five years old. I had to say good-bye to them. Not only did I say good-bye, I said it with the conviction and intention that our paths would never cross again. I said good-bye for the rest of this life, as I knew the journey I was embarking on was completely different from theirs. No drugs, no crime, no violence. It was as if I held a funeral for everyone and everything I knew. I was starting over. I gave away every single material asset, every bit of business and all the money I had acquired. I burned all my clothes. Everything related to that life was extinguished. I was starting from scratch.

What I understand today is that all these things simply came into my life as an exchange for energy. In physics the first law of thermodynamics states that energy cannot be created or destroyed; it only transforms from one form to another. Although I did not realize it at the time, I had simply cleared everything from the past to create space for a new future. However, another challenge lay ahead: I had no idea what that future looked like.

I had no high school diploma and the only legitimate job I'd ever had was a paper route in elementary school. I had a poor vocabulary, no friends and no employable skills. What the heck was I going to do?

My mental chatter was at an all-time high. I had a long way to go, but instead of getting overwhelmed I just started with the basics. Getting up in the morning, brushing my teeth, showering and putting on a pair of jeans and a sweatshirt was a major task for me. Some days I was successful, other days I was not. I was recovering from depression, drug addiction, trauma, and deep emotional wounds that had formed in early childhood.

Yet I persevered. I pushed through, and each week became a little easier and better. Slowly I began to go outside again. I went for walks, spent time in nature, and people-watched in parks and sidewalk cafes. Eventually I began to exercise, cook and be social again. My vibrant smile was beginning to return.

I had always been athletic and interested in exercise and the human body. I also was passionate about quantifying and better understanding what I had experienced. I wanted to know why I did what I did, why I made the choices I made, why I became the person I had become. I began to spend my days at the library reading and learning about the human body and mind. I found that the more I studied the more questions I had. I wanted to learn why we as humans behave the way we do. Why do we choose to live the way we do? How and why do the mind and body experience sickness, health, misery and joy? Why do some people make lots of money while others barely get by? Why do some people get stressed easily and others seem to never get bothered? The list of questions went on and on.

After months of spending several hours a day at the library, I grew even more inquisitive. I was surrounded by the greatest minds in history and I was devouring their information, knowledge and wisdom. As a result, my desire for knowledge and wisdom grew exponentially. This was when I first knew I was destined for a life of serving others.

Although the thought of this terrified and overwhelmed me, I believed I had found my calling, and I was going to follow my purpose. I didn't know what shape my journey would take, nor did I know where I'd end up—but I knew it didn't matter. In life we must learn to manage our fear because it will always be there on some level. I would spend the next 10 years studying in school and traveling the world, learning from some of the most innovative minds in health, healing and human potential. I was on my way to becoming a dedicated student of life and a hunter of human excellence.

What I learned was that the quality of questions we ask of life is directly related to the quality of experiences we will have. If we ask shallow questions, we'll have shallow experiences. But if we ask deep and challenging questions, our lives will be rich and full. I thought that our external circumstances determined our quality of life experience. Money and material goods make our lives comfortable and give us more choices. Today, I live a comfortable life thanks to these things. However, money and stuff do not create a happy and fulfilled person. Happiness and fulfillment can only come from within. The act of asking questions is the catalyst that invokes a higher quality of answers and therefore a higher quality of life. Today I wake up every morning and ask myself questions about the possibilities for my life and the people I serve. One of my favorite questions to ask myself is: "How can I be more aware of the infinite opportunities that surround me and my life right now?"

Education and Experience

Education is a social process. Education is growth.
Education is not a preparation for life; education is life itself."
—John Dewey

As I journeyed through school I excelled in all areas of study. I had a diverse course load and studied hundreds of subjects formally and on my own. I explored kinesiology, psychology, sociology, pathology, astronomy, biology, criminology, ecology, geology, microbiology, neurology, pharmacology and physiology—to name just a few. I was observing nature and the natural rhythms of people, places and things. I even explored business, economics, communications and negotiations. I studied everything I could. I went beyond every "-ology" and at times was overwhelmed by the task at hand. Yet I always came back to the basics: one word, one page, one chapter, one book at a time.

Today I have read and referenced more than a thousand books and articles. The more I investigate the more certain and inspired I become. The patterns and laws of different fields are so similar at their foundational levels that I began to see the underlying patterns unfolding. These foundations stand the test of time and must be realized within each of us to experience our purest and highest state. These are the foundations of this process to access your inner power, create unwavering certainty and fulfill your dreams in every area of your life.

I formally obtained degrees in Exercise Science and Kinesiology. My dedication and commitment to being a student of life culminated with my graduation. I was the top student in my class and graduated with honors and distinction. In India, I was taught ancient yogic teachings and learned that the human spine was literally the "walking stick of god" (or Brahma Danda). They also imprinted within me that the central nervous system within the human spine was the vehicle through which the power of the entire universe manifests in physical form. This was so powerful to understand at such a young age I wanted to learn how to further access that power and teach others to live from it. I learned that chiropractic was the only regulated health profession that specialized in doing precisely that. I received a professional degree from the prestigious Canadian Memorial Chiropractic College becoming a Doctor of Chiropractic, graduating on the dean's list with clinical honors.

My postsecondary path was continually enlightening. The more I studied the traditional curriculum of these programs the more I realized how contemporary science prompted more questions than answers. These university curriculums could not fully tell me why I experienced what I experienced in my life. I kept coming back to the same questions I'd had before starting school: Why did I make the choices I did? Why did I try to take my own life? How did I create certain perspectives of the world? How did I lose myself? How did I heal myself? How had I created a completely different life? My studies, useful as they were, only provided post-hoc solutions for treating the body and mind's improper functions. I was not satisfied. Was this what the best education in the country could offer me?

I went searching for more answers and created my own curriculum alongside my formal education. I made connections around the world and learned from many innovative minds: doctors, healers, professional athletes, sages, billionaires, and personal growth and development visionaries. My postsecondary education provided a wonderful foundation from which I could grow. I had the best understanding of human anatomy and physiology that Western science could provide. To answer many of my questions I found myself diving deeper into mathematics, force dynamics and quantum physics. I was combining physics, my life experiences, and my formal scientific education to unlock the answers to my growing list of questions.

CHAPTER 2

THE NEW SCIENCE OF LIVING

A Quantum Understanding of Life

"If quantum mechanics hasn't profoundly shocked you,
you haven't understood it yet."
—Niels Bohr

Before we begin this next section, know that things may get a bit heady. It's normal to grapple with the concepts, especially if you haven't studied them before now. However, it's important to have a basic understanding of the quantum world because it's going to lay a solid foundation for the following sections, where your personal transformations will begin. I will keep this as short, simple and sweet as possible. Thank you for your patience and understanding.

All my life, I'd reacted to experiences in one of two ways: I'd either love them or I'd hate them. Why was it that some experiences I embraced fully and others I tried to avoid at all costs? I was constantly searching for something outside myself to fulfill a feeling within myself. I believe

I was searching for the source of happiness. After all, isn't that something that most of us are searching for? I sought pleasure and luxury and avoided strife and challenges—a common theme in this world. Yet my life was filled with pain and nearly void of real pleasure. How did this ratio relate to my downward spiral and the loss of my self-identity and handle on life?

Your Greatest Power Lies Deep Within You

"What lies behind us and what lies before us are of little importance compared to what lies within us.
—Ralph Waldo Emerson

When we observe a state of optimal health, happiness, fulfillment and abundance the mind and body are in a perfect state of dynamic homeostasis. In other words, there is a dynamically changing balance with all the systems, organs, and cells of the body. The hormones and chemicals are being released in perfect proportions. Every cell is constantly being reorganized and regenerated optimally.

Conversely, disease is *dis-ease*. It's a lack of ease, homeostasis or dynamic balance within the body and mind. Cells and tissues are not reorganizing optimally and therefore are breaking down and degenerating. If this process continues for months or years the system will be given a name: X, Y or Z disease.

I was searching for a way to understand how one's state of health, fulfillment, abundance and well-being thrived or diminished. This search began when I was 19, when I spent my days with my head buried in books at the local library. To fully understand it, I had to gain a thorough understanding of the cellular world. Within every human being there is a master control system—the nerve system. The nerve system consists of the brain, spinal cord, peripheral nerves, and the dazzling array of neurotransmitters. In fact, the nerve system is so vast and diverse that it is virtually impossible to determine where the nerve system ends and the rest of the body begins. The majority of nerve fibers are located between the brain and pelvis: that's why most people will experience symptoms or diseases in the cells predominantly supplied from these areas. It is also why the best healers in the world focus on these areas of the body to heal and grow from the inside out.

Why is it so important to understand the nerve system? The nerve system is the communication highway that transports vital information to all cells and tissue. This information powers cells and tissue and tells them how to function, adapt and reorganize. There is a constant flow of information between your brain and body. Life requires a source of power, and the more power that's flowing through your nerve system the more extraordinary your life becomes. It's as simple as that.

Every time you move your body, your brain sends a specific neuro-chemical impulse to specific cells and tissues, informing them of what to do and how to do it. Then another message is sent back up your nerve system from these cells to your brain. The nerve system is like a power-ful computer that processes millions and millions of bits of information every second of every day. When you're thinking, expressing an emotion, doing a task, digesting food, or performing any mental or physical process you can possibly think of, the nerve system is in direct control. This power supply is the source of life. If it's flowing at 100%, you are living at your ideal state mentally, emotionally, physically and spiritually. In this state you are rocking an extraordinary life. Anything less than 100% is less than your best life.

Please bear with me here as I elaborate on this concept. Think of your nerve system as the computer system of your body and mind. It's constantly processing information from your external environment to make the appropriate adaptations in your internal environment. For example, if it's hot outside and your core temperature begins to rise, your brain will send messages through your nerve system to organs and cells, telling them to release heat via your sweat glands. You begin to sweat, and as a result your core temperature comes down—and you return to your state of homeostasis. Conversely, if it's cold outside your brain would tell your body to begin shivering to increase your core temperature through rapid muscle contractions, thus maintaining that ideal state of dynamic homeostasis.

Human beings have six primary senses through which we are constantly processing information. Every second of every day you use some combination of seeing, hearing, smelling, tasting, feeling and intuitively sensing millions of bits of information from your external environment so you can comprehend, process and respond appropriately. These senses are simply an extension of your nerve system, and they are responsible for creating the lens through which you perceive, interpret and respond to your world.

When I first learned this I was amazed. We all have this incredible technology within us, a built-in computer system with a more powerful information processor than anything else in the world. So if our life experiences are 100% related to what we neurologically perceive and process, then our nerve system must play the major role in creating our reality. The bottom line is this: how well your nerve system processes information from your environment ultimately determines your state of health, well-being, wealth, choices, behaviors, and whether you're accessing your inner power and fulfilling your dreams—or not.

Your Internal Resonance = Your Real World Results

"If you take the game of life seriously, if you take your nervous system seriously, if you take your sense organs seriously, if you take the energy process seriously, you must tune in and turn on."
–Timothy Leary

Now let's take this one step further. In order to better understand the world within our minds and bodies we must understand what influences us. At the macro level we see ourselves as a large mass of matter with a head, arms, legs, feet, etc. Zooming in one level, we see a bunch of organ systems: digestive, endocrine, cardiovascular, etc. At the next level we see groups of organs: the heart, lungs, liver, etc. When we get in even closer, we see that these organs are made of specialized tissues. These tissues are made of specialized cells, which in turn are made up of molecules. Molecules are made up of atoms. And finally, atoms are composed of subatomic particles: protons, electrons and neutrons. The behavior of our subatomic micro world determines the level of organization in our macro world—our body, our lives and experiences. Epigenetic science has now validated that the resonance and vibration of our inner world (subatomic particles) directly influences what we achieve in our outer world (real life results).

If we observe the behavior of subatomic particles we learn that these extremely small entities coalesce to create a specific frequency. You see, these subatomic particles have a very particular vibration and tone at which they resonate. For example, let's observe water. When we boil water we are increasing the tone of the atoms and creating a different level of organization within the H_2O atoms. Now, if we decreased the vibration and tone of these same atoms the level of organization would change yet again. Eventually, the water would change states and become ice. Do you see how the internal atomic vibration changes the external manifestation of water?

The same idea applies to your mind and body. If you increase the speed at which your subatomic particles vibrate, the level of organization within your cells and tissues increases. This is associated with a system that is closer to an ideal state of dynamic homeostasis—and thus optimal and extraordinary living. You will increase the ability to create real-world results and manifest your greatest desires. Conversely, if you decrease the speed at which your subatomic particles vibrate, the level of organization within your cells and tissues decreases. This is associated with a system that is closer to a less optimal state of homeostasis—resulting in negative symptoms, disease and an uninspired life. A low vibration from within repels high vibrations in your outer world, which are extraordinary results. This is as simple as understanding that a specific cause always results in a specific effect or result, physically, mentally, emotionally or spiritually.

It was clear to me that as I was journeying through my life I was moving toward a less optimal state. My entire nerve system was polluted. I had completely lost my inner state of balance. As a result, I became angry and depressed, and I continued to make poor choices. I wouldn't listen to my inner voice or anyone else for guidance, as I was disconnected from my source of power and inspiration. Our nerve systems are the master controls, and the energy that flows through them is our ultimate source of power, purpose and inspiration. This power is beyond your mind and body. As I became increasingly disconnected from my source of power and inspiration, eventually I reached a tipping point and had to make a clear and definite choice. I had to find a way to re-connect to the source of power that created me from two tiny cells. In order to do that I had to face my state of extreme dis-ease and stop trying to mask it with pharmaceuticals, recreational drugs and worldly distractions. If

I was going to survive, I had to choose life.

As I progressed on my journey I learned that not only was I made up of atoms and that their vibration and tones created my state, I learned that the entire fabric of life is made up of protons, electrons and neutrons. Perhaps my greatest "aha" moment in life occurred when I realized that everything in our world is composed of subatomic particles and that their behavior ultimately determines our reality and destiny. This single fascinating moment of understanding has enabled me touch and transform the lives of thousands of people throughout the world.

If you take the time to understand and apply the laws that govern these powerful yet tiny structures, your life will also transform in extraordinary ways with mathematical certainty.

Integration

"The moment one commits oneself, then providence moves too. All sorts of things occur to help. A whole stream of events issue from the decision, raising in one's favor all manner of incidents and meetings and material assistance which no one could have dreamed would come his or her way."
—J.W. Von Goethe

When I was growing up I chose to create a certain lens through which I saw the world. I chose to have a certain set of experiences by making specific and crucial life choices. These choices resulted in me *creating a state within my body and mind.* Some of my experiences were desirable and pleasurable and many were less desirable or even extremely painful and difficult. How did all of this come to be?

43

What I've learned through physics, anatomy, physiology and as a healer is that every experience we have—whether physical, mental, emotional or chemical—can be broken down to a basic subatomic vibration and tone. The same ingredients that comprise us also make up the entire fabric of the experiences we call life. And it is our nerve systems that act as intermediaries between our atoms and the atoms of our experiences to appropriately interpret and perceive them.

The flexibility and adaptability of your nerve system is what determines your ability to process and integrate information from your environment. Integration is the process through which your nerve system takes the subatomic vibrations of your experiences and adds them to the tone and vibration of your present subatomic state.

In other words, each time you integrate an experience your cells and tissues become slightly more complex. Their level of organization increases and they become more dynamic and animated. You will have taken a small step in the right direction. You'll be that much closer to mastering your life and fulfilling your dreams. As a result, you'll have access to greater inner power, health, thoughts, purpose, choices, relationships, certainty and clarity. You will be able to create and manifest your greatest life. This will happen because you'll essentially become more whole and alive!

What I had realized was enormous. **Our ability to integrate experiences was simply the process of growing and adapting.** In other words, integration is a form of evolution for living organisms. In fact, biological systems integrating experiences through nerve systems over thousands of years is the core concept of evolution. When you integrate an experience, you learn at an atomic and cellular level, changing your biological make-up ever so slightly. At one point in human history, our most complex inventions were a hammer and chisel. Today we fly in planes and communicate over the Internet. These evolutions have come about through integrating our life experiences.

The fastest integrators in life are healthy children. I was watching a little boy at a coffee shop one afternoon. He was learning to stand up. At first he was on all fours, then he was on his bum, but he couldn't get upright. However, each time he tried he would get a little closer to fully standing. Dozens of attempts and almost one hour later he was able to stand for a few moments at a time. His nerve system was taking in everything from his environment and his brain was telling his body how to move, shift and balance with every attempt. After dozens of attempts—i.e., experiences—his body and mind were synchronizing the right sequences to eventually get to a full standing position. I was watching real-time integration lead this child's progress in an essential life skill. Integration was occurring at a subconscious level both cellularly and atomically. These microscopic occurrences greatly influenced his conscious mind and awareness as he began to stand.

Facilitating Integration

"We all have extraordinary within us, waiting to be released."
—Jean Houston

How do we fully integrate an experience?

Remember your nerve system is like your body's computer. It processes information and experiences just like a computer processes strikes of the keyboard or movements of the mouse. Just like a computer's processor, your nerve system has a specific bandwidth. It processes some information very well and other information not well at all. Experiences and information that are within our bandwidth are processed and integrated easily. These experiences range from falling in love to mastering a new skill—anything you'd view as a pleasurable or positive experience.

FULL LIFE EXPRESSION

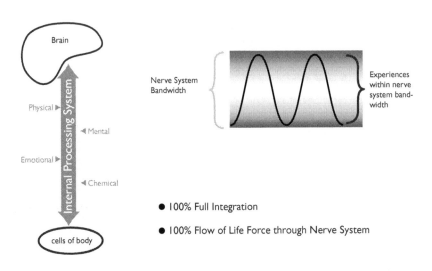

- 100% Full Integration
- 100% Flow of Life Force through Nerve System

Diagram 1

On the flip side, any experiences that are beyond your bandwidth will not be perceived as positive or pleasurable. These experiences will be perceived as hardships and come with pain or stress. If you can't fully integrate challenging experiences, these atoms and particles will lock within segments of your nerve system to create areas of tension, pressure and interference. As these areas of interference continue to build the communication pathways between your brain and body will begin to break down and diminish.

As a result, your body's cells and tissues won't receive 100% of the master messages, so they won't know how to function properly. Your power supply begins to fade. This will also alter the proportions of hormone and chemical release, negatively affecting your physiology and mental and emotional states. What you'll have is a mind and body that are fighting the natural ebb and flow of life. This disruption in flow will ultimately lead to a dis-eased mind and body if you don't address it.

LESS THAN FULL LIFE EXPRESSION

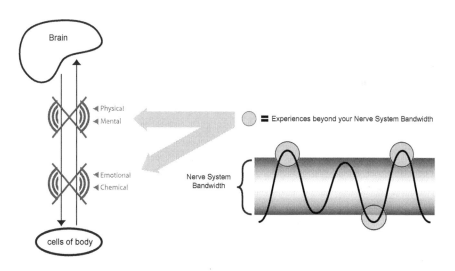

Diagram 2

Remember: A great deal of people in this world function with computers that simply cannot handle the bandwidth that life's experiences require. Imagine having a nerve system that had the processing capacity of an old Commodore 64 computer from the 80's. If you attempted to download songs, surf the Web or check your email, the computer system would slow down immensely and even begin to break down. The information is outside its bandwidth. It's too large.

This is similar to what happens to people. If your bandwidth is too small, you won't have the ability to handle a great deal of experiences.

Loads of information will build up and create miscommunication from within, moving you further from your ultimate desires and destiny. However, the beauty of this amazingly advanced system is that every experience, once fully integrated, will begin to upgrade your nerve system's processing capacity. It'd be like trading in your old computer for a shiny new one with a faster and more efficient processor.

When you don't learn and grow from your experiences, they wait patiently at a subatomic level around your nerve system and act as areas of potential energy. This is potential for new learning, growth and evolution. If these pockets of atoms aren't processed, they have a significant negative impact on the quality of your health, well-being, choices and perspectives. The natural ecology and momentum of life wants you to grow and learn. If integration doesn't occur, your mind and body will begin to speak to you. This is because you're stuck in a pattern or rut and you'll move against the natural flow of what your life is meant to be. If your brain isn't properly communicating with your body's cells and tissues, they start misbehaving. If these old experiences aren't processed they will begin to express themselves physically, mentally, emotionally, or spiritually. Physically they may show up as symptoms, sickness or disease. Mentally they may show up as more self-critical mind chatter. Emotionally, these old experiences may be expressed as depression or anxiety, and spiritually as a loss of self, identity or purpose.

And it doesn't stop there. These old, unprocessed experiences will also show up in your outer life in terms of how you communicate with others and your focus, choices, actions and behavior. As your inner world changes, your outer world changes. The ways you relate, connect and communicate with others will change radically, affecting your relationships, work, career, family and your ability to manifest abundance into your life.

Tune IN and Turn ON

"Extraordinary people survive under the most terrible
circumstances and they become more extraordinary because of it."
—Robertson Davies

Remember that the purpose of your nerve system is to transfer information from your external environment into your subatomic matrix, facilitating your growth and evolution. When you're not doing this, you become stuck in a pattern. When your nerve system is stuck in pattern it cannot effectively process new information because it's constantly trying to process old information.

When I was a teenager, the stresses and demands of my lifestyle built up, and my nerve system got bogged down with un-integrated past events and experiences. Eventually, my perception system became distorted as well. Remember, the nerve system is your sensory perception system. It is the lens through which you see the world.

Think of it this way: If you experience some trauma in your life, such as a major car crash, and you do not fully integrate that experience, you become locked in that pattern neurologically and physiologically. When you think about getting into a vehicle your entire physiology will begin to relive that car crash. Your heart rate may speed up and you may feel nervous or anxious and completely contract. Your perception system gets locked at that level of awareness and you draw conclusions that cars are dangerous and people do not know how to drive—and perhaps you will no longer get into a vehicle. Now compound this with trillions of experiences throughout your entire life that may not have fully integrated: You now have the paradigms, levels of awareness and consciousness that you'll use to navigate through your life. This is the basis of how paradigms of racism, discrimination, poverty, war, and so on are developed.

Compounding this, your nerve system doesn't know the difference between past, present and future. Researchers at Stanford University have confirmed these findings. One study measured the neurological firing of athletes' nerve systems as they performed activities like sprinting. Later, the same athletes lay down on beds and were asked to close their eyes and visualize every action, movement and thought that came with the task they'd performed previously—but without contracting any muscles. While performing this visualization process, they were connected to a neurological feedback machine to measure their neural firing. The amazing finding was that the nerve system fires exactly the same way in both scenarios. The nerve system does not know whether the athlete is actually sprinting down the track or just imagining it.

It's been scientifically proven that the nerve system doesn't know the difference between past, present and future, or the difference between real and simply perceived events. The Chicago Bulls used this information to create an NBA dynasty in the 1990s—Michael Jordan incorporated these findings into his training with a sports psychologist, which gave him a neurological edge for extraordinary achievement. His accomplishments as an athlete speak for themselves.

So what does all this mean for you and your life? If an experience from years past was not fully integrated, your nerve system will fire every day as if that experience is still occurring. Like a record player that skips the same verse over and over, your nerve system will run the same pattern over and over in an attempt to integrate it. That and many other un-integrated experiences will create the lens through which you see your world.

Over the past 20 years as a healer, inspirational speaker, author and student of life, this is what I have learned about myself and most people in this world. We go through life creating certain perspectives, paradigms and points of view. These are the result of experiences we have not fully integrated. We are stuck atomically, cellularly, neurologically, chemically, hormonally and consciously. If we were abused as children we feel that most people cannot be trusted. If we were raised in an area of crime and violence we feel most people are dishonest and will take advantage of us. If we were told that money doesn't grow on trees we will feel the universe is not abundant and believe in scarcity and competition. We must grow, integrate and transcend these lenses if we want to move to new vantage points, paradigms and worldviews. This is the start of how we create a more extraordinary life. Change must begin from within.

As a child I felt threatened and unsafe. These were my perceptions, and subatomically this is where I resonated. I had thousands of experiences that supported and solidified this perspective, and I felt the entire world functioned this way. My nerve system was locked in a pattern of trying to process these negative experiences and feelings, yet it sought to integrate them daily so I could grow beyond them. On a cellular level this is how I felt every day—I was in a low-grade survival state. These perceptive neural patterns then led me to develop a specific paradigm of life: *People in this world cannot be trusted and I must be extremely vigilant.* Our paradigms lead to certain beliefs about life: *The world is a rough and unforgiving place.* These beliefs lead to thoughts about how we must deal with life: *I've got to be tough and strong to take care of myself.* These thoughts lead to emotions and choices that facilitate our actions and behaviors. These behaviors become our lives. This loop feeds back on itself and our behaviors lead to new experiences that are of the same vibration or resonance as the original experience.

Remember, you will attract experiences and people of the same subatomic resonance and repel everything else. Ultimately this stunts our growth and evolution. It forces our nerve systems to perpetuate the same perceptive patterns and get stuck in a paradigm. As a result, our systems keep playing the same verse over and over again, leading to the same successes and failures in our lives.

This is how it breaks down:

Nerve system pattern

↓

Paradigm

↓

Beliefs

↓

Thoughts

↓

Emotions

↓

Actions

↓

Behavior

↓

Your life
(More emotions)

↓

New experiences

As a healer I have seen that people who have not integrated experiences from their past are stuck in that pattern and state of consciousness. Have you ever wondered why some people who were chronically sexually abused as children go on to sexually abuse children when they become adults? As children these people detested and were traumatized by the experience and the perpetrator. Why on earth would they go on to do it to other children? It is because this is the verse that keeps playing through their nervous systems, over and over again. They have not fully integrated the experience. They have not fully overcome these extremely challenging experiences. And until they do, those experiences collectively will be the vibration and lens through which they see their worlds and create their experiences.

The same can be said for people of authority. I have seen countless executives and managers who are liked and respected by their employees. I've also seen many people in positions of authority take advantage of others. It usually begins with an experience at a young age in which they gave up their inner strength and power to another person. They were controlled and taken advantage of, leaving them feeling less worthy and meaningful. This pattern runs deep within the bureaucratic models of our culture. If these people don't integrate their experiences with age, those experiences create their lenses and help define their whole personalities. When these people are put into positions of authority, they lack the ability to create symbiotic relationships and lead in an authoritarian fashion, dictating to the masses and further disempowering people.

In life you can choose to be right or you can choose to be happy. When you choose to be right, you shut down your life and diminish the opportunity for more growth, evolution and integration. When you accept that you don't know everything, you open yourself up to new possibilities. You become a student of life and accept that every person, place and experience will enrich your life in some way, regardless of how easy or challenging it is to integrate. You begin to change from within—and this is the start of mastering your life. This is the start of rocking an extraordinary life mentally, emotionally, physically and spiritually. This is the start of accessing your inner power and creating unwavering certainty to fulfill your dreams. Anything that can be conceived in your mind can be achieved in your life. It all begins with you making the choice to just do it.

Seeing the Blessings in Difficulty

"All of us are on our own paths, doing exactly what we know how to do at the moment, given the conditions of our lives."
—Unknown

I feel truly blessed to have the life I've created for myself today. I also feel fortunate just to be alive. Although I flirted with danger and death far too many times in my youth, I am in a deep place of gratitude for every experience in my life—together, they make up the journey that brought me to where I am today and where I am going tomorrow.

As far as I can remember, back to my earliest memories, all I've wanted was to feel at peace within myself. Regardless of whether we're aware of it, I believe that is the journey we are all on. When we are at home within ourselves, happiness and success come naturally. Yet many of us go down a different path. I was no exception, since from a young age I chose to see the world from a place of fear instead of trust.

For most of the first 18 years of my life, I experienced so many hostile situations and frightening interactions that my nerve system had a very hard time processing them. The patterns became so deeply carved that the only way I thought I could cope with the life I'd created was to sedate myself with material goods, entertainment, drugs and other useless distractions. The distractions provided temporary feelings of happiness and relief, but inevitably would only make things worse. This is a common practice for people who prefer to keep themselves so distracted and busy that they don't have to look at what is most important and real. Fortunately, these false ways of living always will catch up with us. We all will have the opportunity to face our inner demons so that we may conquer and grow beyond them. You just decide when you'll do it.

Growth opportunities come in different forms. I am grateful that a stream of synchronous events got me to leave Vancouver for India. The contract on my life turned out to be the catalyst for my healing and growth. It was in India that the seeds of transformation were planted within me. When I returned, the tension between what I innately knew to be my authentic infinite self and the way I was living—from my lowest finite self—became more excruciating. Events climaxed on the night when I tried to take my life, and I was granted a second chance, an opportunity to live life better.

I had so much to process and integrate that my system literally shut me down. Medically speaking, what I experienced was a nervous breakdown and helplessness with suicidal depression. The doctors wanted to give me drugs. That was a no-brainer for me: drugs were a huge part of what got me to that place, and I didn't see how more drugs would get me out. I wasn't interested in creating a delusional state of false happiness and well-being. I was completely disconnected from myself because everything I experienced was far too great for a teenager to integrate. Yet my system still wanted to learn from it all.

The Intelligent Power Within

*"Do not go where the path may lead, go instead
where there is no path and leave a trail."*
—Ralph Waldo Emerson

What I know now, as a healing doctor, is that when we lie down on our backs we completely decompress our spine and nerve system. This allows most of the nerve system, from the brain to our sacrum, to completely decompress and unwind. As a result, the nerve system goes through the natural rhythmic, somatic waves necessary for integration. In fact this is the primary reason why we sleep each night. It is to process and integrate the events of the day, week or years and facilitate cellular reorganization and regeneration. My system had to go through this for months and it was so full of information that it didn't want any more experiences. My nervous breakdown truly was a breakdown of my nerve system. In this state my cup was full; I was completely catatonic.

The day I arrived at my parents' house and told my mom, "I'm tired, I need to rest," I made the biggest understatement of my life. Since I felt thoroughly safe, I let my defenses down and was able to sleep for more than three straight months. When I wasn't sleeping I would innately lie flat on my back, which is the ideal sleeping position for integration. I had so much unprocessed information throughout my nerve system, I had to decompress and integrate for months. The first month was truly a dark, painful and arduous journey into my soul. I connected with every demon within me—and they were not pretty. Although I never acted on them again, I was consumed by thoughts of suicide. I simply did not want to be on the earth any longer. I felt ashamed, disgraced and horrible for whom I had become. The inner pain and angst was immense. I was helpless and had no thirst for life.

As I progressed it was amazing to witness what I experienced. My entire system began to retrace every unintegrated event I had had since birth. It was the purest form of core healing. First came childhood memories of Scotland and then early memories of moving to Canada. Experiences I had never even thought about were in the forefront of my mind as I began to integrate them on the subatomic and cellular levels. As the weeks progressed I moved into my school-age years and began to process every challenge that I experienced during that time.

The biggest challenge was processing the experiences I'd had from ages 13 to 18. I had seen and experienced things that were straight out of Hollywood thrillers. Everything I saw and was a part of reverberated through my entire system. Every cell and tissue experienced the pain and angst of every event. I had no idea what was happening as these thoughts, fears and challenges flashed through my conscious mind as if I were sitting at a bus stop watching cars drive by in slow motion. Every feeling and emotion was fully expressed at a cellular and atomic level.

I spent most of that time in an ocean of tears; at other times I suffered excruciating physical, mental or emotional pain, screaming at the top of my lungs for help. Other times I was vomiting and voiding. I was seeing, feeling, sensing and experiencing everything. I was integrating a massive amount of information. In five years I had experienced and accomplished what would take most a lifetime of work and energy to achieve. I had careened recklessly through life and my experiences had finally caught up with me.

As months passed I noticed that my ability to integrate was growing and the process was becoming easier. My internal computer was becoming more efficient and I was gaining clarity. Physically my body felt newer every day; it was as if I had to relearn to walk and move again each morning. My appetite was steadily restored. I began to talk with my family. I knew I was well on my way to fully rediscovering myself when I asked Raj, casually and with genuine interest, how the Canucks were doing (for the uninitiated, that's Vancouver's professional hockey team).

These months were absolutely pivotal for me and were a time of deep core healing. At the time I had no idea what was really occurring, yet I somehow found a way to be in a place of trust. Memories and thoughts of India even resurfaced. When I looked in the mirror I could barely recognize myself—I looked healthy, robust and relaxed. I began to smile and laugh again. I started to like myself again. My entire nerve system had rewired and I had grown physically, mentally, emotionally and spiritually.

The greatest gift from all of this was that my direction in life had been solidified. I wanted to dedicate my life to serving others and to make a grand difference in the world. I wanted to see others fully express the light that burned deep within them. I wanted to be a part of something so much bigger than myself. I began to dream of a new life.

PART II

"Life is full of beauty. Notice it. Notice the bumblebee, the small child, and the smiling faces. Smell the rain, and feel the wind. Live your life to the fullest potential, and fight for your dreams."
—Ashley Smith

The Strategies that Will Transform Your Life from Ordinary to Extraordinary

Today my intention in everything I do and all I am is to inspire and teach people to express their full potential and be fully alive. I believe that life is a gift, and what we do with our lives is a gift back to the world.

The lessons and strategies I've learned throughout my life have helped me get from where I was to where I am—and they'll play a vital role in where I go next. They provided a framework of how I was able to survive in an urban underworld. Where I went wrong. How as a high-school dropout I was able to fully integrate my postsecondary education and become an honors and dean's list student graduating at the top of my class. How over the past decade I have been able to transform lives as a healing doctor through my thriving Centre for Optimal Living. And finally how I have inspired thousands throughout the world as an author and inspirational speaker.

What I Offer

The only thing that is certain in life is that everything is uncertain. Change is the flavor of life. It is never a question of *if* change will occur; it is a question of *when*. However, no one can change anyone else. I do not believe that anyone can even fully persuade another person to change. We are the gatekeepers to our own door of change, growth and possibility. The choice to open that door is one that we all make within ourselves.

If you decide to open that door, become a student of life and apply these universal laws to your own life, I feel confident that many of the amazing things I have personally experienced and seen in the lives of tens of thousands of people will also occur for you. You will be able to connect to your core self. You will feel your true nature and deepest values surface. Your feelings of self-confidence and self-worth will enhance. You will define yourself from within and feel a more profound sense of peace. People's opinions will matter less and the dualistic nature of life will become more balanced. You will actually have a desire and thirst for more change and growth. Your internal voice and vision will become much louder and clearer than the opinions of others.

Your relationship with yourself and others will also begin to change. You will access your inner power and begin to see more clearly through the veils of life. You will begin to adopt behaviors and embark on endeavors with unwavering certainty that is a greater expression of your infinite self. You will be able to create and attract more abundance into your life. You will enhance your ability to fully experience inner happiness, joy and self-actualization. This is mastering your life. Welcome to this extraordinary journey of fulfilling your dreams. Get ready to *rock it*!

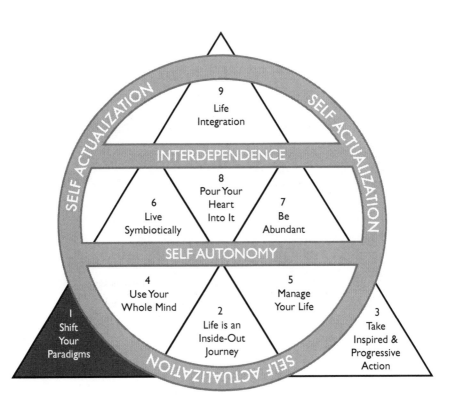

CHAPTER 3

STRATEGY 1 — SHIFT YOUR PARADIGMS

*"A human being is part of a whole, called by us
the 'Universe,' a part limited in time and space. He
experiences himself, his thoughts and feelings, as
something separate from the rest, a kind of optical
delusion of his consciousness. This delusion is a kind of
prison for us, restricting us to our personal desires and
to affection for a few persons nearest us. Our task must
be to free ourselves from this prison by widening our
circles of compassion to embrace all living creatures
and the whole of nature in its beauty."*
—Albert Einstein

When I was a child and teenager I failed to fully embrace the principle
of widening our circles of compassion. I created my lens of the world,
which was based on my perceptive neural patterning. I truly felt that my
lens and my way was "the way." I thought I had it all figured out and
nobody could convince me otherwise. It was not until my early twenties that I learned about this notion of paradigms.

A paradigm is a specific worldview, frame of reference, model, assumption or perception. It's the way we perceive, understand and interpret our world. An easier way to understand your paradigm is to see it as the road map that you create when embarking on different endeavors. As a child, I viewed the world as hostile. In this paradigm it would take an immense amount of strength, effort and force to achieve anything, as I would have to constantly strive to break through that perceived hostility.

The reality is that we all have thousands of these road maps within our neural systems. These paradigms answer specific questions for us on a daily basis. They tell us what is real for us and show us what we actually value, and they plant the seeds of creation in our physical world. Everything we experience is filtered through these lenses.

My challenge was that I was completely unaware I was creating these mental maps. Therefore, the thoughts, attitude, behavior and life I created were based on a completely false set of assumptions.

We all are constantly learning new skills and more efficient ways of accomplishing things. Every time we integrate new information we grow, learn and see new possibilities. As we do this we begin to develop a new awareness of what is real and how things could be. This is what I call a paradigm shift. When we learn and grow we create new vantage points and begin to see and create things differently. In order for us to fully express that inner fulfillment and happiness we must continue to make paradigm shifts throughout our lives. These shifts also allow our human will or spirit to fully emerge, creating and painting our ideals of who we are and what we want to achieve and become.

Achieving Clarity

"Your paradigm is so intrinsic to your mental process that you are hardly aware of its existence, until you try to communicate with someone with a different paradigm."
—Donella Meadows

You cannot create a paradigm shift until you fully understand your present paradigm. Many people I've met have attended many self-help programs and corporate or personal-growth seminars. Generally those programs that roused motivation but didn't instill commitment for inner change were unsuccessful. This is because they violated a fundamental law—they attempted to change outward attitudes and behaviors only. For example, they'd say the key to being healthier, wealthier and happier was acting a certain way or saying certain things. These programs failed to recognize where people were resonating. They failed to recognize that shifting one's perspective is an inside-out job, not an outside-in job.

To learn our present paradigm we must observe what is real for us and what we value. We then must accept that this is merely our lens and not necessarily the inherent way of the world.

Paradigm shifting is an idea that facilitates the growth and evolution of who we are as human beings. Achieving clarity is an "Aha!" experience. It can happen while we're solving a problem, gaining a new understanding, or (if we're so fortunate) having an epiphany. It is when the light within us becomes brighter.

When I was immersed in my postsecondary education and traveling during the summers, connecting with and being mentored by doctors, healers and facilitators of human potential, I had significant paradigm shifts. I learned that every major breakthrough in science first began with a break from tradition and old ways of thinking. For a new paradigm to be created an old paradigm must be let go. We only have the capacity to hold so many paradigms, so we must create the space for new ones.

During this time, I also learned that Newtonian sciences were the primary paradigms from which I was being taught, even though they are nearly 300 years old. I was intrigued—especially since many of my questions about my journey and life were not being answered. Newtonian sciences are necessary and must be understood and taught, and just because something is old does not make it wrong or outdated. However, I began to use this particular paradigm more as a foundation from which to grow. I created a new paradigm, one that stemmed from Albert Einstein's work: the relativity paradigm, quantum physics, force dynamics, and the nutty world of subatomic particles.

Embracing Change

"We don't see things as they are, we see things as we are."
—Anaïs Nin

All paradigm shifts, even if they are in a dark direction (like the one I chose as a child), move us from seeing the world one-way to seeing it another way. They are the catalysts for powerful change—and in life the only constant is change. Being adaptable to change and shifting my paradigms has created new sources of attitude, behaviors, relationships, skills, connection and consciousness.

Some paradigm shifts occur instantaneously and others develop over time. My biggest paradigm shift came during a life-threatening crisis. I went from valuing nothing within myself to valuing everything life has to offer. I suddenly saw my priorities in a different light. From what I've observed throughout my life, I feel that most fundamental shifts occur when people step into a new role, such as student, husband or wife, parent or grandparent, supervisor, athlete, leader, etc. I have also observed that a great deal of strife among family members, couples, friends or colleagues arises during these transition periods. That's because many people enter into an agreement with another person when everything feels wonderful, as they have each created a similar paradigm. As life changes, new paradigms develop—a fundamental necessity for growth. The challenge occurs when people do not communicate their new paradigms and assume nothing has changed, when, in fact, everything has changed.

Speak Your Truth

> *"The Wright Brothers' first flight was not reported in a*
> *single newspaper because every rookie reporter knew*
> *what could and couldn't be done."*
> —Edward R. Murrow

Throughout human history there have been countless shifts in the collective consciousness. Every paradigm shift that emerges from a universal truth stands the test of time. However, every shift will go through three stages. The magnitude and depth of the shift will determine how long the paradigm will remain in each stage.

The three stages of a paradigm shift:

1. It will be ridiculed.

↓

2. It will be opposed, perhaps even violently.

↓

3. It will be accepted as self-evident.

Take, for example, one major paradigm shift in human history. In 1543 the scientist Nicolaus Copernicus finally published his magnum opus, a book called *De Revolutionibus Orbium Coelestium* (*The Revolution of Celestial Spheres*). This work was not only the starting point of modern astronomy; it was the defining epiphany that began the scientific revolution. Copernicus had known for decades that his theories were relevant, yet they presented such a significant paradigm shift that he knew many people wouldn't be able to grasp them. He deeply feared the repercussions of making his work public. However, one of his close friends eventually persuaded him to publish his work. Inadvertently, he published the book the same year that he died.

The crux of Copernicus's work used simple geometry with no experimental evidence or even a telescope. He demonstrated that the sun was in fact at the center of the universe, not the Earth (as was believed at the time). He also demonstrated the observed motions of other celestial objects in the universe. He claimed Earth and other planets and stars revolved around the sun, instead of the sun and other celestial bodies revolving around the Earth.

For six decades his work was ridiculed as preposterous. Yet, as time went by, a handful of dedicated scientists began to believe that his work was correct. In 1616 this momentum caused the Roman Catholic Church to issue a decree suspending Copernicus's work. They claimed that the Earth moving around the sun was completely false and that it opposed and contradicted the true sense and authority of Holy Scripture. The Church edited his book to omit his major findings.

In 1663 the revolutionary scientist Galileo Galilei, who was propagating Copernicus's life work, was placed under lifelong house arrest for defying the Holy Scripture. (Ironically, while under house arrest, he would become the first person to prove Copernicus's theories with the newly-invented telescope, talk about synchronicity.) The next phase of strong opposition was in full swing.

Today it is common knowledge that it is indeed the planets, which include the Earth, that rotate around the sun and not vice-versa. This is known as Copernican Heliocentrism, and it is accepted as self-evident.

For a more recent example of a major paradigm shift, look to the late 1970s. Personal-computing entrepreneur Bill Gates made the bold statement that "every household in America will have a personal home computer" in the future. This was a time when some major institutions still did not have computer systems. The idea that every home would have one seemed outrageous. Again, his statements were initially ridiculed. As this shift passed through opposition it eventually became self-evident that most homes would indeed have a computer. Today, it's even been taken another step further—people now have personal computers in their pockets in the form of smartphones. This paradigm shift has changed so much in the world.

Share Your Talents

"New opinions are always suspected, and usually opposed, without any other reason but because they are not already common." —John Locke

Right now there is an emerging paradigm in healthcare. When I began to learn the nature of atomic particles and their relationship to cells, the nerve system and matter, I knew there was something more to understanding neural vibrational fields and energy. This was almost 15 years ago. I didn't fully understand this new paradigm, yet I was very intrigued by it and began researching it.

At the time, energy healing was ridiculed as quackery, so I kept my research private. As the years progressed I began to develop some stronger understandings and worked with some innovative doctors to better understand the sacred geometry of human beings. Today as a healing doctor at my Centre for Optimal Living, I work tonally with the nerve system, facilitating integration. I deeply understand the relationship between the mind, body and spirit and how it works through symptoms, sickness and disease to optimal health, radiant vitality and living. I have seen thousands of people's lives transformed from this energy healing work in my practice and others throughout the world.

I have known for several years that the future of healthcare and peak performance will be centered on energy healing. It will lead to the disappearance of mortality and morbidity from cancer, cardiovascular disease, anxiety, depression and other major illnesses. But I also know that people don't yet fully understand this new paradigm of health and life, as it's still being ridiculed and strongly opposed. Many researchers and scientists are now studying this work and I feel strongly that in the next 25 to 35 years energy healing will be the primary form of healthcare. Similar to how a computer is in almost every home today, people will stop relying on drugs and surgery and seek energy healing during times of both disease and wellness.

Though it's not yet accepted by the mainstream, energy healing is far from a fringe practice. In fact, the famed Dr. Mehmet Oz said on *Oprah* in 2009 that the future of healthcare will be energy medicine. Again, every breakthrough in science first began with a break from tradition and old ways of thinking. For a new paradigm to be made, an old paradigm must be destroyed. Today, more and more people are questioning the traditional healthcare system and are demanding a higher level of service.

Paradigm shifts are not limited to science. People who harness their inner power, momentum and dedication are the ones that bring powerful paradigm shifts to fruition. It is the constant that drives evolution, science, health, personal transformation and consciousness.

The Be, Do, Have Paradigm

"Nothing splendid has ever been achieved except by those who dared believe that something inside of them was superior to circumstance."
—Bruce Barton

Many unfulfilled people I've come across are lost in the *Have, Do, Be Paradigm*:

- They believe that when they *have* something, such as more health, money, love, or time, they will finally be able to *do* something.

- That *doing* may be going on a vacation, buying a new house or car, starting a relationship, opening a new business, and so on.

- They believe that, in turn, this *doing* will allow them to *be* something they desire, such as happy, wealthy, healthy, or fulfilled.

They are committed to the Have, Do, Be Paradigm despite the fact that it's in direct opposition to the reality of the universe.

As stated in the law of vibrational resonance, the level at which one is resonating sub-atomically, molecularly and cellularly will create a specific inner ecology. This environment within us seeks to resonate with like forces outside us. There is a direct relationship between the resonance of our inner ecology and our outer experiences (reality). As a result, we can never *have* anything until we *become* that resonance from within first.

The consumerism of Western society leads us to believe that if we *have* certain things we will feel and become whatever the ads imply: happy, healthy, rich, and so on. This is incorrect. Instead of Have, Do, Be we should embrace its opposite: the *Be, Do, Have* Paradigm.

Adopting the Be, Do, Have Paradigm applies this law and will facilitate your personal growth, experience and evolution at an exponential rate. You will become, do and have the things you desire at a much faster rate. This is a creative paradigm shift that has stood the test of time. Its purpose is exactly that: to facilitate your creation, to allow you to bring your gifts to the world, and to live in your ideals.

To apply this principle, first you must *be* whatever it is you desire—happy, healthy, energetic, abundant, or compassionate from within.

This may take some time, as you have to shift from your present paradigm. You must ask yourself some questions:

If I had X, what would I feel? How would I walk, talk, and relate to others? How would I behave and act? **Essentially, who would I be?**

The key to being is to connect with your feelings and emotions as if you already have "X". I learned about this powerful truth studying translations of ancient prayers recorded in Aramaic, the language of the Essenes (scribes of the Dead Sea Scrolls). This paradigm has been around for so long, yet we still fail to fully use it. The translations stated that one must "Be surrounded by your answer- Be enveloped by what you desire, that your gladness be full". This is essentially saying that feeling the emotions is the language of being and it's used to direct the focus of our consciousness. It's that state of being that we're in that is the source of creation, not something that we do a specific time of day.

You must now become that in order to shift your inner resonance and ecology. Once you figure this out you can start doing the things from this place of "being-ness" or emotional resonance. What would you do if you were being (emotionally feeling) this powerful, conscious, and abundant person that you truly are? Over time you will discover and realize that all these things you are *doing* will actually bring you the things you want to *have*.

To put this powerful principle into action, simply look at what you want to *have*. Now ask yourself who you think you would *be* if you *had* that—then go straight to being. When you decide who to be and then choose to be that person right away by feeling the emotions you desire, you'll manifest the results in your future experiences so much faster.

Give More to Become Extraordinary

"Things do not change, we change."
—Henry David Thoreau

Most people fail to recognize that their "not being happy or fulfilled" is connected to their not having enough time, money, energy or love. The people who are happy and fulfilled always seem to have enough time, money, energy and love. They are in vibrational resonance with the exact things they value. Their inner and outer world is more harmonized. Whether one is happy or in despair the law of vibrational resonance is ALWAYS in complete balance. Although people can be manipulated, the universe can never be manipulated or fooled.

Experiences in life are created from our neural lenses. They are the "eye" through which we see our world; they are our state of mind. For example, happiness is a state of mind that will reproduce itself in the physical form for you to see. This is because all states reproduce themselves. This is important in practicing this paradigm because your state and actions must be sincere. Otherwise the universe cannot reward you—remember the law of vibrational resonance is ALWAYS in balance. Therefore, nature requires that your mind, body and spirit be completely united with your thoughts, words, emotions and actions for the process of creation to work. In fact, success and fulfillment are nothing more than living from a place where your thoughts, words, emotions and actions are 100% aligned.

In my early twenties I really struggled with this paradigm. On a vibrational level I knew that all people were connected to each other and nature, yet I was having a very challenging time practicing the Be, Do, Have Paradigm. I worked at it for several years before I finally became successful at practicing it. When this paradigm finally "clicked" for me,

I came up with a unique little trick. I figured that in order to give something to someone else, I first had to possess it myself. So whenever I needed to "be" something, I gave it away to someone else. I wanted to be happy and fulfilled, yet I had a hard time feeling it, so instead I helped others feel happy and fulfilled. I wanted more love in my life, but I wasn't sure what that emotion felt like, so I helped other people experience more love in their lives. I utilized the people, places and things around me and poured my heart into the process, giving others everything I desired. It worked and still works for me today.

Several years ago, before I created a vast amount of abundance in my life, I helped others create it in their lives. It's important to know that I never did any of this for personal gain—I sincerely want every person I cross paths with to experience these amazing qualities. As people began to receive them, I would shift to a deep place of gratitude and achieve a new inner resonance. What I have, I give, and what others have, they give. That is why whatever we give away will always be returned with greater magnitude: it is the universal law of reciprocity. Paradoxically, this powerful law of reciprocity is invoked only when we help others without *expecting* anything in return. We must do it free of attachments.

When you practice this, your mind and emotional guidance system will come to new conclusions—you will conclude that you must have whatever quality you're giving to others, because otherwise you wouldn't be able to give it away. This new thought leads to new emotions, choices and actions, which will create new experiences. You will now *be* that which you desire. This allows your most powerful creative process to fully emerge, your higher and connected infinite self.

When you give more, you'll *be* more and create more, and hence manifest more in your physical experiences. Imagine what the world would be like if everyone practiced this paradigm. That super cool world is a dream of mine.

Become Your Greatest Self

"Success is the sum of small efforts repeated day in and day out."
—Robert Collier

When I began my journey to reach as many people as possible through speaking internationally and writing this book, I knew what it would require from my professional and personal life. Before I began, my wife Kate and I sat down and talked about the changes that this would bring to our lives. I learned from friends who are in places that we're going. We discussed what it would look like and how our lives would change. We talked about moving into a new paradigm before it even happened. I had to know I had her love and support unconditionally. With it, I could fully apply the Be, Do, Have Paradigm as our lives were changing.

Our paradigms are deeply rooted within our character and consciousness. Our subatomic makeup is the essence of what makes us, from our micro cells to whole macro selves. Our vibration sub-atomically determines the flexibility of our nervous system and how conscious and aware we are. These are the foundational elements of our nature and character.

Your Life . . . Your Choice

"Be more concerned with your character than your reputation, because your character is what you really are, while your reputation is merely what others think you are."
—John Wooden

It's important to know that these paradigms are the lenses through which we see our world. They are how we create the natural laws and principles that govern our values and character. As we expand our paradigms and consciousnesses we develop deeper and deeper principles, which are fundamental truths with universal application. When these truths are fully integrated they empower people to create a diverse array of practices to deal with multiple situations, changes and obstacles. Integrity, fairness, honesty, patience, dignity, service, nurturance, growth, impeccability and encouragement are the natural by-products for the person embodying these deep principles. And profoundly the people, places and things in this person's world will also embody these vibrational traits.

As I have progressed on my journey I have found that I care much less about what others think of me and I care a lot more about what others think of themselves and their worlds. This includes how I can serve them best in their relationship with me. My realm of paradigm shifting has moved far beyond myself to encompass everyone around me and the world we live in. Profoundly, as more and more people continue to embody higher vibrations and realms of consciousness, the people, places and things in their worlds will also begin to change and evolve.

Exercises to Facilitate Paradigm Shifting

"We have an innate desire to endlessly learn, grow, and develop.
We want to become more than what we already are. Once we yield
to this inclination for continuous and never-ending improvement,
we lead a life of endless accomplishments and satisfaction."
—Chuck Gallozi

Shift your paradigms with these exercises and begin to access your inner power:

1. Think of a time in your life when you felt stuck, lost or frustrated with a situation, conversation or experience. Make a list and write with great detail how you were feeling and why. Now imagine that other people are watching this experience—except imagine that each person has a video camera. Each camera has a slightly different lens, perspective, personality, level of awareness, education and experience. Now imagine that you can walk up to them and see the experience or situation from another point of view, including the actual people in the experience. Walk up and take notice of several different points of view. Now write down all these other perspectives that could be observed from these cameras. Be very detailed and know that anything is possible from a new lens. This exercise will open you up to the possibility of seeing things in more than one way.

2. Think of a time in your life again where you could not see the gift or learning opportunity in the experience. Shift your point of view (your paradigm) and think about the experience through a new lens. Write down how you are a better person because of the experience. Write down what you have accomplished and achieved as a result. Be very specific and clear. When you can

see the blessing in the experience, write down what you are grateful for. Write down the names of all the people and places related to the event and write a sentence of gratitude to every person and every thing.

3. Think of something in your life you would like to have. This can be anything: a tangible object like a new house or car; a quality like better health; a relationship, like a lifelong partner or a family; or an achievement, like an athletic feat or a new career. Now think of what it would feel like to have it. Write down what you would look like, how you would feel, dress, behave, act, think, speak, relate to others, carry yourself, and so on. Most importantly connect with the feelings and emotions of having it while experiencing everything from the last sentence.

Read this list EVERY DAY and allow your emotions to feel and experience this person—being in emotional resonance is the key.

Now, what would this person do? Make a long list of what you would do while being this person. The more hours you can spend each day being this person the faster you will start doing the things that will allow you to have what you desire. Be patient, persistent and do not stop until you attain it.

4. Think about whatever you choose to have in this world. Make a long list: happiness, prosperity, love, compassion, and so on. Every single day choose one of these "haves" from your list and give it away to somebody by allowing them to fully experience it from your words, actions or behaviors. Do this sincerely and purely for the grace of giving. All these "haves" will return to you in great magnitude and will transform your life.

79

5. Each day you will connect and converse with people who may or may not have similar perspectives or opinions as yourself. Understand that the way you see the world and your life is simply your perspective and lens. Rather than trying to impose your opinion into the minds of others, be open to contemplate different ideas and perspectives. Cultivate curiosity not judgment. Test other opinions for days or weeks before you begin to come to conclusions. This is a powerful way to transcend to new paradigms quickly.

6. Open yourself up to the "Beyond Body Beyond Mind" paradigm. Although you are just beginning this process ask yourself, "what is beyond my body, what is beyond my mind?". Sit in a place of quiet contemplation and curiosity with these questions every day. Ask yourself, "What and who is this power that controls my body?" "What is this power that animates my cells?" "Who is this within me that is observing my mind?", "Who am I?", "What is my purpose?". Remember, the quality of your life is dependent on the quality of questions you ask yourself. Over time powerful and profound answers will begin to surface. Be patient, persistent and diligent.

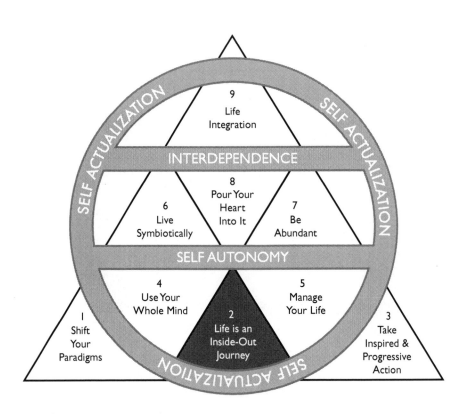

CHAPTER 4

STRATEGY 2 — LIFE IS AN INSIDE-OUT JOURNEY

"A man travels the world in search of what he needs
and returns home to find it."
—George Moore

Those who know what they value and are able to live life by those values will become the leaders in their chosen fields—and in life. Our values guide every choice we make. Therefore, they guide our destiny. When I was a teenager I was unclear about what was most important to me and what I truly stood for. As a result, I was unable to lay a foundation for my self-esteem, worth and ability to make conscious decisions from within.

Have you ever found yourself in a position in which it was extremely difficult to make a decision? Where you couldn't see the opportunity to bring your voice and vision to the world? It was simply because you did not know what you valued most within that situation. All thoughts, choices and decisions come from value clarifications.

Inspiration is Living "In-Spirit"

"You are what your deep, driving desire is. As your desire is,
so is your will. As your will is, so is your deed.
As your deed is, so is your destiny."
—Upanishads

Years ago, when I began speaking professionally, many people I knew found it strange that I wanted to be an inspirational speaker. I quickly learned that many of these people were confusing me with a motivational speaker. I have absolutely nothing against motivational speakers. If that's the kick-start people need to begin changing their lives, it's a wonderful spark. However, what I do as a healer at my Centre for Optimal Living, as an author and as a professional speaker, is offer people the opportunity to begin changing their lives from the inside-out. I help inspire people to live their purpose, vision and mission in life. Motivation comes from the outside world and inspiration comes from within.

You might be in a state of sickness or disease. You might have emotional trauma, anxiety, lack of abundance or high stress. Even if you're feeling great and looking for a proactive way to continually build optimal health and more abundance, be more adaptable to change, and fulfill your dreams—no matter where you are on that spectrum of optimal living and abundance or disease and despair, the journey is an inside-out process.

There are no express lanes or quick fixes to life. "Get happy and successful" overnight programs don't last. I have had the opportunity to work with many people from all walks of life. People who are searching, people who are in angst or pain, people longing for success and happiness, creative people, talented people and trusting people. I have worked with CEO's, executives, entrepreneurs, teachers, athletes, homeless people and multiple generations within families. In all my experience I have never seen lasting solutions to problems, enduring success, inner fulfillment or happiness that came from the outside-in.

However, I have seen people become immobilized or turn into victims by following this paradigm. These are people who focus on things outside of them as the source of problems in life. They make other people and their situations "wrong" by perceiving them as weak or lazy and taking no self-accountability. I have seen people in romantic and business relationships try to solve their unhappiness by trying to change the other person without taking any personal responsibility. The natural law that life is an inside-out journey makes everyone accountable and responsible for everything they can do and change. After all, we cannot change anybody else, but we can change ourselves.

The Infinite Intelligence Within

"Intelligence is present everywhere in our bodies . . .
our own inner intelligence is far superior to any we can try
to substitute from the outside"
—Deepak Chopra

Life truly is a process, right down to the atomic and cellular levels. Ninety-eight percent of all the cells in your body are brand new in approximately four years through cellular reorganization and regeneration. Yes: every four years you are essentially a brand new person. Most people have a challenging time understanding this: "If I'm brand new every four years, why do I keep feeling so much crappier as I age?"

This is how it works: Your brain is constantly sending messages to all the cells within your body through your nerve system. If a cell or tissue is damaged, the brain will not send messages to reorganize these cells. In fact, an immune response will be set in motion and the immune system will discard the damaged, decayed or dead tissue. As this is occurring, your brain will also send neural impulses to facilitate new cell growth. If you've not been processing or integrating your life experiences, your nerve system will not be sending 100% of the correct messages to your cells, because of miscommunication. If you're in a dis-eased state, your cells will generally be regenerating at less than 50% of their optimum.

Think of every time you have cut yourself. You put a Band-Aid on the cut and, magically, a few days later the cut is healed. The Band-Aid did not have much to do with this process. It was an inside job. The nerve system sent platelets to the cut area and they stuck together like glue, causing the blood to clot and preventing further bleeding. This clot eventually hardened, forming a scab to protect your body against infection. The scab also protected the area so the nerve system could facilitate the reorganization and regeneration of new skin cells, and it acted as a sensor—if you were to brush up against anything and disrupt the healing process, you'd be alarmed with a mild pain sensation telling you to change your position. Blood vessels are also reorganized and the nerve system invokes an immune response so white blood cells can attack any foreign invaders that may have gotten into the wound. Eventually, in about 10–14 days, the scab fell off. But if you picked the scab off, your healing process would have been prolonged as new skin cells would've been torn off as well. It could have also resulted in a scar.

I'm still humbled today by the intelligence of the human body—consider the entire process that occurred internally just for a minor little cut. One can only imagine the greatness of the powerful intelligence coursing through our minds and bodies via the nerve system, handling everything in our internal world.

Your Life of Particles

"A discovery is said to be an accident meeting a prepared mind."
—Albert Szent Gyorgyi

When I was a student in college, I spent countless hours with friends trying to quantify the magnitude of not only the innate intelligence that regulates our inner world, but the universe's intelligence, which regulates our outer world. There were many late nights and one memorable Thanksgiving evening, when a friend and I spent the entire night outside sitting in his parents' hot tub, gazing at the stars and eventually watching the sun rise. We would question and challenge each other and ourselves, and we'd do our best to find universal answers. I was on a quest to learn the essence of life, its energy source, and consciousness; find universal truths; and lift the veil on some of life's mysteries. This quest has changed everything in my life and I am forever grateful.

Today is an amazing time to be alive because so many experts are discovering the answers to these questions. In fact, as I write this book there is an experiment occurring on the French-Swiss border called The Large Hadron Collider (LHC). The LHC is built along a 27 km-long (17 miles) circular tunnel that is designed to smash together beams of subatomic particles at just under the speed of light. Researchers are hoping to see signs of even newer physics in the aftermath of the collisions, which should unlock more of the mysteries of the universe. Personally, I discovered through metaphysics, physics and force dynamics that a recurring theme that kept arising was this notion of "light." Light from the sun has always been used as an energy source, and great scientists have used it as a measure of different phenomena. I would eventually learn that the light we see with our eyes and the light that powers the human mind and body from within are actually the same thing.

To better understand this I need to give you a quantum physics crash course, so please bear with me. Every atom and its subatomic components may function as either a wave function or a particle. As wave functions, atoms exist in the form of a possibility, but cannot be observed in nature. These waves are like oxygen in the air: we know they are there, but we cannot see them. As particles, however, these atoms take physical form and we can see, feel and touch them. Remember, everything we can see, feel or touch is made up of atoms. For example, your body, your clothes, the home you live in, the vehicles, buildings, plants—everything around you. The specific vibration of atoms determines the physical properties and how the matter will manifest.

When two particles that complement each other come together, they will actually destroy each other; as a result, the energy is transformed into light. It's important to know that complementary particles will have equal yet opposite mass and charge.

So why the heck is this so important?

Again, everything within the universe is composed of subatomic particles. We can better understand ourselves and how we create our world by understanding these tiny little entities. As a result of the fact that we're composed of these particles at the foundational level, human consciousness behaves identically to complementary particles.

Molecules of Emotion

"Nothing real can be threatened. Nothing unreal exists."
—A Course In Miracles

Everything in the universe is created with an energetic complement because the universe is always in perfect equilibrium and balance. There is brightness and darkness, up and down, future and past, happiness and unhappiness, elation and depression. These polarities are nothing more than complementary particles. What's amazing is that when these sub-atomic particles come together in the middle of the infinity sign (∞), they actually annihilate each other and form something that is greater than the sum of its parts. They actually form light, the power source within every living being.

The human mind or consciousness is constantly creating complementary emotions—those with an equal or opposite charge (such as trust vs. fear, abundance vs. poverty, sadness vs. happiness, past vs. future, good vs. bad). The goal is for these complementary emotions to synthesize each other to create perfect balance and more power and light within the human mind and body. Similar to complementary atoms birthing light, these complementary emotions from consciousness also birth light within us. Light is what powers our cells and tissues, and as an emotional state this is called "love." Fritz Albert Popp, a leading bio-physicist, also found that light emissions would orchestrate the body when energy reaches a certain frequency of coherence. This coherence expresses as a full mind, body and spirit: a person beaming with radiant life and radiant vitality from making a resonant coherent jump. This jump is an internal quantum shift or leap to a new level of awareness and consciousness.

Expressing Your Full Potential

"No universe with intelligence is pointless . . . intelligence could persist for eternity—perhaps in the form of a cloud of charged particles (of light)—through shrewd conservation of energy."
—Freeman Dyson

Everything in the universe is in perfect balance and proportion. Therefore, all particles are created simultaneously to maintain this balance—including every emotion. Everything one perceives as being negative or positive is in a perfect state of balance or equilibrium. This is the duality of life. We cannot have health without disease, happiness without sadness, up without down, or light without darkness. If that were the case, we'd have no contrast to fully experience all of life, which is known as the full quantum state. We need both sides of the equation to see the entire picture. Imagine if you were observing a painting that had no contrast. It was either fully dark or fully light with no contrasting shades. It would look like a blank slate, and you couldn't see the deeper underlying picture. The same is true of life. If there were no contrast or duality we couldn't see the entire picture, or full spectrum, of life.

The problem we run into as humans is that our senses mislead us into the imbalance, only accepting half of the equation of reality. We get caught up in either the negativity or the positivity of life's experiences, resulting in a distorted perception that is not in equilibrium with the universe or ourselves. As a result, we cannot integrate and end up dissipating our potential energy and light. This takes away our power from within and we cannot be centered to our highest self. We also cannot find the fulfillment and presence within ourselves, as we get locked into only seeing the world from a fragmented point of view.

INFINITE EXPERIENCES

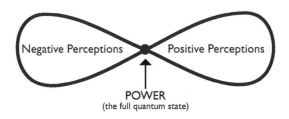

POWER
(the full quantum state)

Diagram 3

The diagram above is the sign of infinity. Life has an infinite field of experiences and opportunities. On the journey of life, for every positive experience there is an equal and opposite negative experience to balance the equation completely. On the right is everything you view as positive and on the left is everything you view as negative. To be caught in the veils of the left or right side of the equation is to deny the full spectrum of life; the power and light within you will not be ignited.

The center of the infinity sign is where both sides of the equation meet. This is the ultimate source of power within a human being. This is where complementary emotions will annihilate each other and birth something that is far greater than each—your full potential, your inner light. This is the full quantum state of life that is present in every experience, facilitated by the lens within you. This is beyond your finite body and mind. Therefore, having control of your perceptions within facilitates the balance in your life. When in balance the two experiences annihilate each other and birth your true essence, light. This is your true inner power, infinite and omnipotent self within you. It's the full quantum state.

91

Pure Powerful Presence

*"Without love there is no life, and the life is of
such a quality as is the love."*
—Emanuel Swedenborg

When we are trying to be positive thinkers or are caught in the negativity of life, we are unable to be present, because from within we're only attuned to our finite bodily senses, which live in space and time. When you are constantly living in the past or future, you cannot be fully present here and now. If you are consumed by memories of the past, your dominant emotional state will be guilt. If you are consumed by the imagination of the future, your dominant emotional state will be fear. Neither of these is real, because they are not in the here and now.

The circle in the middle of the infinity sign is pure timeless presence. In this state, every person is perfect and in a state of pure inner power. Nothing from the outside can influence this state of presence, as everything in life can be seen from a place of perfect equilibrium and balance. If you are living in this state, your light will be shining very brightly and you'll be fulfilling your wildest dreams.

So does this actually mean that there is no place for positive or negative thinking? No, it absolutely does not mean this! In fact, positive thinking is vitally important to move from despair or depression to the center point of power. Similarly, healthy skepticism plays an important role, too—if a person is in a state of manic excitement or elation, skepticism will move him or her back to the center point of power and pure potential. The reality is that there are 4,600 human traits within every single person. Half of these are perceived as being positive and the other half are perceived as the equal and opposite negative trait. Every single person expresses all positive and negative traits. When you embody this from within, you'll experience a feeling of liberation.

This is not to say that achieving balance is easy. Some people always try to be positive to every person they know and meet. Unfortunately, these people end up negating themselves because it's impossible to get rid of the polarity within us. People who put on a façade of unending upbeat positivity simultaneously create chaos in their private lives or personal health. I have seen it happen thousands of times. Through the process of life integration I am able bring them to a greater state of balance and presence.

This may be challenging some of your belief systems because domestication tells us that we need to be upbeat and positive. However, there is something within you that is far greater than this upbeat and positive mindset. It is your pure potential and power as a human being. It is the center of that infinity sign. Every single experience you have in life is pulling or pushing you toward your center, your balanced, infinite and whole self. Therefore, we all are positive and negative, kind and unkind, happy and unhappy at different times. In fact, the measure of love in a marriage is the degree to which your partner brings you back up to power when you're feeling down and grounded back to power when you're up in your ego and elation.

I spent several years of my life trying to be a full-time positive thinker. I read many books and spent a lot of time, energy and money on positive-thinking programs and people. The reality was that I was avoiding half of who I truly was. No matter how hard I tried, I still knew I was lying to myself, because deep down inside I knew I did not have that fulfillment I was so desperately trying to obtain.

Thousands of articles and books later, world travel, and 20 years of being on this journey of mastering my life, I now realize that I don't have to do this. We are given all our balanced qualities for a reason; in fact, it's the biggest reason in life that I know of. It is so we can manifest our destiny! It allows us to own our disowned parts and express our repressed selves.

You are not here to experience half of your potential for living. Moving beyond your body and mind to access your inner power and fulfill your extraordinary dreams requires that you embrace both sides of yourself. You are here to be a whole being. Experiences and traits that fall on either side of this equation are here to simply teach you that.

Your Life is Rooted in Your Values

"If God is omnipotent, then every occurrence—including every human action, every human thought and every human feeling and aspiration—is also his work."
—Albert Einstein

Did you know that every perspective you have and decision you make is based on your internal value system? It's true! Every person has a hierarchy of values. The things that are most important to us are at the top, and at the bottom are the things that don't matter to us at all. Anything in life that supports our highest values from within we deem as being "positive" and are attracted to; anything that challenges our values we deem as "negative" and are repelled from.

In life we have conscious and unconscious voids. These voids are anything that we perceive as being absent from our life—money, friendships, family, love, acceptance, health . . . you get the picture. These perceptions of what is missing in our life, the voids, collectively become the vehicle that drives our perception as to what is most important, our hierarchy of values. These underlying voids within us drive our public actions and behavior.

As you know by now, life is an inside-out process. To experience inner fulfillment we essentially must fill our perceptually empty voids. Each of these voids has a hierarchy that in turn determines the hierarchy of your values. What you perceive or put your attention on and how you act or intend upon them will determine your destiny. The greater the void, the higher you value it, and therefore the more you focus and act upon it. The more important a value is to you, the more discipline, dedication and order you will have in relating to it. The less important a value, the less discipline, dedication and order you will have in relating to it.

One of the best ways to understand this is to think of people who have almost lost their lives. Before their near-death experiences many people never stopped to think about how blessed or lucky they were to simply experience the gift of life. The human mind is an interesting creature in that it may need to confront the loss of something to realize its magnificence. Because I almost lost my life, over the past 20 years my health, well-being and life have become my main priorities. The void of losing my life was so great that I value it so much today. So much so that when I wake every morning I devote the first few hours of the day to personally improving my life from the inside-out. I exercise, meditate, visualize, journal and practice gratitude. Every day I am focused, disciplined and dedicated to these rituals, as they bring my health and life to extraordinary. When I show up at 100% I can then serve and give to the people, places and experiences of my world 100%. It all begins from within.

To birth light within us and transcend the positive and negative infinity cycle of life (also known as the rat race), all we have to do is live according to our highest values. Based on where you are resonating today this will allow you to tap into your power, potential and inspiration. If you decide to live according to your lowest values you will step out of your power zone and will need constant motivation from other people, places and things to keep you engaged.

Nothing in Life is Missing

*"You have so little faith in yourself because you are
unwilling to accept the fact that perfect love is within you,
and so you seek without for what you cannot find within."*
—*A Course In Miracles*

When I was 18, I lived in a mind and a body that were diseased and ill. My perceptions told me that my health and well-being were deeply missing. This became my greatest void and, as a result, my greatest value. It's an oft-repeated observation that many people don't realize what they have until it's gone. I witness this with many of my clients, from their health and wealth to their relationships, careers and families. Even today one of the things I value most is my health, well-being and personal growth and development. As a result I treat my mind and body like a temple. I train more than 25 hours each week as an ultra-endurance athlete. I'm the director and healer of a busy Centre for Optimal Living. I'm an international speaker, author and strategist empowering the lives of people around the world. Many people have a hard time seeing how I manage to do everything. I am deeply inspired to do everything I do. I require little outside-in motivation, as it is all driven from within me. The reality is that none of these things were ever missing from my life. I simply had to release the blocks to the power; unwavering certainty and inspiration that lives within me so my life could unfold in its perfection.

When you prioritize your values your life will become purposeful and powerful. The gift is that you will also begin to realize that nothing in your life is actually missing—there are no voids. Whatever you see as missing has simply manifested in a form that you do not recognize yet. All private voids will become public values. Your values will determine the destiny of your life. If you are displeased with your life, simply shift your focus and values from the inside-out and what you act and intend upon will create a new destiny. Life is an inside-out job!

Shifting Focus

"If we did all the things we are capable of doing,
we would literally astound ourselves."
—*Thomas A. Edison*

Similar to changing and growing at a cellular level, life even on the outside is a process that is facilitated from the inside-out. When we are able to fully adapt and grow within ourselves we create a solid foundation and new principles for the way we approach life. A natural by-product is creating the life we intend to live.

I am always fascinated by people who are amazed when they see wonderful things happening in the lives of other people, families or organizations and say, "Wow, how did they do that, and how can I do it?" Most of the time I find they are asking for the secret weapon to relieve the pain and experience the joy. There are many physical and social Band-Aids in life, but quick-fix skills, techniques or treatments tend to mask the acute effects of a more systemic, underlying, chronic problem. They will work for a short while, but over time many other acute symptoms will appear. The more people look for solutions outside themselves, the more that very approach will contribute to the underlying concerns. Your life will not be built on a solid foundation and it will be at risk of falling apart at any time.

What I have found in my life and in dealing with thousands of people as a healer and strategist is that every problem we experience can be addressed from the source, from within. In fact, the way we observe a problem actually is the problem. I have been in contact with people who have been dying of terminal illnesses. Some of these people are alive today and others have passed. The fundamental difference I observed is that the people who are still alive chose to see an opportunity where others saw an unbeatable challenge. The courageous people who looked for opportunities worked from the inside-out. They focused on integration. They were able to learn and grow. They shifted their values. They gave their systems a chance to reorganize. They took accountability for the actions, emotions, thoughts and behaviors that got them there and learned about how they could change them to get them out. They were able to shift with the ebb and flow of life and successfully process their experiences and step into their power.

Transform Past Wounds into Present Wisdom

"Problems cannot be solved by the same level of thinking that created them. We must raise our level of awareness."
—Albert Einstein

I have experienced many challenges and hardships throughout my life. When I experience a challenge today, I accept that it cannot be solved on the superficial level that created it. I must process and integrate it and bring myself to a new level of awareness and understanding. Doing so will create an opportunity to learn, grow and overcome the challenge. Times of challenge offer opportunities to learn the greatest lessons of life. If I cannot see the gift or learning opportunity in a challenge I simply say, "I presently do not have the awareness or understanding to fully embrace this experience, so simply observe it and who I am being. In time I will move to new vantage points to fully integrate this opportunity."

If you want to have better co-workers, focus on being the type of colleague you'd like to work with. If you are unhappy with your marriage, focus on becoming the partner you would like to be with. If you have a symptom, sickness or disease, focus on being the person with radiant health and vitality. If you want others to trust and respect you, focus on becoming a more compassionate and loving person. What we focus on inside ourselves projects into our subatomic matrix, changing our cellular make-up and physiology and creating new magnetic attractors.

These attractors act as vibrational magnets that create a life based on where you are resonating. Your future life will be attracted to you similar to the way metal filings are attracted to a magnet. Think of your future life in the weeks, months and years that lie ahead. That is your future self and it creates a future pull that has a very specific magnetic field. Your atoms and cells create specific physiologies that are like magnets. These inner magnets will be attracted to certain outer magnetic fields and be repelled from others. Accepting that life is an inside-out job allows your free will and choice to shift your inner world to create and live a more profound outer life.

Living from the End

"The world is only in the eyes of the maker.
Do not believe it is outside of yourself."
—A Course in Miracles

There is a powerful yet subtle difference between working toward an outcome or result versus thinking, acting and feeling from it. Working toward something is akin to being open-ended, vague and even on a "flaky" journey that has no end in sight. Sure, you may be achieving small goals and accomplishments along the way, but you'll always be stuck in the mentality of needing to *go somewhere*, as opposed to creating the inner state of power and unwavering certainty that is in the experience of achieving it.

I spent more than 14 years studying martial arts, and on many occasions we attempted to break solid concrete or wood blocks with our bare hands or feet. There was a palpable difference between those who were successful and unsuccessful in achieving this mind-boggling feat. It had everything to do with their ability to live from the end.

As a young boy I was stuck in my ego and full of attachments to how I wanted to break those blocks. Every time I attempted to break a block, I ended up injuring myself and being unsuccessful. After many years of lifting heavy weights and developing a chiseled, strong body on the outside, I was still weak and disempowered from the inside. From this place I still found myself unsuccessful and frustrated. (Especially since people with half my outer strength were accomplishing.) I learned that it had nothing to do with what was on the outside and everything to do with where I was within myself.

After many years of practice, my sensei (master teacher) taught me how to connect with that power within myself. Instead of focusing on breaking the block I focused on a place beyond it. Within myself I already had to know that my hand was at this point of completion and had transcended the space. That space between my hand and the bottom of the block became secondary because I was already living from that point of completion, rather than focusing on the difficulty of getting there. This is the secret to living from the end.

When we make our future dreams a present fact, our entire inner ecology and physiology transforms. This is the essence of living from the inside out. It's living with the feelings and emotions of our desires already fulfilled. This is because life does not follow our predictions; instead, it answers to our emotional expectations. In short, the focus of our inner awareness becomes the reality of our outer world experiences. We must move beyond choosing a new reality to *becoming* that new reality from within, consciously and emotionally.

All of life is entirely an inside-out job. Life is a journey, and working from the inside out allows us to taste the juiciest fruit along the way. For authentic happiness and fulfillment we all must work on mastery and hold ourselves accountable for the change we can create in every situation and experience.

Once you embrace life as an inside-out process, you will experience changes within yourself first. Over time these changes will spill out into the world. You'll create a harmonious relationship with yourself and then with others. This is a continuous process of renewal and regeneration based on natural laws that govern human growth and evolution.

Start Living the Inside-Out Journey

"Life's challenges are not supposed to paralyze you,
they're supposed to help you discover who you are."
—*Bernice Johnson Reagon*

Do these exercises to empower yourself to live from the inside out:

1. Everything that's happened in your life, no matter how challenging, has served a greater purpose. Every person, place, thing and experience has two sides to its equation. When you can see life for what it truly is in its fullness and vastness you realize that everything has light and love, and you can be grateful.

Look over your entire life and find every significant experience that you felt was negative in some way. That is, you felt it did not help you and was not aligned with your life's purpose, mission or destiny. Then ask yourself how this experience served you or somebody else at the time. Now ask yourself how that experience has helped you become the person you are today. Write this down, making a long list of how that experience has assisted your life. Do not stop until you feel a deep sense of gratitude for every experience.

This is the key. You must continue making this gratitude list until every cell in your body is in a place of gratitude. Be patient; it will happen.

You will see that everything is in perfect equilibrium and has always been guiding you.

How will you live your life knowing that everything in the universe is conspiring to help you fulfill your destiny? Write down how you will now live your life.

2. All your ideas, thoughts and behaviors can be expressed or repressed depending on what you perceive as missing in your life. These perceived voids drive your values and therefore occupy your attention. Your hierarchy of values determines how you see and act upon your world. This is how you create your life.

Make a list of the top 4 things for each of the following (repeat items in different sections if applicable):

- The space in which you spend the most time
- Where you focus your energy
- How you spend your money and invest your time
- The thoughts that dominate your mind
- What your daily intentions are
- What you spend time focusing on and visualizing
- What inspires you
- Your goals
- What you accomplish every day

Look through your lists to find the things that occur multiple times. The things that occur most frequently are the highest on your value list. The things occurring less frequently are lowest on your value list. This may be a surprise for you.

You can begin to fulfill your dreams and live from your infinite powerful self by simply changing the things that dominate your space, focus, time, money, and thoughts.

For example, if you've never had aches and pains or a disease or illness, but you know you're not the poster child for radiant vitality and optimal living, you likely don't make your health a top priority. It has never been a significant void and you've been able to simply cruise by without giving it much thought. But today you notice you've put on some extra weight and decide you would like to value your health as a greater priority to start looking and feeling healthier. You may want to read some magazines and books on health and vitality and put them on your coffee table. You may want to go online to get more information so you're focused and engaged on health and vitality. You may want to put inspiring pictures or posters in your home or set them as your desktop wallpaper. You may want to hire a personal trainer or join a fitness club. You may want to go to the sports store and buy training clothes and equipment. The list is endless—just know that the more something occupies your space, time and energy, the more you will begin to value it.

The same can be said for aspects of your life you want to change. For example, you may have been an athlete your entire life and everything that occupies your space is related to that. One day you decide that you want to know more about art and music. All you have to do is remove the things that create triggers for being an athlete and replace them with the things that will keep you focused on art and music and watch how your knowledge, interest and values begin to shift to the things that occupy your space and time the most.

What do your values have to be so you can create your ultimate destiny—so you may be the best person you could possibly be and have the greatest impact in your lifetime? The choice is yours and it all lies deep within you!

3. With these new items occupying your space, time, focus and energy, begin to let yourself bask in the feelings and emotions as if you've already become that which you desire. Spend time every morning and every evening in these states. Think of these feelings and emotions as muscles that require constant exercise to become stronger. As your inner world changes, your outer world will mirror those changes. Spend as much time as you can each day living from this place within yourself.

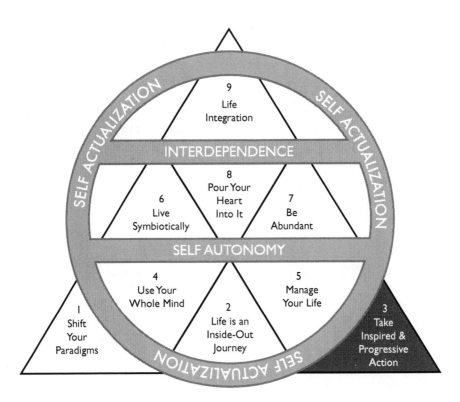

CHAPTER 5

STRATEGY 3 — TAKE INSPIRED AND PROGRESSIVE ACTION

"Whenever a warrior decides to do something, he must go all the way, but he must take responsibility for what he does. No matter what he does, he must know first why he is doing it, and then he must proceed with his actions without having doubts or remorse about them."
—Carlos Castaneda

Over the past several years, one of my favorite pastimes has been training as an ultra-endurance athlete. I derive so many benefits from training and racing in these challenging events. One of the amazing things I have found is that I am able to step out of my body and actually take on a new perspective of myself. For example, during one of my major races, a 100-mile ultra-marathon, I was able to see where I was in relation to the entire mountainous course. It was as if I could see myself running through the trails from the perspective of being in a helicopter above the mountains.

We all need to find things that deeply inspire us because they help us grow, evolve and step into our power zone. It doesn't matter what they are, whether sports, art, music, or anything else that you feel called to. These are the activities that give you a longer, more fulfilling life.

By engaging in inspired activities we become more self-aware and are able to share our gifts with the world. They allow us to gain a greater ability to remove ourselves from our feelings, moods, and thoughts. This creates an ability to observe the most important paradigm we have, our "self paradigm." This is our basic blueprint of how we watch and create our world. Why did I respond that way? Why did that hurt my feelings? Why do I behave and act the way I do? These are just a few of the questions that we can answer through self-awareness.

When we engage in inspired action, our new self-awareness allows us to continually address who we are becoming. Yet, if we choose not to begin taking progressive action we allow the paradigms that others create for us to dictate our lives. We begin to see ourselves from the paradigms, opinions, and perceptions of other people. The most common linguistics I have observed are cross-cultural and tend to fall into a couple categories:

- "Why are you acting like that?"
- "You look so tired."
- "I can't believe you actually did well."
- "What's wrong with you?"

These are merely the projections of the self-doubt, weaknesses and character flaws of the people giving the opinions. The challenge is that, for many people, these opinions come from people they respect—partners, parents, siblings, bosses, co-workers, or friends. We must take into account the things others say, but we also must filter them carefully.

Living our lives based on the opinions of others forces us to judge ourselves more and more. We begin to think we're not good enough, strong enough, smart enough, and attractive enough. We begin to live life reactively and we regress. We stop living life from the inside-out and start letting everything external to us dictate our lives.

What happens then? We become powerless. We become reactive to our physical environment. If the weather is poor we feel lousy. If the weather is nice we feel great. We begin to follow the "herd mentality" of humanity and do what others are doing without deciding whether those things are actually what we want to do. Herd mentality is what I call one of the diseases of humanity. The remedy is to become a critical thinker. Reactive people behave, act and are driven by feelings, their environments and their circumstances. These people's lives are emotionally driven from the outside and based on the behavior of others. Living this way inadvertently gives influence and control to others' character weaknesses.

Pain is Inevitable; Suffering is a Choice

"In spite of your fear, do what you have to do."
—Chin-Ning Chu

When we become more self-aware, we become more proactive in changing our paradigms, thoughts and actions. This allows us to take initiative and to take responsibility for our lives. Living life in this manner allows us to make decisions and take actions based on what we value most. We begin to live according to our value system—from ideas, behaviors, emotions and thoughts that are rational, well-planned and internalized. It is only at this stage that we begin living life from the inside out.

In order to better understand my own life I wanted to reach way back and learn what created my father's paradigms as a child during the early years of India's independence. During my studies, I became greatly interested in Mohandas K. Gandhi, the man who helped achieve India's independence and its eventual separation from Great Britain and Pakistan. I have studied his life in great depth. Gandhi said that nobody can take another person's self-respect if it is not given to them. People who take inspired and progressive action do not give away their self-respect. What we experience is based on what we permit ourselves to do, not what we permit others to do to us or on our behalf.

Taking inspired and progressive action will affect every area of your life. In fact, this behavior will transform your life from ordinary to extraordinary. So many people told me that only after a year of being an endurance athlete I would never be able to complete races that lasted more than 20 hours. Instead, I listened to the voice and vision from within and ignored the naysayers. When you are guided from within you will challenge the small minds and opinions of others because you are stepping out of herd mentality. As an ultra-marathoner I have participated in races that lasted more than 21 consecutive hours, with breaks no longer than two minutes. During a race of this magnitude it was as if I was living life in fast-forward. I experienced the duality of life's thoughts and emotions fully. There are times of ease and comfort and times of extreme angst and pain. There is joy and elation, and there is sadness and sorrow. There are thoughts of trust and confidence and thoughts of fear and doubt. When I felt great, running was effortless. When I was in extreme pain, discomfort, doubt or anguish, I would step back mentally and simply observe myself. I knew I was far greater than what I was feeling. I made a conscious choice not to suffer.

You may not believe that suffering is a choice. I assure you that if an experience is internalized, integrated and observed, you will learn and choose not to suffer. I was running 100 miles non-stop at a pace that got me a podium finish. It was inevitable that I would experience pain. Yet, suffering was still a choice. I did not let it affect my character. Times of greatest challenge forge our character; they give us the freedom to handle more and inspire others to do the same. Choosing to transcend suffering and painful circumstances inspired me to lift my life to new levels.

When you choose to do something that is inspired from within, that idea, action and behavior is extraordinary for you. Following through on that inspiration will create a radical change in your life. On the other side of that accomplishment you will become a different person. You will be more powerful, purposeful and inspired. You will create more results in every area of your life. After I completed that 100-mile race I knew that I could accomplish anything in my life. All of a sudden there was no limit to what my life could become. If I could think it, I could achieve it. The inspiration and progressive action you take is just a confirmation to the world that you want it badly enough despite the pain and discomfort that may arise. You will become the person that is worthy of that accomplishment. Gandhi said, "We must be the change that we want to see in the world." He also said, "Our greatness lies not in remaking the world but in continually remaking ourselves." There will always be challenges and obstacles in life. Yet know that whatever your mind can conceive, you can achieve.

Quitters Never Win—and Winners Never Quit

*"We are continually faced by great opportunities
brilliantly disguised as insoluble problems."*
—*Lee Iacocca*

Throughout my years of study I learned that to be successful in life I had to choose to take action, no matter what. The faster I acted the faster I would learn, grow and reap the rewards. I would be able to choose my responses to circumstances and create new experiences. When I first began my postsecondary journey I was taking a first-year university course in English. Although I had all the necessary prerequisites, the professor was not my biggest fan. I was still in the process of getting cultured and learning how intellectual people interacted and spoke. It was a foreign and scary world for me. I had a very poor vocabulary and still spoke with a lot of slang. My formal introduction was something like, "Yow, check this out!" It did not go over well with this professor.

When I handed in my first paper I got a big fat "F" for FAIL. I went to my professor's office to see how I could improve, but she let me hear it with absolutely no filters. "What the hell are you doing in my class?" she demanded. "This is not university-level writing. I can't even look at this. You are pathetic—what a joke. It's so bad I don't even know where to start."

I stood there speechless. I wanted to sink my fist into her face. My entire body began to tremor like a volcano erupting from within. I was not accustomed to anybody talking to me like that. I didn't want to do anything I would regret, so I just ran out of her office without saying a word. The tears were pouring down my face as every derogatory word I could spew at her and action I could take against her ran through my head.

I walked out the school doors and decided that university was a joke and wasn't for me. In my first month I was going to quit. I thought of every reason why I shouldn't have gone back. Yet I could not deny what she was saying to me. I disagree with her delivery and communication style, but she was right: my writing was pathetic and clearly not at a university level. Thankfully, I channeled my rage and anger through an intense workout at the gym and meditated in a hot steam room to integrate all of it. The next day I woke up and looked myself up and down intensely in the mirror. I finally stopped at my eyes and gazed deeply into myself and thought: *No way, I am better than this. I'm not letting somebody else dictate my destiny.* I was not going to be reactive. I got inspired. I took action. I took action immediately that morning.

I went to the head of the English department. Synchronously, he was available. I told him how poor my essay was and how I wanted to improve. He listened to me for almost an hour. He recommended a "how-to" writing book and said I should keep a pocket dictionary on me at all times. I read the book cover to cover in two days. It was the first book I had ever read all the way through. That book was the first of many great empowering gifts, as I began to systematically improve my writing over the next year. He also told me that I would expand my vocabulary by looking up every word I heard but didn't know the exact meaning of, and then writing down its definition.

The dictionary task was daunting. After all, I was still a high-school drop-out trying to fake it until I made it. I was writing down dozens of words every day. Each night I would put the words into sentences to ensure I fully understood their meanings and applications. I would also pronounce them so I could begin to use them in my everyday conversations. Every time I had a break I would walk around the school and look for groups of different people that I thought looked very intelligent. I would sit closely and eavesdrop, writing down every word that I did not

113

know. I did this throughout my entire ten years of postsecondary education. Even today when I come across a word I don't understand, I find myself acting like a dictionary, breaking it down into its roots and then trying to fully understand its meaning.

I learned a powerful lesson when I received that F. I chose not to react to my professor and not to let her opinions of me dictate how I thought about myself and become my self-fulfilling prophecy. I got inspired. I took action. I took action immediately. I did it proactively and progressively over the next ten years. I took initiative and I took control. Today when I look back at that emotional day when that teacher shared her lens of me, I am in a deep place of gratitude. She had given me a phenomenal gift. She said it tactlessly, but clearly that was required to drive me to change. Her words drove me to strive for more and led to the synchronous events of the next day and ten years of postsecondary education. Becoming an honors student, graduating at the top of all my programs on the dean's list with distinctions, winning several awards, scholarships and creating this book may never have been possible if I did not take action that day.

Taking inspired and progressive action allows us to create a path and make commitments to ourselves. That in turn allows us to become more conscious and self-aware. We learn our strengths and let them grow. We become aware of our weaknesses and can create change. We essentially build the strength of our character based on our own experiences and lenses. We become more on-purpose by harnessing our power and commitment to personal growth, mastery and evolution.

Life Mastery Wheel

*"The greatest danger for all of us is not that our aim is
too high and we miss it, but that it is too low and we reach it."*
—Michelangelo

It is vitally important to be crystal clear on what you desire in every area
of your ideal life. In my personal development programs, at drsukhi.com,
I define 10 distinct areas in which we all must take inspired action if we
are to fulfill our greatest potential:

- Intellectual life
- Physical life
- Character
- Emotional life
- Spiritual life
- Family life
- Social life
- Financial life
- Vocational life
- Quality of life

Mastering these 10 areas of life will enable you to create and live your
life in your ideals. I encourage you to become a member of this amazing and growing community by taking inspired action right now, if you
haven't already. You will get the latest and greatest information that I have
tested both personally and professionally for more than two decades. To
join, simply go to drsukhi.com and enter your name and email address
in the opt-in box. Every week you will receive relevant high-value con-
tent, coaching and inspiration. You will also be able to connect with me
personally. Living beyond your finite body and mind and accessing your
inner power to fulfill your dreams will become your new reality.

Get a Crystal Clear Vision

*"When the voice and vision on the inside becomes louder and clearer
than the opinions of others on the outside, you've mastered your life."*
—John Demartini

Jack Canfield is one of the creators of the internationally renowned
book series Chicken Soup for the Soul. Before anybody knew who Jack
was, he had a vision for the original book. His idea was bigger than
most people could conceive. In fact, many people in the publishing
world thought his idea would be a grand failure. He took inspired action
by writing the book and then going to New York to sell it to a publisher.
He lined up meetings with 22 publishers in three days. Every single
publisher rejected his proposal.

Despite the massive rejection, Jack's vision was so clear that he did not
give up. He went to Book Expo America and began pitching his book
to more publishers. He was rejected another 120 times.

Now, I want you to fully appreciate the tenacity of this man and his
partner. They had been rejected more than 140 times. Most people
would have given up after their fifth or sixth rejection. He went beyond
30, 50, 75, and 100 rejections. In fact, he was rejected 144 times—and
then one publisher actually said "yes."

One important part of taking inspired action is doing it consistently and
progressively, regardless of what's going on in the people, places and
things around you. You must take steps that proceed forward, advancing
toward your ultimately destiny. If Jack Canfield never took progressive
action, you and I probably wouldn't know who he is. Today, Chicken
Soup for the Soul has more than 200 titles, with 115 million copies in
print in 47 languages. I have read many of his books. Perhaps his great-

est gift to the world is that his books have touched so many lives and hearts.

You have that much power within you. You have the power to see your ideas through to fruition in the physical world. It is impossible to transform your life without touching the lives of the people around you.

The Key is Vibrational Resonance

"If you limit your choices only to what seems possible or reasonable, you disconnect yourself from what you truly want, and all that is left is a compromise."
—R. Fitz

It is a universal law that, when done properly, taking inspired and progressive action will enable you to make what you want in any area of your life to actually begin wanting *you*. Does this sound powerful? It's one of the most powerful tools that completely transformed my life and the lives of people like Jack Canfield. My intention is to teach you how to use this law starting right now as you take inspired action to fulfill your dreams.

When it comes to applying universal laws and principles, there is a caveat: you must adhere strictly to the designated criteria if you're to be successful in creating desirable results. Conversely, working against the criteria can bring you an immense amount of frustration, heartache and pain.

The first step is to have the right thoughts of what you want to create. You must know what it is that you desire. Now, 99% of people in the world will start and end here. Most of them will also refer to this as "positive thinking" or "forward creation." After investing their time and energy into positive thinking exercises and not getting all their desired outcomes (or perhaps none at all), many people get frustrated and give up. Their conclusion usually sounds something like, "That crap doesn't work."

The Law of Vibrational Resonance states that you will attract into your life the people, places and things that are of the same vibration or tone as you. In other words, like attracts like and repels everything else. Your thoughts are not your internal subatomic vibration; they are the first step in changing your internal thermostat. This is why positive thinking does not work for very long. Personally, I was a student of the positive thinking movement in my late teens and early twenties. Several years and hundreds of books later, I learned why it wasn't working. The idea that we create our reality solely by our thoughts is a crippling half-truth.

Quantum physics tells us that we are made of tiny subatomic particles that vibrate at a certain frequency. This science has also shown us that other people, places, events and things are also made of these same basic structures that also vibrate at a specific frequency. This means that everything in life is composed of energy. In other words, with a high-powered microscope you would see that the entire world is made up of atoms moving and vibrating throughout space. One of the best illustrations of this is in the movie *The Matrix*. There's a scene close to the end of the first original movie in which the entire matrix collapses and Neo (Keanu Reeves) sees everything as pure vibration and energy. Therefore, nothing is actually still—everything is in a constant state of flux, change and resonance.

Get In Tune

"Energy is an eternal delight, and he who desires,
but acts not, breeds pestilence."
—William Blake

Everything you have experienced in your life and everything you will experience is from the resonance within you. This is because the frequency at which you're resonating can only attract to you the things that match that frequency. This has a lot more to do with positive and negative thinking. Whether you're aware of it or not, like gravity, the Law of Vibrational Resonance is always in effect.

When I first learned about this law I was absolutely furious. *Do you mean I wanted all those crappy things to happen to me when I was growing up?* I thought. *I would never want anyone to go through what I went through growing up, especially not a child.* I kept thinking this law was incorrect. It wasn't until I understood it fully that it finally made sense.

Most people do not want illness, disease, tragedy, poverty, abuse, fear or isolation in their lives. They have not intentionally created their realities. Most people also believe that success and fulfillment are byproducts of where you live, who you are, and your status, accomplishments or level of education. The truth is that the Law of Vibrational Resonance could not care about any of this.

Life's All About Energy

"Energy cannot be created, nor can it be destroyed,
it can only be transformed from one form to another."
—First Law of Thermodynamics

Everything in the universe is energy, including you and me. In fact, you have enough power in the form of energy within you to light up an entire city for a month. Can you believe that? Yet we have been conditioned not to use our natural internal resources to improve and transform our lives.

You are reading this book right now and you will be a different person when you finish it. I ask you right now to stop giving away your power! I stopped giving away my power when I was 18—and as a result, I've transformed my life. If you've experienced any hardships or challenges in your life that you didn't welcome, it was simply because you were unaware of what you were doing.

When you learn to take inspired and progressive action daily and tap into your true power and true resonance, you will manifest your desires and your ideal life. You can begin to shift your resonance right now by simply thinking about the things in your life that you are grateful for. Think about every area of your life, no matter how big or small, and start being grateful for it. When your system is brought to a new reso-nance you can begin to change your thoughts and focus on what you'd like to master in all 10 areas of your life.

Get Your Energy in Motion

*"Passion is energy. Feel the power that comes
from focusing on the things that excite you."*
—Oprah Winfrey

The next step in this powerful process is to begin to "feel" what it's like to actually have the things you're focusing on. This means that you must put strong emotions behind your thoughts. This is vitally important—you must feel it to your core. Most people who think they're applying this law completely are actually being incomplete in this area. Emotions are the doorway to accessing your power! Remember:

Emotion = Energy + Motion

The universe will now respond to this shift in your resonance by repelling the people, places and things that are not of this resonance and attracting the ones that are. Sound simple? It is! But don't confuse simple with easy. Inspired action must be taken daily, consistently and progressively. You can't just think about your ideal life for a week or two, generate a few emotions, and wait for the universe to deliver what you desire. This is your life: what is it worth to you? It must be a daily practice.

There are caveats to this. What I've learned from experience is that the greater our desire to achieve or change something in our worlds, the more elusive our power may become. This sounds contradictory. Why is it so? Sometimes, our attachments are strong because they're anchored by ego. The ego gives an illusion of power, when in fact its energy and tone is weak and powerless.

On the flip side, the most powerful human state is love. Begin to love all that you are and you'll love what you do and who you're becoming. From this place, a one-degree shift in focus will attract that which your heart desires.

Connect Within

"You can be anything you want to be, if only you believe
with sufficient conviction and act in accordance with your faith;
for whatever your mind can conceive and believe, you will achieve."
—Napoleon Hill

Your thoughts will begin creating pictures and words that will connect you to your heart, and that will build feelings that will become emotions. The heart actually has 15 times the vibrational frequency of the brain—this is why the ego is weak and thoughts are not enough. You must be willing to live every day as if everything you desire to create an extraordinary life and the ensuing results are guaranteed to you. Every day you must focus on this. Doing so will allow you to transcend needing it and, instead, simply become it. If you feel within yourself that you still "need it," the resonance within you has not reached the threshold for it to manifest.

When you connect within you will be inspired, which is living "in spirit." Take progressive action from this place and you're empowered to leverage the Law of Vibrational Resonance; do not stop until you are living your life in your ideals in all 10 areas.

Do not concern yourself with others and what they may think. Dr. Amen is a child and adult psychiatrist, self-help advisor and author.

He has a rule that I love called the 18/40/60 Rule. He says when you're 18, you worry about what everybody is thinking of you; when you're 40, you care a lot less about what others think of you; when you're 60 you realize nobody's been thinking about you at all. Are you picking up what I'm putting down here?

Transforming the World

"Miracles occur naturally as expressions of love.
They are performed by those who temporarily have
more for those who temporarily have less."
—A Course In Miracles

It's important to understand that we are not observers of this process called life. We are participatory agents playing a vital role in how the universe unfolds. As conscious participants we're actually part of everything we observe and witness. Scientifically it is still not fully clear how the world around us responds, but we do know that the universe is altered by the presence from within each of us.

From moment to moment we are participating in the universe's creation. That's because we're wired to create. On a quantum level we're all connected to each other through some kind of quantum net or soup. And the miraculous thing about this is that small changes in our individual lives can create extraordinary shifts in our world and even on the entire universe.

A great example of this is the "butterfly effect." In chaos theory, this effect states that a butterfly that flaps its wings in Tokyo can lead to a hurricane in Brazil a month later. The reality is that butterfly effects are being created every day; we just need to connect the dots to witness their presence.

Our inner worlds and outer experiences are intimately related. This is well documented in the acts of prayers and meditation. A friend of mine is deeply connected to Transcendental Meditation (TM). In the summer of 1993 he was a part of a group that tested this idea for eight weeks in Washington, D.C. as part of a national demonstration project to reduce violent crimes and improve governmental effectiveness.

In the first week there were about 500 TM practitioners, and in the final week there were close to 4,000. Researchers found that by the end of the eight weeks there was a drop of nearly 25% in homicides, rapes and assaults. Profoundly, the crime rates decreased more substantially as more people practiced TM. The greater the number, the more leverage the power within each person created.

There have also been other experiments using prayer for peace, where statistically significant declines also occurred. Things like traffic accidents, emergency room visits, violence and crime all decreased. As you can see, when we move beyond our finite body and mind and step into our infinite power, that vibration not only transforms our lives, but it also transforms the people, places and things around us because we are all intimately connected. The take-home point with all these experiments was that all these people were not focusing on decreasing crime or violence; they were simply focused on creating peace within themselves. That's it! And that state of peace within all of them created a similar state within other people who had no idea what was occurring. As their internal states changed, their outward behavior also changed. It's impossible to transform your life without transforming the lives of those around you.

The interesting thing that also occurred in all these experiments is that once they stopped, all the violence and crime returned. And in some cases it returned to even more intense and greater levels. This is why we can't just take inspired action once and hope all the ducks of our extraordinary life will line up for us. We must continue to tune in and connect to that power within ourselves daily and progressively. Choosing our reality and life is not something we do for a moment. Personally, I work it more than a full-time job. Because once we stop feeling as if our new reality no longer exists, the effects of our decision are over as well.

The piece I want you take from this is that reality making isn't something that we choose to do: it's something that we are for every moment of our entire lives. Because our feelings and emotions are the way we choose and we're feeling with emotions every second of every day. Therefore, we're constantly creating our lives and destiny whether we know it or not.

Extraordinary people forge their own paths in life, and you, my friend, are extraordinary. That's why you're reading this book. You need to base your choices, decisions, dreams and actions on your ideals—not the goals, desires, opinions, and judgments of your friends, parents, spouse, children or co-workers. Stop worrying about what other people think about you and follow your heart. As you begin to take action toward mastering your life you will begin to care a lot less about what other people think of you and care a lot more about what others think of themselves. That is a truly powerful and inspired place to live from.

Start Taking Inspired and Progressive Action

"You weren't an accident. You weren't mass-produced. You aren't an assembly-line product. You were deliberately planned, specifically gifted, and lovingly positioned on the Earth by a Master Craftsman."
—Max Lucado

Exercises to take inspired and progressive action:

1. **Map your Life Mastery Wheel** to see how well you're navigating through life. Take out a sheet of paper and draw a large circle similar to Diagram 4. Divide that circle into 10 equal parts and label each with one of the 10 areas of life that require inspired and progressive action. Within each area determine how well you are fulfilling your ultimate destiny for that part of your life. For example, in the area of physical health if you're expressing radiant vitality, health and fitness you would give yourself a 9 or 10. If you're health is average you'd give yourself a 5 and if it was horrible you'd give yourself a 1 or 2. Think of the hub of this wheel as 0 and the outer edge as 10. Once you know where you are for your physical life shade in the portion of that pie up to that number. Continue this shading process for all 10 areas of life. Now look at your wheel. Is it symmetrical like the one on the right of Diagram 4 or is it asymmetrical similar to the wheel on the left of Diagram 4? The Life Mastery Wheel will give you a reality check as to where you need to focus more time and energy to take action. How well would your wheel roll down the street? That's how well you're moving through life.

LIFE MASTERY WHEEL

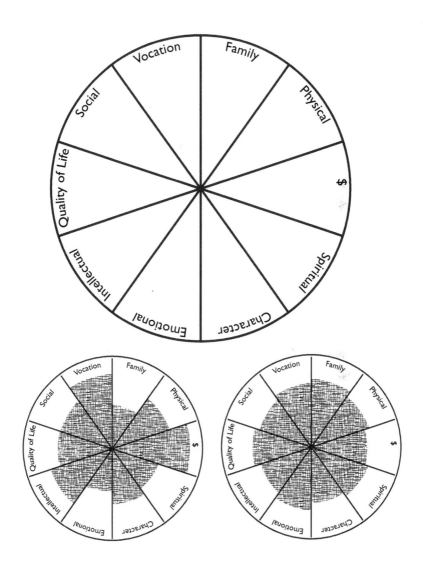

Diagram 4

2. **Get crystal clear about what you want.** Now that you know which areas of your life you need to improve this should be clearer. If you are vague, too general, or have doubt you will not manifest your deepest desires and fulfill your dreams. You must get out of your way by knowing what you want before you begin.

    Find a quiet and relaxing space. Lie on your back with your arms to your sides, palms facing the sky. Close your eyes and begin taking long, slow, deep breaths, expanding your diaphragm with each inhalation. After a few minutes, begin to ask yourself what you desire in all 10 areas of your life. Pick one area to focus on each day.

    Listen quietly for the answers. They may come in the form of words, stories, pictures, feelings or emotions. Keep a journal close by and write down everything once you feel you have fully explored that area of your life. After 10 days you should know exactly what you desire for every area of your life.

3. **One area at a time, form pictures of you living your life in your ideals.** This is similar to remembering an experience from the past, but this time you are using forward visions of your new future.

    Now that you have a picture in your mind, you must connect to it emotionally by feeling it, taking it from your head to your heart. The experience must feel so real and compelling that you can touch it. You must feel that it's already in your possession. You must see and feel every tiny detail: you can touch it, smell it, taste it. It becomes a part of you and you experience the joy of it, right here, right now. Use all your senses to generate the emotional fuel to allow it to manifest in the real world. This is what will allow you to shift your internal thermostat to become a vibrational match.

4. **Internalize the feeling within you.** This will allow your desires to be a part of you. As you continue to go deeper and internalize, you will shift from a place of needing to a place of deserving your desires. You will know you are there when every cell within you can be in a place of gratitude and you can emanate a feeling of thanks.

5. **Be open to all forms.** The universe will not manifest your desires out of thin air and they likely will not fall into your lap (although it's possible and I have personally seen it happen). The universe will open up pathways and opportunities that will allow you to create your ideal life. Therefore, you must continue to take inspired and progressive action until your requests are fulfilled. You must do this with 100% faith, knowing that what you are asking for is coming. You must be living with 100% congruence at every possible level. Do not waver; the universe is always watching.

Apply this to all 10 areas to master your life. By combining your focus, thoughts, feelings and actions the universe will reward you every single time, with no exceptions. Be patient and make the time to practice this daily. You will begin to rock extraordinary health, wealth and happiness in no time, because that is your ultimate destiny.

6. **Harness the power of prayer.** When I was 18, I sat at the edge of my deathbed and began to pray. I wasn't really sure what I was praying for or how to do it, but I innately just found myself

praying. As strange as it may sound to you, today I still find myself getting on my knees and praying. If you want to tap into that infinite power within yourself and make this world more of an extraordinary place, prayer is a powerful tool. Each day pray for yourself and the world around you. Create the feelings and emotions within yourself during your prayer. Peace, love, inspiration, gratitude, enthusiasm and compassion are the most powerful emotional states.

For more support and guidance in mastering this powerful process, please visit www.drsukhi.com.

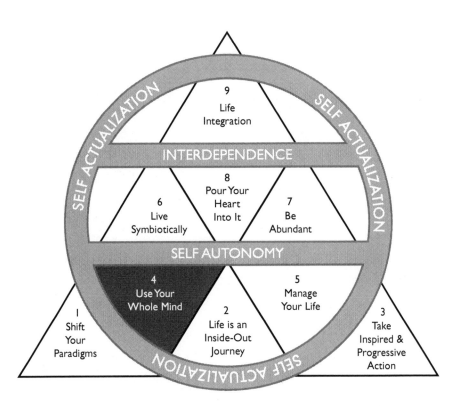

CHAPTER 6

STRATEGY 4 — USE YOUR WHOLE MIND

"Whatever you hold in your mind will tend to occur in your life.
If you continue to believe as you have always believed,
you will continue to act as you have always acted.
If you continue to act as you have always acted,
you will continue to get what you have always gotten.
If you want different results in any area of your life,
all you have to do is change your mind."
—Unknown

I've always been interested in why people behaved the way they did, made certain choices, took certain actions—and ultimately how they created their lives. This fascination forced me to delve into how our minds actually functioned. What I've learned is that the mind is an extension of the brain and is the most amazing computing system known to humanity.

Our brains are made up of two separate halves. Each of these hemispheres is connected by a thick band of nerves called the corpus callosum. This neural band acts as the network connection between the two powerful information processors, allowing them to communicate. These two sides of the brain create two separate minds that see and interpret the world completely differently. Essentially, they create two separate people and worlds.

The right brain creates a mind that solely uses feelings. It uses large spatial orientations with "big picture" ideas. This mind allows imagination to rule. It sees symbols and images, the present moment, philosophy and religion. It can "get it" and derive a bigger meaning. This mind believes and appreciates. It is predominantly feminine energy. It will know the entirety of an object; it sees the whole. It sees function and is fantasy-based and intuitive. It presents possibilities and takes risk. Some extraordinary people like Albert Einstein, Thomas Edison, Leonardo da Vinci, Michelangelo, Oprah Winfrey and Bill Gates are all right-brain thinkers.

Conversely, the left brain creates a mind that solely uses logic. It is very detail-oriented and believes that facts rule. It sees words and language, the past and future, math and science. It can comprehend only what it sees; it cannot derive meaning. This mind knows and acknowledges through order. It is predominantly masculine energy. It will know an object's name. It sees the parts. It is reality-based, formulates strategies, is practical and is very conservative and safe.

When I learned this I finally realized why the questions I asked about life could not be fully answered.

In 1981, Roger Sperry won a Nobel Prize for his contributions to understanding the brain and mind. In 1973 he conducted "split-brain" experiments and concluded:

> The main theme to emerge . . . is that there appear to
> be two modes of thinking, verbal and nonverbal, rep-
> resented rather separately in left and right hemispheres
> respectively and that our education system, as well as
> science in general, tends to neglect the nonverbal form
> of intellect. What it comes down to is that modern
> society discriminates against the right hemisphere.

I was amazed to learn that over 90% of our educational system develops only one side of our existence, the left mind. This holds true for
college and university education, as well. The right mind has to just
figure things out for itself. In fact, research has shown that the majority of children live in their right brains before entering school. By the
time these children become adults, they'll use just 2% of their right
hemisphere. This is one of the reasons I am a strong advocate of healthy
children working with healers who cultivate balance within the entire
nerve system. It allows them to continue to develop and grow their
entire mind, creating a perfect balance and expression of their right and
left hemispheres.

Find the Balance

*"We know too much and feel too little. At least we feel too little of
those creative emotions from which a good life springs."*
—Bertrand Russell

To deny one of our powerful mind processors is to deny half our existence. We have all met people who are very logical, only see the facts and
do not take risks—these people are living from their left brain. We have
also met people who are extremely creative and see the possibilities and

big ideas of life—they are living from their right brain. If these two people met they would likely comment on each other's character flaws. But they are both simply looking in a mirror and seeing parts of themselves they have not fully realized or expressed. I believe that the consciousness we exhibit is the collective consciousness of whatever cells are functioning, and that both of our hemispheres complement one another as they create a single seamless perception of our reality of the world.

Life is about pursuing dynamic homeostasis or dynamic balance. If the cells and circuitry of the left mind are functioning well we would use face recognition to identify people, if it was not functioning well we could use our right minds circuitry and observe mannerisms, voice, and the gait of ones movement. A massive lesson for me was to continue to use my entire brain and mind. When somebody sets foot into my Centre for Optimal Living, I spend a lot of time in my left mind, getting the facts. I then shift to my right mind to see what is possible. I strive for a dynamic balance between my analytical knowledge and creative art. When I use my right and left minds equally, the transformations I've been able to help create in other people's lives have been humbling.

Optimal Living Begins with Great Health

"The doctor of the future will give no medicine,
but will interest patients in the care of the human frame,
in diet, and in the CAUSE and prevention of dis-ease."
—Thomas Edison

Western medicine is deeply rooted within the confines of the left brain. It has evolved and grown immensely. In times of emergency, crisis and trauma, it is the best system available to handle illness and disease. However, the public is beginning to evolve beyond this paradigm. People want more preventive care—and even wellness care—to take a more proactive approach toward optimal living and vitality. I believe for medicine to be fully realized it must move into the right brain and find the balance, as we have only seen half of what it has to offer. It is through this journey that we will be able to fully eradicate the epidemics of disease.

Medicine specializes in the treatment of symptoms, sickness and disease. This left-brain approach is based on managing diseases primarily through drugs and surgery. It treats the effects, not the cause. In this model there is no preventive or wellness care. Even early detection and specialized testing is still disease management. There is no service in this model that improves the health and well-being of the patient. Within this model people are told to go out and live their lives however they want, and if they get a problem they can then reactively manage it.

There is a direct correlation between the amount of money that is put into this system and the prevalence of disease, morbidity and mortality. Yes, you read that correctly. The more money put into our present healthcare system, the more diseases people are getting. That's because it is a disease management system disguised as a healthcare system. The third leading cause of death in North America today is medicine. That includes properly prescribed drugs and surgeries. This is the limitation of a left-brain creation. Albert Einstein said that the definition of insanity is doing the same thing over and over and expecting different results—let's stop the insanity.

Wellness care and optimal living is completely different. It embodies the left and right brain simultaneously. The education and services under this model actually increase the expression of a person's health, vitality and quality of life. Whether a person feels fantastic and has radiant vitality or is diseased and ill, they can benefit from wellness care. This model focuses on the cause, not the effects, of illness and disease. This model empowers and educates people to take accountability for their own health and life. Wellness care vastly transforms the quality of a person's life. It recognizes that the power that created all of us from two tiny cells inside our mother's body must be cultivated and fully expressed to live an extraordinary life. I have transformed the lives of tens of thousands of people through wellness care. Specifically, I have created 5 pillars of radiant health and optimal living that I encourage every person to practice to be their best.

5 Pillars of Radiant Health and Optimal Living:

1. Optimal mindset
2. Optimal nerve flow
3. Optimal nutrients & minerals
4. Optimal biomechanics & movement
5. Optimal stress & toxin reduction

Pure health, healing and the full expression of life come from the perfect balance of living in both minds. This has been my journey: to diligently strive to live in balance and harmony within my whole mind, expressing the strengths and qualities from both sides. If you do the same, it will completely change the way you look at and think about your world. It will radically transform what you create and the value you provide to the world. You will have the ability to be cognitively flexible enough to welcome change (right hemisphere), and yet remain concrete enough to stay committed to your journey (left hemisphere). Your life will become extraordinary.

The Whole is Greater than the Sum of its Parts

"A man is literally what he thinks."
—James Allen

When you use your whole mind, you can begin living with images, pictures, and paradigms of the end of your life as the frame of reference or criteria for examining your present life. Who you are and what you are doing today, tomorrow, next week, next month, and next year can all be seen in the context of the whole. This allows you to see what really matters most and keeps you accountable to stay on purpose toward living the life you actually see for yourself. This ensures each day is lived meaningfully and continually contributes to your bigger vision.

As biological creatures we are incredibly powerful beings. The neural networks in our nervous system communicate with other neurons in circuits, and their behavior can become highly predictable. For example, the more conscious attention we give a particular circuit (specific behaviors/attitudes/thoughts/outcomes), the more these circuits or patterns will run without any environmental input. Therefore, what you focus on continually creates a groove within your nervous system. And the more one focuses on it the deeper that groove becomes and the more challenging it is to jump out of it. When this is positive, we call the neural groove "being in flow." When it's negative, we call the groove a rut.

The whole nervous system and mind is also a "seek and find " instrument. It is designed to focus in on and discover whatever we are looking for. If I am looking for blue in the world then that is what I'll find everywhere. We'll even begin to lie to ourselves and turn other colors like purple into blue as well. At first this process is slow, but once that neural groove becomes deeper by staying focused on blue, we'll begin to see it everywhere. Give this a try by looking around your present surroundings.

The Right and Left Minds

"Perception is but a mirror, not a fact.
What I look on is my state of mind reflected outward."
—A Course In Miracles

The two hemispheres not only think about things in different ways, they also process emotions and body awareness differently too. The right mind is all about right here and now. It truly doesn't have a care in the world as it just skips down the street like a young child filled with joy and enthusiasm. It's that part of us that is extremely friendly, full of joy and happy. On the flip side, the left mind is caught up in the details and nitty-gritty of life. It keeps life on a very tight and rigid schedule and is oh so serious. In fact, it judges absolutely everything as being good or bad, right or wrong—especially ourselves.

Emotionally, the right mind loves the richness of this present moment and fills it with gratitude. It's loving, compassionate, and eternally optimistic. There are no judgments here because everything is seen on a continuum of relativity. It completely accepts things as they are. It's pouring rain outside: "That's cool." It's freezing: "Who cares, life is awesome." The right mind accepts life as it is. It knows who is taller or shorter, richer or poorer, but it makes absolutely no judgments, as it knows we are all equal co-creators of the human race.

The right mind thinks out of the box and is wide open to new possibilities. It doesn't care about the box that was created by the left mind. It is creative and appreciates chaos, as it knows that it's the first step in the creative process. The right mind is in tune with the body, intuition and that gut feeling. It celebrates freedom and couldn't care less about your past or become afraid of a perceived future that may or may not materialize. It honors your cells and sees your body as an amazing vehicle and gift that you use to navigate through life. Therefore, it cares about your body, your mental health and your relationships with all other people and the universe.

This highly conscious right mind even knows that every cell within us (except red blood cells) has the same infinite intelligence as the original zygote cell that was created by our mother's egg and father's sperm cell during conception. So it knows that we are the life force of the 50 trillion geniuses that are creating our being and life. The right mind knows we are intimately connected to each other in this very complex and intricate fabric of the entire cosmos called life and that is why it lives life to the beat of its own drum because it knows that anything and everything is possible.

With no boundaries or limitations the right mind knows we are all brothers and sisters and we're here to make this world a more conscious, loving, kinder, healthier, peaceful and extraordinary place.

As amazing and as powerful as our right minds are, the left mind is equally as amazing when used in perfect balance and harmony with the right. The left mind can take all the energy, information about the present time and all of the infinite possibilities created by the right mind and mold them into a purposeful, manageable plan of action. How great is that?

The left mind can communicate these ideas with the external world, including yourself. Yes, the left mind is also responsible for all that "mind chatter," but with the right mind it can be used to maintain your identity and purpose, and keep you separate from the eternal flow. Therefore, you become a single solid that's separate from the whole. This may sound counterintuitive, but it gives us contrast and with contrast we can contribute to the greater whole in new ways by seeing it with new eyes and a new perspective. This is what drives human growth and evolution, allowing us to reconnect with the whole in even deeper and more profound ways.

While our right mind values humanity, our left mind values the economy and finances. The left mind also describes, judges and critically dissects everything in life. It lives by constantly contemplating and calculating everything. It's also a perfectionist and does an amazing job handling the areas of home and corporation. The left mind is also a great multi-tasker and thrives in performing as many tasks as possible all at the same time.

To create mastery in your life and move beyond the limitations of your finite body and mind, you must learn to fully express both minds in a harmonious, dynamic and balanced way. To prevent the left mind from becoming manic and overly controlling and the right from becoming lazy, you must cultivate and nurture the garden of both your minds.

The Power of Using Your Whole Mind

"Imagination is everything. It is a preview of
life's coming attractions."
—Albert Einstein

When you use your whole mind you have the power to shift between your left and right brains. Depending on the circumstance each side has its strengths and weaknesses. Yet once you deepen your ability to use both sides and turn each one on and off you can handle present situations better and create a preview of how your life may unfold. The intelligence and power that continually creates you from within is always trying to guide you in your life. When you begin to open this communication channel you will become more accountable for the choices and actions you take and where they will ultimately lead you.

I had a powerful experience of this when I was 17. I was attending the funeral of a friend who had just been murdered. Hundreds of people came. His family was devastated and very emotional. There were people of all ages and from all walks of life, from educated professionals to high school drop-outs and criminals. I can remember standing silently and observing everything. His mother walked over to my friends and me and started screaming at us. "You did this! You killed my son. He's gone—you are all a disgrace!" My friends just laughed and ignored her. I took her words to heart. What was she saying? I cared about her son. He was one of my close friends and I had spent the past week in tears, mourning his death.

Even at that young age I had an ability to shift my vibrational field to that of another person so I could truly empathize with them. This is what I did. I took on the lens of his mother and observed and felt everything she did. I completely stepped out of my left brain and into my right brain. My posture and physiology changed, I was feeling, sensing and observing, and I saw the present and my future self.

Every day we make choices that lead to roads with many forks and twists. I saw myself at my funeral. I was 18, still a kid. I saw my family, my friends, everyone that was important to me. I felt their pain, angst and sense of loss. I heard what my legacy was. They'd say I was a kid who had a lot of potential but simply made the wrong turns when I came to forks in the road. Deep down inside I knew this was not my legacy. I knew I was destined for so much more. This, along with several other synchronous events and experiences, allowed me to see the whole, to see my entire life. It was clear that I had made many mistakes and had to change my ways.

That day gave me a preview of my life's potential coming attractions. This is the gift of our right mind. Then I had to come back to the present and integrate all of it, straddling the division between my right and left minds. Unfortunately I delved too deep into my left mind again, and I let my ego control and continue to push and use force rather than stepping into power and flow.

Deepening Your Power

"The sky has never been the limit. We are our own limits.
It's then about breaking our personal limits and
outgrowing ourselves to live our best lives."
—Unknown

In life we all have many responsibilities. For me, I see being responsible as choosing how to respond to our surroundings (the sensory stimulation to our nervous system) in every moment. There are certain physiological programs that run a specific circuitry within us once they are triggered. For example, I used to have a temper that was as short as a wick on a firecracker. I would explode and lose it in seconds if that program was triggered by an external source. Once that circuitry was triggered, my brain would release chemicals that surged through my body, giving me a very real physiological experience.

Here is the gift of science: after that initial trigger that released those chemicals, within 90 seconds the chemical component of that anger gets completely dissipated from the blood and my autonomic neural response is over. This means that physiologically after 90 seconds I should no longer feel angry.

Now I don't know about you, but in my days of darkness sometimes I would remain angry and violent for several days, not a mere 90 seconds. Today, I know from neuroscience that if I remain angry after 90 seconds it is because I am making the constant and conscious choice to continually let that circuitry run by hooking into it with my left mind. But if I tune into my right mind and become fully present again and let go of the past or future, I can choose to unhook from that neurocircuitry and allow that reaction to completely melt away.

By understanding how your right and left mind influence you, you open the door to greater empowerment. Today I can connect and converse very well with an extremely left-minded, cerebral person as well as the complete opposite right-minded person who lives in the ether. For example, if one communicates with facts and figures I'll match that energy by going cerebral; if someone comes at me with ideas of possibility and potential I'll dance there with them. Always know that you have far more control over which one of your neural circuits run than you previously may have believed. I believe that finding some balance with your minds and choosing your circuitry to match the moment will allow you to own your power and make choices far more consciously.

The challenges, heartaches and letdowns in my life continue to serve me as powerful and valuable life lessons, simply because I choose to move to the right and see with eyes of compassion and gratitude. For me, developing and strengthening this muscle of becoming a nonjudgmental witness of myself and life has been one of my most daunting tasks. Yet with practice and patience I've become a student of mastering this awareness, and I invite you to join me.

Today when my mind runs judgmental, counterproductive or seemingly uncontrollable neural loops, I wait exactly 90 seconds for the emotional/physiological response to process and integrate. After 90 seconds

I speak to myself and I say with sincerity, "Thank you for the gift of these thoughts and emotions, but I'm no longer interested in thinking or feeling them, so stop bringing this shit up!" Sound harsh? It's actually quite effective. I'm simply asking my being to stop hooking into a specific circuitry.

At times the emotional response is so strong that this conversation with myself is not enough. Extreme responses take extreme measures. This is when I'll add a kinesthetic component. I'll go for a hard run or bike ride, or I'll lift heavy weights. During that time I'll use some pretty harsh language with myself to step back into my power. This may not be for everyone, but it works very well for me. What I've noticed today is that I rarely have to use these extreme measures because the circuitry of being happy, healthy, whole and powerful wants to naturally run.

Creating Your Life

*"You can never learn less; you can only learn more. The reason
I know so much is because I have made many mistakes."*
—Buckminster Fuller

There are times in our life that call for us to use our left mind and times that call for us to use our right mind. Having the perfect balance and flexibility to move between the two is what makes autonomous, happy and whole people who can overcome any challenge and create what we authentically desire.

Over the years I began to see my life in a completely different light. I saw that I wanted to have loving and kind relationships. I wanted to learn about the ways of the world. I dreamed about attending a university. I even grabbed books and walked around my house pretending that I had important things to read and write about. I wanted to authentically connect with people. I wanted to live beyond what Western society had glorified in my left mind.

When I look back now, I realize that all things in life are actually created at least twice. First we create an idea within our right mind. If we follow through on it, we then create its physical manifestation with the left mind. Building a home is a perfect example. My father is now a real estate developer. When we sit together we look at a piece of land and begin to create ideas within our right minds of what the homes could look like. Then we make a few simple sketches and further develop our ideas. This eventually leads to a blueprint and construction plans with our left minds. An immense amount of time and energy is spent before any physical structure is built. Over time, these ideas in our minds will manifest as buildings that people in the near future will call home.

Theodore Roosevelt said that all the resources we need are in our minds. Everything in life is created in our minds first. Every business, style of parenting, garden, painting, book, seminar, health condition—the list goes on and on. When you harness your entire mind you combine your right brain's visuals and big ideas with your left brain's logistics and facts to actively create a life that you love from the inside-out. When you harness the power of your whole mind you will begin to take more action and create new paradigms and perspectives. You will become more aware as the inner wisdom and guidance system deep within you fully emerges. You will become more of *you*.

Transform Your Life by Changing Your Mind

"It's not enough to have a good mind;
the main thing is to use it well."
—Rene Descartes

To fully use your entire mind it is important to understand how you process information and develop your belief systems and ideas, which ultimately lead to the choices you make. Cell biologists have taught us that our programmed perceptions directly shape our biology and behavior, as well as the character of our lives.

So what are the primary sources of our perceptions? Some are inherited, the reflexive behaviors we commonly refer to as instincts. Moving your hand away from a hot stove or your immune system fighting off an illness are examples of instincts. These instincts are acquired from nature and shape the smallest part of our perceptions and way we view the world.

The second source of perceptions that control our lives are life experiences that get downloaded as memories into our subconscious mind. These memories shape how we will view life, and they begin very early. In fact, they are first acquired through our mother's emotional patterns while we're still in the womb. A complex array of biochemistry and maternal emotional signals, hormones and stress factors all cross the placental barrier and influence fetal physiology and how the fetus develops. For example, when a mother is feeling joy and elation, the fetus will as well. When the mother is in a state of fear, the fetus will experience fear. If a mother has thoughts of rejection toward her baby, the nervous system, which is an extension of the brain and mind, will develop patterns with emotions of rejection. During the ten months in the womb, emotional information downloaded from the mother's perceptions shapes half of a person's personality. Can you believe that? Half of our personalities are formed before we've even entered this world.

(If you or someone you know had a particularly stressful pregnancy or time in the womb, it can be reprogrammed in your mind. I will share more about this shortly.)

Perhaps the most influential time of life that shapes our nerve system and mind through perceptual programming occurs from birth to age six. During this time a child's brain is constantly downloading. It's recording sensory experiences and learning motor programs such as sitting up, walking and speaking. In this six-year period, the child's sensory systems are fully engaged, downloading enormous amounts of information about the world and how it works.

When I began to retrace the path of my life it was clear to me how much fear and hostility I downloaded at these ages. I was born in a racially prejudiced community and spent most of my first 18 years in an environment plagued with crime, violence, and drugs. Most of the work I had to do in my late teens and twenties to master and transform my life was to replace and reprogram these subconscious lenses of the world and the way I believed it worked.

We're heavily influenced by our early experiences because up to the age of six we're on an accelerated pace of learning behavior patterns from the people, places and things in our environment. Children download this information through the six senses (sight, smell, taste, hearing, feeling and extrasensory electromagnetic perceptions). It's important to understand that these downloaded perceptions, whether they are real or perceived, will become the fundamental subconscious programs of the mind and nerve system. They will shape the character of every person's life.

Let's take this conversation a little deeper so you can fully understand the magnitude of why we make certain choices and decisions and take certain actions, which create behaviors. Science has shown us that nature contributes to this accelerated learning by enhancing the subconscious mind's ability to download massive amounts of information. In brainwave studies, readings from EEG's (electroencephalographs) on adults and children reveal that nerve system activity is directly correlated with different states of awareness or consciousness. Specifically, there are at least five frequency levels associated with brain states.

Gamma brain waves are the fastest frequencies (greater than 35 hertz, or Hz) and constitute a state of peak performance, focus, concentration and cognition. Beta waves are the second fastest (12–35Hz) and are associated with a strongly engaged mind, seen in a person conversing, giving a speech or teaching. Gamma and beta states represent a state of arousal.

Alpha brain waves are slightly smaller (8–12 Hz) and are associated with calm consciousness. People who have just completed a complex task, intense workout or a hard day at work and are now sitting down to rest or taking a walk in the park are likely in this state.

Theta waves are the second smallest frequency (4–8 Hz) and are associated with states of imagination and reverie. This is a state of daydreaming, and most people have experienced it. Think of a time while you were driving on the highway and realized that you couldn't recall the last 10 minutes of your drive. This theta state is where people often get great ideas and epiphanies. I experience this often as an ultra-endurance athlete; after several hours of physical exertion this low-frequency brain state predominates. It's what runners refer to as a "runner's high." The smallest frequency brain activity is called delta (0.5-4Hz). When we go to sleep at night we will descend from gamma or beta to delta and enter a sleeping, unconscious state.

Discover Your Beliefs

"We are made by our beliefs. As we believe, so we are."
—J. Wolfgang von Goethe

Why is it so important to understand these brain wave states to fully utilize our whole mind? EEG vibrations will shift from state to state during normal, healthy processing throughout an adult's life. However, in developing children, EEG vibration rates and states evolve over time. Science has shown us that during the first two years of life, delta is the predominant brain state. During ages two to six a healthy child's brain wave will increase to primarily being in theta. During this time children will mix their imaginary world with the real world. The calm, conscious state of alpha does not become predominant until after age six. By the time a person reaches age 12, he or she will express all frequency ranges, with the predominant state being the focused consciousness of beta. Welcome to the teenage years!

The crucial fact here is that children aged six and younger operate at a state below the level of consciousness. These delta and theta states are known as hypnagogic trance. This is the neurological state that doctors and healers like me utilize to directly replace old patterns of physiology, beliefs and behavior into the subconscious nerve systems and minds of our clients.

If you could observe the mind of a child under the age of seven, you would notice that her perceptions and beliefs of the world are directly downloaded into her subconscious, without her analytical self-conscious mind filtering or discriminating them first. This is because that analytical self-conscious mind doesn't fully exist yet. Essentially, before the age of seven we live in our right mind. At the age of seven we flip the switch over to our left mind. This is profound—it means that all our fundamental ideas, beliefs and perceptions about life, our roles in it and what's possible are learned at a time when we do not have the capacity to choose or reject the beliefs or ideas. In other words, we were all programmed subconsciously with specific neural patterns before we could think critically about the information. We spend the first several years downloading these programs and spend the rest of our lives running them in our worlds. That is, unless we are not completely fulfilled with our lives and actually do something about it.

Reprogramming for Success

"In order to succeed, your desire for success should be greater than your fear of failure."
—Bill Cosby

When I was in university, a sociologist and economist taught me that if you wanted to know where you were going to be in the next 20–30 years all you had to do was look at your parents. In all areas of your life—your health, wealth, career, family, etc.—there is a 95% probability that you will be exactly where your parents are. This is because most of what we download as children comes from the people, places and things in our environment.

The science of epigenetics has shown us that these downloaded neurological patterns are so powerful that they will actually override our genes. Take, for example, swimming. For ten months *in utero*, each of us lived and grew in a fluid-filled environment where we instinctually know how to move and shift in water—just like dolphins. In fact, when we are born we have the innate ability to swim like dolphins; it is an instinctual reflexive pattern. You may be asking, "Why, then, do we all need to learn to swim?" or "Why are some children afraid of the water?"

If you are a parent, you likely feel a healthy sense of concern for your child's safety when he or she is near a body of water. If you are frantic, stressed or fearful in your physiology or behavior as you pull your child away from the water, she or he will download a new pattern. Your physiology or behavior has just taught her or him to be fearful and that water is dangerous. This pattern will override the instinctual ability to swim, and it makes your child susceptible to drowning.

You may be thinking that this is a disempowering understanding of why we create and live the lives we do. However, the great news is that whatever has been programmed into your mind and nerve system can be deprogrammed (and your nerve system subsequently can be reprogrammed). This has been my personal journey over the past 20 years and I have empowered the lives of so many people professionally. At my Centre for Optimal Living this is my focus and intention, and online I perform live life integration sessions to people all over the world. People are now able to heal, grow, develop personally and create their lives in their ideals from the comfort of their own homes. The secret to this is to gently and efficiently bring people back into a theta state, stop the old patterns from running, and replace them with new empowering programs that will help them express their full life potential. I have developed a very powerful, honoring and innovative process to facilitate reprogramming for success.

To learn more about life integration sessions visit www.drsukhi.com.

The Self-Conscious Mind

*"There is nothing training cannot do. Nothing is above its reach.
It can turn bad morals to good; it can destroy bad principles
and recreate good ones; it can lift men to angelship."*
—Mark Twain

The final source of perceptions that shape our lives and derive the actions from our subconscious mind is our self-conscious mind. Your self-conscious mind is the collective synergy between your left and right mind. It has the capacity to morph and mix objective information with imagination and creativity into a process that generates unlimited beliefs and behavioral variations. The power of our self-conscious mind is that it allows us to reach into an extraordinary force in the universe: the ability to express free will.

Stopping the Monkey Chatter of the Left Mind

*"First they ignore you. Then they laugh at you.
Then they fight you. Then you win."*
—Mahatma Gandhi

To master your life, you must pay very close attention to "self-chatter." The first step in this process is to make a conscious choice to say that internal verbal abuse is not acceptable and will not be tolerated under any circumstances. You will be pleased to learn that this internal abuse center of our left mind that lives in doom, gloom, fear, jealousy, greed, etc. is the size of a peanut. (Yes, it's really that small.) This peanut area thrives on gossip, whining, complaining, and sharing about how horrible life is, akin to a group of monkeys chattering or complaining.

Now you're not going to let a group of peanut-sized monkeys push you around, are you? How do we keep these voices in check?

I've found that my peanut-sized life destroyer needs a little discipline from my conscious right mind on a regular basis. My authentic self keeps an open line of communication and usually has the greater say in most matters. Yet I often do find that these little monkeys challenge the authority of my higher voice and constantly try to push my buttons.

Paying close attention to our internal self-talk is vitally important. Yet we have to take that a step further and decide that this internal abuse is not acceptable and must stop. To do this, you must constantly cultivate and nurture the garden of your extraordinary mind. The key is to keep an open line of communication between your left and right minds' personalities.

The egotistic storyteller of the left mind will pause for moments when your authentic voice from the right speaks, but then it will continue with those self-sabotaging neural loops. The key is to invite new ideas and new circuits of thoughts from the right mind. Eventually these new neural right-mind loops will begin to replace the old left mind's monopoly over you. Be persistent, patient and diligent.

Today I find that the consciousness of my right mind is eager and excited for all of us to take a huge leap forward for humanity. By fully expressing our whole mind, by tuning into our right minds, I believe this planet can transform into the extraordinary, peaceful and loving place that we all desire it to be. You are one of the single minds within this organism we all make up called humanity. You decide who you want to be and how you show up in this world, and that contributes to the greater whole of humanity. Using your whole mind will enable you to fully show up and own your power.

Exercises to Use Your Whole Mind

*"Concerning all acts of initiative and creation, there is
one elementary truth-that the moment one definitely
commits oneself, then Providence moves, too."*
—J. Wolfgang von Goethe

The following exercises will enable greater cerebral flow between your two brain hemispheres and processors so you can access your whole mind in a more purposeful, powerful and productive way.

Step 1

One of the most empowering ways to gain greater control of the most powerful muscle, your whole mind, is to consciously decide which emotional and physiological loops you want to hook into. We must limit the amount of time we let ourselves bask in the neural circuitry of self-sabotage, anger, fear and despair. They have such immense control over our emotional and physiological circuitry that they can literally destroy our lives.

Whenever you get hooked into a self-sabotaging loop, the first thing to do is honor it. Yes, honor the pain, fear, etc. Once you honor those feelings, shift to a place of gratitude and thank your mind and every cell within your body for having the ability to fully experience that circuitry. After the physiological response has integrated (90 seconds), you have a choice. You can let that neural loop continue to run or you can come back to the present moment.

Coming back to the present moment will remind you that everything is perfect. If this doesn't work it simply means that multiple neural loops and circuits are contributing to your emotional and physiological state. Break the loop by thinking about something that brings you great joy. This may be a pet, a loved one, a child, or an activity or experience. It can be anything: get creative. Then bask in the feelings of pleasure. This may take seconds or several minutes. This activity—basking—is essentially moving you away from your left mind into your right mind. Once you arrive there and are feeling a little better, think about one thing you would love to do in your life, right now. Then think about what it would feel like to be doing that. Bask in this feeling some more (essentially overriding the old pattern).

The focused human mind is the most powerful tool in the entire universe. Our left mind has the capacity to allow us to fulfill our deepest dreams and desires. The left-brain is the head coach of our 50 trillion cells and it directs the vibration and tone of every atom, cell and tissue in the body. When your cells are healthy, wealthy and happy, you and your life will be too.

Step 2

Many people believe that our thinking mind and compassionate heart are light years apart. The truth is that they are seconds away from each other. Today I know that the feeling of deep joy and inner peace is a part of our neural circuitry that lives within our right brain, and it wants to fully express itself. In fact, it's always running and is just waiting for us to tune in and hook into it. These feelings of deep joy and inner peace live in the present moment. It has nothing to do with what we bring in from the past or project into the future. Another step in controlling your whole mind is to be present, right here and right now. The more you run this neural circuitry, the stronger it will become.

Remember that both the right and left brains are constantly working together to generate our perception of reality. This means that our right brain is always on, whether you're aware of it or not. The key to becoming present is to tune into the subtle feelings and physiology that are moving through your body right now. Close your eyes and tune in. Do you feel tired, lazy, energetic, happy, sad...? Whatever you feel is the present moment. Do not let your left brain come in and assess and judge what you're feeling. The right brain says it is what it is, no judgments. Practice this exercise throughout the day: it only takes seconds, and eventually you'll be able to activate this circuitry of deep inner peace and joy on demand.

Another way to strengthen your present right brain muscle is to ask yourself what it feels like to be doing whatever it is you're doing, right now, especially if you're eating or drinking something. We have strong sensory receptors in our noses and mouths that allow us to experience different aromas, flavors, textures and temperatures. Try to observe all these sensations during your meals. Don't get caught up in the past or future of the left mind. If you do, come back to the present moment of the right mind. Have fun with your food and think about all the minerals and nutrients it's providing your 50 trillion cells so you can fully experience life.

If you're having a hard time doing this, pay closer attention to the foods you're eating. Refined sugars, caffeine, dairy, wheat and chemical additives have a tendency to make this process much more challenging. I recommend removing them from most meals. On the flip side, foods high in the natural chemical tryptophan (bananas, turkey, halibut, and salmon) will cause a rapid release of the neurotransmitter serotonin, which will cause you to chill out and feel mellow. That makes it much easier to remain present.

Another way to become present is to light a scented candle of an aroma such as lavender, vanilla or anything you love. These scents tend to decrease the stress response of the hormone cortisol and, as a result, increase the neurotransmitters serotonin and dopamine. Light a scented candle, close your eyes and bask in the feelings of that aroma. Feel that deep feeling of inner peace and joy it brings. All these techniques will strengthen your circuitry to become more present and empower you to access it more easily anytime or any place.

Step 3

Albert Einstein said, "We must be willing to give up what we are in order to become what we will be." To have more control over your entire mind is a process of letting go and loosening the shackles of our ego-driven left mind. Yes: this is much easier said than done. Your desire for inner joy, health, wealth and happiness must be far greater than your attachment to your ego or your need to be right. But the following techniques will allow you to do just that.

1. Sit down with a piece of paper and a pencil. Without giving it too much thought, start sketching. Think of pictures and whole things. There is no right or wrong here, just art.

2. To continue expanding your right brain, close your eyes and visualize your ideal life. Think about all 10 areas of your life: your family, social life, finances, spiritual life, career, character, physical life, intellectual life, emotional life and quality of life. Think about big ideas of what's possible—do not concern yourself with the "how," only the "what." Dream. Dream very big. And when you think you can't dream bigger take each of these

areas to an extraordinary place. Write down a list of at least 10 possibilities under each area of your life mastery wheel.

3. Try a left-brain activity. Get 10 pieces of paper. Write down one area of the life mastery wheel, such as "Financial Life," at the top of each page. List at least 10 dreams all over the page with a felt marker. Over the next week go through magazines, books, and websites to collect pictures, inspiring words, quotes, and anything that resonates with those dreams. Paste them all over that page, front and back, just like a collage. Repeat this with the other nine areas of the life mastery wheel.

4. Then try a right-brain activity. Every night before going to bed, look at all 10 pages and bring the feelings and emotions into your heart as if you were actually being, doing and having those things in your life right now, today. As you lie down and begin falling asleep, keep these thoughts, ideas and emotions running through your physiology until you're sleeping.

5. Repeat step four when you wake up (except, of course, the part where you fall asleep). Throughout your day observe your actions, choices and behaviors. Begin to question why you're doing what you're doing—why you're making the choices you make, having the thoughts you have, and taking the actions you take. Pay attention to whether those choices, thoughts and actions are aligned with your dreams. Realign everything you do to stay on purpose with your highest potential.

To quote the poet Carl Sandburg, "Nothing happens unless first a dream."

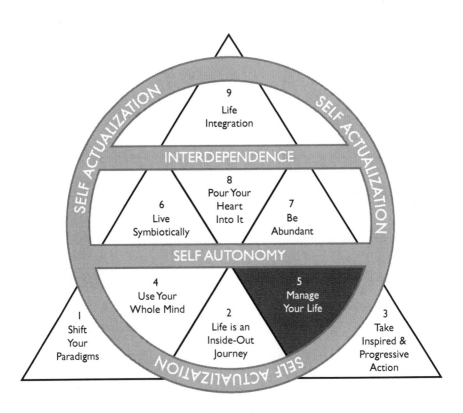

CHAPTER 7

STRATEGY 5 —
MANAGE YOUR LIFE

*"Life is meaningless only if we allow it be. Each of us has
the power to give life meaning, to make our time and
our bodies and our words into instruments of love and hope."*
—Tom Head

Once you're able to see your world more from your whole mind, you
will be able to imagine, envision and tangibly create things that you
presently cannot see with your eyes or touch with your hands. But once
you have developed your road maps or paradigms you can begin to take
progressive action in seeing them to fruition. When you're able to manage yourself, you will express the values and principles that lie deep
within you into everything you do. This creates the space for your free
will to emerge.

Managing your life can be functionally sound when you begin to understand what matters most to you. This means you'll have to understand
your core principles. I've learned that the more I study the traditional
sciences of the left mind and the quantum sciences of the right mind,

the universal emerging principles of life begin to surface. The further I delve into the hundreds of -*ology*s the more common they become.

I feel these principles are universal, constant, omnipotent and omnipresent in all people. They do not change, react or get angry. They will not leave us or die. They have been present for at least all of recorded history and are still present today. They are not quick fixes or short cuts.

These principles are deep fundamental truths that are consistent and precise through the entire fabric of life. They are much bigger than any person, place or thing. Most important, we can actually validate them every day through our experiences.

The challenge we face is that we're limited by our ability to process everything from our experiences and the fabric of life. We all have a neural bandwidth that creates specific patterning, lenses, ideas, paradigms and consciousness. Therefore, our knowledge and awareness of these underlying principles is somewhat limited. The limitation comes from nature, universal laws, and our own lack of personal awareness.

Defining Life Centers

"While values drive behaviors, principles govern consequences."
—Steven Covey

The key process in being able to see more clearly is to begin peeling back the layers of your own limitations. By simply being aware of deeper principles to live by, you create an environment that facilitates learning through integration. Over time the lens through which you see your world becomes clearer. Principles do not change; what changes is your ability to understand and live by them.

Your paradigms form from a deep inner guidance system. If you have accessed your inner power and are self-aware, you won't be affected by other people's behaviors, attitudes or opinions. Your principles and centeredness won't be shaken by environmental circumstances or situations. Newer paradigms of autonomy and actualized living will emerge.

These universal principles lie deep within you. These principles are your center; they are your foundation. Outside, you have other commitments and connections to other centers. These centers are the 10 components of the life mastery wheel; family life, vocational life, social life, financial life, intellectual life, physical life, your inner character, spiritual life, emotional life, and your overall quality of life. There are many centers outside yourself. The constant movement of where you invest your time and energy will influence your life. The dynamic balance you achieve in expressing your fundamental principles through the 10 centers of your life is paramount for managing your life.

LIFE CENTERS

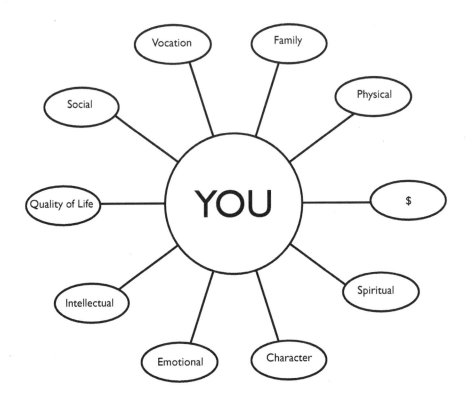

Diagram 5

I encourage you to create a life-management diagram similar to the one above. Place a circle in the middle and write "ME" in it—this is your hub! Now place as many sub-centers around your hub that you feel are important to you. Every sub-center can fall under one of the ten life mastery centers. Then prioritize them in terms of your commitment to each one, ranked from 1 (least important) to 10 (most important).

Leadership plays an instrumental role in managing your life—we all must lead our own ships. You can take the opinions and suggestions of others, but ultimately you must make your own decisions. Leadership is actually a philosophy for living. It is an art; as such, it utilizes the right mind. Once you ask yourself the important right-brain questions of what you would like to experience or create, you can shift into managing and creating. Management is a left-brain activity and is the execution of the ideas.

Know Your Commitments

"Commitment unlocks the doors of imagination, allows vision, and gives us the "right stuff" to turn our dreams into reality."
—James Womack

Effective life management gives you the time and energy you need to express your deepest principles into your outer centers of life. Expressing your human will is the embodiment of living from the inside out. As a healer I have experienced many things that contradict the left-mind medical consciousness. I have seen people living in severe states of illness and disease. The people who overcome these challenges and learn from them are the ones who had a human will that was power-fully expressed. They refused to believe what the left-brain model had told them. They created a new paradigm, harnessed their whole mind and took inspired action. They took the necessary steps to begin heal-ing themselves from the inside out. Most importantly, they believed in something that was greater than their physical self. They knew that the power that created the entire universe lived within them and was expressed by their connection to the human spirit. They allowed their deepest principles to be fully expressed. They managed their life better to facilitate better integration.

To manage your life, you must continually prioritize your inner and outer commitments. Life is a constant balance of energy and time. Each day you have a finite amount of both. Expend too much energy and you'll begin to deplete yourself, get stressed, and fail to fully integrate your experiences. You'll stop growing, learning and evolving. If you continue along this journey you will begin to live in a mind and body that is dis-eased. Conversely, if you do not expend enough energy and have too much time, you begin to slow your life's evolutionary process and will not share your gifts with the world. A dynamic balance is key.

Having the ability to simply say "no" and let go has been a powerful lesson for me. In order for me to transition from my teen years into an adult and student of life I had to let go of many things. I had to say "no" to the only friends I knew in my life. People I had deep connections to, people who I trusted and loved, people who literally had saved my life. I had to say "no" and let go of all the material assets I had accumulated to try to make myself happy from the outside. I had to say "no" to the only life I knew, a life I was extremely good at. I had let go of virtually everything. As challenging as it was, saying no created the space for me to begin making a new life with new centers and commitments outside of myself. It allowed the facilitation and full expression of my deep principles into everything that I did. I was able to manage my life in becoming a student and to getting where I am today.

Your Priorities Become Your Life

"What comes first, the compass or the clock? Before one can truly manage time (the clock), it is important to know where you are going, what your priorities and goals are, in which direction you are headed (the compass). Where you are headed is more important than how fast you are going. Rather than always focusing on what's urgent, learn to focus on what is really important."
—Unknown

Despite having a busy schedule these days, I still find time to manage and prioritize my life so that I can maintain balance yet still pour my heart into everything I do. The key is always in finding the balance. We must keep the balance between our inner and outer worlds. Know your roles and responsibilities. Know what is important to you. Many people put health, family or personal development at the end of their lists—and others don't have them on their lists at all. These are fundamentals of what it means to be a human being. For me, these make up the foundation from which everything else grows.

Managing your life means shifting priorities—sometimes one area will take precedence over others, which is natural. Many people believe that success in one area of life means they're a failure in some other area. This does not have to be the case. I've found that throughout my life I've had to prioritize, so I spent more time and energy in certain dimensions. As my priorities changed, as I grew and evolved, the time and energy in my life centers would also change and evolve. Yet, I would always strive to create balance in everything. Ultimately, success and happiness come from within us—the only way to achieve outer success is through inner peace, power and flow.

The way to think about it is that you're not prioritizing your schedule, but instead scheduling your priorities. Visit them daily and have weekly, monthly and annual forecasts.

I was a postsecondary student for ten years. During this time I also created my own curriculum, studying the works of many great minds. During the last four years of my formal education, my life was stressful and overwhelming. I had more than 50 contact hours at school each week. My student loans were maxed out, so I had to work as a server and bartender most evenings just so I could pay my tuition and bills. My days would begin at five a.m. and end at midnight. Most of my friends had financial support from their families, so it was unheard of for any student in this program to be working more than 30 hours each week on top of their educational obligations. Where was I going to find the time for sanity?

There was no doubt that my life was out of balance, but I had a plan—and the sacrifice was well worth the investment. In fact, I had a ten-year plan that I divided into years, months, weeks, days and hours. I knew that each day, as overwhelming as they were, brought me one step closer to my ultimate dreams. I was investing in my financial and career centers and would see no return for many years. I maintained my family, emotional and social centers, as well as my quality of life, to the best of my ability. Some weeks were good and others were horrible. I maintained a strong daily spiritual practice and expressed my inner principles for living into everything I did. Although I lost some of my radiant vitality, I exercised most days and bought the most nourishing foods that I could afford at the time. I did my best to maintain the balance in every area because most of my energy was put into my intellectual life.

The key is to do your best in the balancing act of life, knowing that you may never achieve optimal balance. Think of the tightrope walker, constantly engaged in the process of balancing with every step. If they weren't totally engaged, they would fall off. Yet, they also will never achieve perfect balance, as they would become static in a dynamic process. Life is the same. I strived for this balancing "act" and graduated in all my programs in the top of my class with honors and distinctions. By prioritizing my life, this became my actual life. Since I graduated I have continued this process and it has allowed me to achieve a level of health, wealth and happiness in a fraction of the time that I initially planned for. I had a solid foundation of facts, information, knowledge, experience and wisdom so I could share my gifts with the world.

When managing your life, remember that people are far more important than things. We all enter and leave this world with the same amount of material things: zero. We leave our legacy in the hearts and minds of other people. When reflecting on this fundamental principle, recognize that the most important person in your life should be YOU. When I lost myself I couldn't manage anything in my life. I ignored all my responsibilities. I could hardly manage the simplest of responsibilities, such as personal hygiene. It's an extreme example, but it's a common theme in many people's lives, and it's one that can be easily avoided. If you're not showing up for yourself, you can't show up for anyone else. Put yourself first so you can be there for the people that you love and care about most.

You manage your life with a compass, not a road map. It's about understanding and centering your life on principles, which will give you purpose and clear intentions. It also will facilitate more self-awareness and higher levels of consciousness to uphold the integrity of the principles and purpose that you deem most important.

The Power of Neural Conditioning

"In order to live a fully human life we require not only control of our bodies; we must touch the unity and resonance of our physicality, our bond with the natural order, the corporeal grounds of our intelligence."
—Adrienne Rich

For the past two decades I have been mastering one of the most powerful strategies to create massive change for a more compelling and fulfilling future. In fact, in working with thousands of clients I have learned that this is a surefire way to not only better manage the areas of your life wheel, but to create massive change in anything that you desire.

Does this sound powerful? It is the process of neural conditioning, and it changes who you are from the inside out. It will not only shift the way you look at people, events and opportunities, it will change how you feel about them and ultimately adjust your internal thermostat to a greater resonance and frequency.

When you shift your internal thermostat for more health, wealth and happiness you will achieve greater results and fulfill your dreams. In order to fully understand and begin employing neural conditioning, it's vital to understand the basic human drivers or motives in our lives.

One of the most basic of biological instincts is to avoid pain and seek pleasure. In all the centers of your life, that's what you're ultimately trying to create—less pain and more pleasure. We can actually leverage this powerful concept. What if you could associate an undesirable behavior or way of being with an immense amount of pain and discomfort? Well, you can—and if you did it consistently, how often would you repeat the behavior? Not very often, because who truly wants to experience more discomfort and pain in their lives? You could then go on to find a new empowering, productive and on-purpose behavior to replace the old undesirable one. Once you know what that new productive behavior is, you could again leverage this idea and associate an immense amount of pleasure and goodness with this way of being. How often would you engage in this behavior? You would actually crave it because it makes you feel so wonderful.

If you think back and assess your life you'll notice you have created certain ideas, lenses, ways of thinking and behaviors to simply experience less pain and more pleasure. At my seminars in the past I've told a story about "little Johnny" to illustrate this concept. He is a fictional person that has gone through the typical Western cultural domestication. Little Johnny was born into this world with a surgical procedure called "the delivery" in a hospital. His mother was given toxic chemicals that directly affected him during this process. Once he was brought into this world he was taken away from his mother and poked and prodded and given more toxic chemicals called medicine. Apparently the intelligence that created him from two tiny cells in nine months was not good enough for the educated left minds of physicians. As a child in the first few years of life, he was given more drugs and chemicals that supposedly made him healthier against certain diseases. If he had a little cold or fever, his loving parents would then give him more drugs to get rid of the pain. Baby Tylenol and aspirin were just a part of avoiding pain and getting more pleasure. The idea of what these toxins were doing to his mind and body were irrelevant. In fact, by the time little Johnny became a teenager, our culture taught him that he must avoid pain at all costs. He must do whatever it takes to just get rid of it and experience pleasure as fast as possible. Domestication taught him that life is meant to be easy and effortless and that masking pain and getting instant pleasure is what living is about.

As a teenager, little Johnny started having a hard time in school. He also got cut from his hockey team and dumped by his girlfriend. He's feeling pretty sad and bummed out. What do you think little Johnny is going to do? Is he going to look for the lessons and grow beyond them? No way! He's in pain and all he wants to do is get out of pain and into pleasure as fast as possible because that's what domestication has taught him. So little Johnny goes down to the corner store and gets some distractions. Johnny gets "high" and feels fantastic: he has no more pain and therefore no more problems. This artificial pleasurable state goes from a few days, to weeks that turn into months that turn into years and the distractions, addictions and drugs get stronger because he wants to experience higher and higher levels of pleasure. His family finds out and they are adamant that they never raised Johnny to be this way and never condoned these distractions and addictions. I say to them, "Oh really!" You never taught Johnny that life is meant to be painless, and if there's ever a challenge you just find the fastest way to use something from the outside to get to pleasure? As we grow up in this cultural ideology of avoiding pain and getting instant pleasure, we sabotage our lives. If our partners, family, colleagues or friends say or do something that makes us experience pain, we hurt them in return with our words and actions. We hope this will bring us more pleasure, but it doesn't.

We live in a world of people who are addicts—what I like to call "-olics." We are letting pain dictate the choices and behaviors we make. We have all experienced fear, sadness, frustration, anger or boredom. When most people experience these emotions, they look for the fastest way to escape them. There is a massive difference in trying to avoid something versus moving toward something else. When we try to *avoid* pain we actually allow pain to control us. We develop strategies to avoid or attempt to cope with these emotions. We develop addictions such as food, drugs (pushed or prescribed), alcohol, shopping, relationships, sex, television, Internet, violence—the list goes on and on. But these addictions will never change our internal thermostat because we are always being reactive and avoiding something deep within us. In fact countries even do this with each other and we call it "war". This problem is systemic. And it's just another attempt to get out of pain and into pleasure. The challenge with this methodology is that we allow pain and pleasure to control us and dictate our lives. It's ingrained so deeply within us that we don't even realize we're doing it. Little Johnny was raised in our world's consciousness and he's the embodiment of a disempowered and lost person. This may come as a surprise to you, but most people have a "little Johnny" deep within them.

So here's the good news. Now that you have this new awareness you can stop this cycle of control and take your power back. You can transcend the pain and pleasure cycle at any time. One of the keys to accessing your inner power and fulfilling your dreams in every area of your life is to learn how to leverage pain and pleasure so you control them and they can't control you anymore. Now you're in charge of your destiny.

In order to transcend the pain and pleasure cycle and create a more purposeful and meaningful life we have to go through several simple steps. Eventually these steps will become more empowering habits that will get you out of pain and into pleasure—and ultimately into power. And you'll do it all from within, with more elegance, grace and effectiveness. Get ready to start rockin' it!

Transcending the Pain and Pleasure Cycle

"The beginning of a habit is like an invisible thread, but every time we repeat the act we strengthen the strand, add to it another filament, until it becomes a great cable and binds us irrevocably, thought and act."
—Orison Swett Marden

Neural Conditioning: 5-Step Process

Step 1: Get clear on what you desire

The first thing we must do is decide what we truly desire. You would be absolutely amazed at how many people I've worked with have no idea what they actually want in life. Sometimes they talk to me for 30 minutes about what they don't want before they even start to think about what they *do* want. To change your internal resonance or thermostat you must move toward whatever you desire rather than avoid whatever you don't desire, because avoidance doesn't pave the path for inner change. When you look at your Life Centers you must be very specific in what you would like to experience and possess in each center. Thinking about these desires should create an immense amount of pleasure from within. The more specific, precise and clear you are, the more powerful you will become in moving toward mastering your life.

Several years ago I decided I wanted to meet my ideal life partner, my wife. I knew she was out there, but I hadn't met her yet. I had no interest in dating; I just wanted to get straight to the point. So I wrote down exactly what would bring me an immense amount of pleasure in a wife. I got extremely detailed and specific. I wrote down her height, weight, eye color, hair color, scent, interests, background, values, choices in recreation, level of consciousness, favorite coffee—the list went on for pages. The simple act of writing an exhaustive list brought me an immense amount of joy. The first key to changing anything is getting crystal clear on what you want. When I eventually put this "out there" to the universe, I met my wife, Kate, two days later. It might sound unbelievable—but in fact, the universe acts that quickly when you are clear on what you desire.

Step 2: Create leverage from the inside out

"There is one quality which one must possess to win, and that is definiteness of purpose, the knowledge of what one wants, and a burning desire to possess it."
—Napoleon Hill

The gift of mastering neural conditioning is that we can create massive change instantly. Most people believe that they truly want to change but they just don't have the drive to do it. We are all capable of change, but it must come from within us.

Many people believe that as a speaker my purpose is to motivate people. This could not be further from the truth. When we constantly need motivation to do something it simply means that we have not made it a strong value from within. Motivation comes from the outside in. When you need constant motivation, you haven't shifted your internal resonance and you haven't grown. As a result, the changes in your life will not be sustainable. You'll eventually go back to the place where you started and feel frustrated because you have invested so much time and energy trying to create change. This pattern can occur in any area— from health to wealth to family, and beyond.

Inspiration is a very different animal. Inspiration comes from within you, from the inside out. This is the power of neural conditioning; it creates massive change from within, ultimately changing your internal resonance so the changes are sustained throughout your entire life. Inspiration simply means "in-spirit," the intangible force that drives us and gives us life. Inspiration will shift you to an immeasurable place of power. Many people believe that when they are seeking pleasure they are in their power place, but they are wrong. They are still caught in the dualistic nature of life—by simply seeking pleasure, they will always be susceptible to the other side of the dualistic coin: pain. Most people ride the pain and pleasure cycle of life. I offer you something greater: a state that transcends this lower state of consciousness, the state of pure, timeless power.

If you want to raise your thermostat you must first leverage the duality of the pain and pleasure cycle en route to power. Whether you will create change or not first begins with what pain and pleasure means to you. In fact, for many, the simple idea of changing is painful enough to just avoid the idea of what pleasures could come. For example, someone might say, "The thought of marriage counseling pains me, and after all that work, what if my partner leaves me anyway?" This type of thinking comes from our mixed emotions and the fact that we link pain and pleasure to changing, which creates a neurological state of uncertainty. As a result, we cannot fully commit and utilize all our resources to create massive change.

Each of us has a threshold of tolerance. For many people the idea of changing some area of their life creates more pain than staying in their present situation. We've all experienced this in our relationships, health, career or finances. When eventually the pain of the present situation became greater than the pain of changing, we changed. We reached our threshold and finally decided to take action for change.

The beauty is that we can use internal leverage to shift this threshold immediately. In fact, whenever I work with people the first thing I do is use leverage to empower them to begin making the changes they have been trying to make for years or even decades. Using our internal leverage is so powerful that I can empower people to change their tolerance thresholds in a single session. Consider this bit of wisdom from Anthony Robbins:

The greatest leverage you can create for yourself is the pain that comes from inside, not outside. Knowing that you have failed to live up to your own standards for your life is the ultimate pain. If we fail to act in accordance with our own view of ourselves, if our behaviors are inconsistent with our standards—with the identity we hold for ourselves—then the chasm between our actions and who we are drives us to make a change. One of the strongest forces in the human personality is the drive to preserve the integrity of our own identity.

To create leverage from the inside out is to first bring your awareness to a place where not changing is incredibly painful and changing is incredibly attractive and pleasurable. This is where questions play an important role. Pain-inducing questions will force you to estimate the cost of not changing. Think about a change you want to make in your life. Ask yourself, "How much has this cost my finances, personal health, happiness, family, career, children, emotions or spirituality?" Write down and visualize how your inability to change has negatively affected you and the people that you love most.

The next step is to ask questions that will induce an immense amount of pleasure related to the act of changing. Ask yourself, "How great will I feel? How good will I look? How proud will my family be? How awesome will my life be?" Get tons of compelling reasons to create change immediately. You must have enough reasons to change right now. If you feel you will do it tomorrow or next week, you haven't stacked up enough reasons to change. Keep writing until it's so compelling that you start this instant!

This process is about changing your master control system, your nerve system. This conditioning links negative patterns with not changing and positive and pleasurable patterns with changing. Now you are conditioned from the inside out.

Step 3: Break the old pattern and way of processing

> *"An old belief is like an old shoe. We so value its*
> *comfort that we fail to notice the hole in it."*
> —Robert Brault

One definition of insanity is doing the same thing over and over again and expecting different results. This could not be truer. Most people want to change and improve some area of their lives. In fact, every person should be trying to change and improve some areas of their lives, because if we're not growing we're dying. It astounds me that people continue to use the same modes of thinking, focus on the same things, and ask the same questions—yet expect different results. The area of your life you would like to improve deserves new strategies, new perspectives, new questions and a different focus. This is the key to changing.

Everything that you need to transform your life is lying deep within you. This does not need changing. You should not aim to change who you are. Instead, develop the strategies to access the potential, principles and inspiration that lie deep within you.

Once you are clear about what you want and have developed lever-age, you must use new ways of thinking, asking and acting—otherwise, you'll get the same old results. Deep within your nerve system you have old limiting patterns. Your old way of processing information and run-ning these patterns creates a specific lens of the world. These limiting patterns must be broken to ensure your changes last and that you keep developing new strategies that are efficient, fun and life-transforming.

The fastest way to interrupt a person's pattern is to do something they do not expect or something that's completely different from past experi-ences. As an optimal living doctor, when I first sit down with people most of them want to get into their story of some past wound or trauma. I under-stand this impulse—my own life's story is a roller coaster of extreme ups and downs. But the story does not serve us because it keeps us locked in an old pattern and way of being. Stories inhibit our potential. I used to use my stories to garner sympathy, love and support from others—and this kept me stuck. When somebody gets into their story and gets very emotional with me, I break the pattern quickly. Once, at my Centre for Optimal Living, a woman became hysterical with her stories of past pain and trauma. I got up and said, "Oh, that's an intern at the door and they're going to come in and watch how I perform my initial consultation." I didn't do it because I was rude or uncaring—I did it to interrupt her pat-tern. And it worked: immediately the woman snapped out of her state and regained composure. People who are stuck in a pattern feel they have no control over their lives. When I do something unexpected like that, it proves to them they have complete control and know how to change the way they feel immediately at a neurological level.

I encourage you to think of ways to interrupt your patterns. When speak-ing in public, I often interrupt the audience's patterns by getting them out of their seats and celebrating to upbeat dance music. It instantly shifts their states and physiologies. Most importantly, it breaks the old pattern. You can try this at home. Imagine your favorite sports team winning the championship. Imagine your child just got accepted to a top university. Imagine you just made millions of dollars. These visualizations will move you to a place of enthusiasm and gratitude.

Breaking an old pattern is similar to scratching a DVD with a metal nail. The next time you put the disc in your DVD player, it will not be recognized and cannot play, because the old recording pattern has been broken. This is what must be done with your nerve system. For example, if you had a bad day because your boss or teacher yelled at you, you could keep running this pattern in your mind and continue to feel upset for the rest of the day, week or even the entire month. Rather than let this pattern run, wouldn't it be great if you could scratch it so many times that you couldn't experience the negative feelings and emotions anymore? How about turning the experience into something that is funny and pleasurable?

All the feelings that we experience are simply based on the images we focus on and the feelings and sensations we associate with those images. Go back to a past interaction that made you feel sad or upset. Now let's get creative. In your mind turn this interaction into an old black-and-white movie. Play the movie backward, watching every person take the words they spoke back in. Play it back as fast as you possibly can. Then run the image forward again even faster. Play the image backward and forward as fast as you possibly can, but shift the instigator's clothes to a clown outfit. Give them a large red foam nose, paint their face and give them a curly red wig. Imagine them waddling instead of walking. Silence their voice and replace it with a fast piano tune. Keep playing the scene over and over, backward and forward, right-side-up and upside-down, dozens of times. Do this until the pattern is completely scratched and erased so it cannot be played again. Add in music that inspires you, start to move your body to the rhythms, and smile and laugh.

Now when you think about the original experience it will be replaced by your new sensations. You'll no longer feel sad or upset. If you feel any of the old sensations, continue the process until the old feelings are completely gone and are replaced with the new empowering ones.

Step 4: Replace the old pattern with inspiration

"So show a little inspiration, show a little spark, show the world a little act when you show it your heart, we've got two lives— one we're given, and the other one we make, and the world won't stop. Actions speak louder so listen to your heart."
—Unknown

You have now created change in an area of your life, but to make it a long-term commitment you must replace the old pattern or belief with inspiration from within. If a new pattern does not replace an old one, the old one will find a way to resurface over the days, weeks or years to come.

If you've been following these steps to manage your life and create change, you are clear on what you want, you are getting leverage, you have broken old patterns and have started to replace them. Now you must close the gap with new choices that will give the same pleasurable feelings without any negative side effects. For example, if your change was to quit smoking you must find many new ways to replace the old benefits of smoking. The old positive feelings and sensations must be preserved with new behaviors. If smoking helped you alleviate anxiety or depression, you can alleviate those feelings with other activities, from simple yoga poses to helping people in need.

There were times when I found it challenging to get out of pain and into pleasure by replacing an old habit. In these circumstances I would simply model myself after people who had similar experiences and were able to turn things around for themselves. All people who have made lasting change have replaced the old pattern with inspiration. Inspiration is rooted deep within us and guides us to higher choices, actions and behaviors. Mastery and happiness are the synthesis of what occurs when what you think, say and do become completely aligned. It is vitally important to continue to condition the new patterns until they completely replace the old thoughts, actions, behaviors or ideas. It is through this persistence that the change you desire will become the new you and allow you to keep transcending.

Step 5: Integrate pain and pleasure for power

"All emotions are pure which gather you and lift you up; that emotion is impure which seizes only one side of your being and so distorts you."
—Rainer Marie Rilke

As long as we are caught in the dualistic nature of the pain and pleasure cycle we will not live up to our full potential. The first level of awareness is to continually avoid pain. This is the lowest level of awareness. We will harm others, take recreational drugs and/or medications to get rid of pain, and let our choices and actions be motivated by fear. This state of awareness has created many of the problems we're experiencing globally—from the broken healthcare and educational systems to economic and business problems.

The good news is that we can easily transcend this state by stepping beyond pain and into the realm of pleasure. Once we transcend to this state we will no longer do things to get rid of pain. Instead we will try to make ourselves feel pleasure at all costs. Our goal will be the endless pursuit of pleasure.

This sounds like a wonderful place to live, and it is. However, the universal law of polarity says that one state cannot exist without its opposite. Therefore, even though our pursuit may be constant pleasure, pleasure cannot exist without pain. Our resonance will always oscillate between the two polarities of pain and pleasure. This is something we cannot escape.

INFINITE EXPERIENCES

Diagram 6

You've seen this diagram before—it's a drawing of the infinity symbol. I use the infinity symbol because life is full of infinite experiences and opportunities on both sides of the equation. The space on the left is pain and its exact complement, pleasure, is the space on the right. We cannot experience one side of the equation without having the other lying dormant within us for contrast. We always need contrast in life. If you look at a masterpiece painting you will see different shades of colors.

Some are dark and others are light. It is this contrast that allows us to see the entire painting as a whole piece. Imagine for a moment that the artist did not use any contrast. Instead while painting their masterpiece they used the exact same color with no contrasting shades. Now if you or I looked at this painting all we would see is a sheet of canvas painted one color. Not much of a masterpiece is it? Yet, the artist would argue it is a masterpiece.

Similarly, you are a master painting your own picture on the canvas of life. Deep within your masterpiece is waiting to fully express itself, but you must see the full contrast of your life (good and bad, dark and light, pain and pleasure) to experience your magnificent whole self.

In our lives we all know those super-happy, always positive, outgoing people. They are so upbeat that it almost comes across as being false. As a healer I have served thousands of these people and every single one of them would express the exact opposite intensity of emotions, feelings and thoughts when in the comfort of their own homes. It is as if these people are expressing a manic state of extreme highs and lows. I know many people who live in this emotion-driven state, always seeking pleasure because a deep underlying pain is trying to surge to the surface.

At a young age the size of the polarity is very large with extreme highs and lows. If you look at the infinity symbol in Diagram 7, you can see that one side of the equation is everything you perceive as pleasurable or positive and the other side is everything you perceive as painful or negative. Now imagine that your life is like a pendulum swinging back and forth from positive pleasure to painful negativity. With every moment, experience, hour and day you oscillate between the two allowing the experiences around you to dictate the state within you. For example, if the weather is sunny and pleasant, there's no stress in sight, and you perceive no challenges, heartache or despair, you are on the right side and are in a state of pleasure from within. But if the weather is cold or miserable, you can't find your car keys, your home is messy, you make a mistake at work or have other challenges or obstacles surrounding you, you are on the left side and are in a state of pain and negativity.

THE UPS AND DOWNS OF LIFE

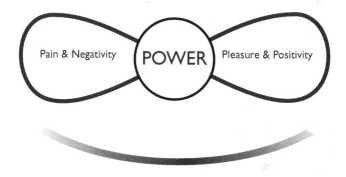

Diagram 7

So does the world around you get you up or down? Happy or sad? Vibrant or dark? If you let the experiences outside you dictate the state within you, I'm sorry to say this, but you are a disempowered person. You are not a master of your destiny. You are not connected to your inner power, you have little certainty and your ultimate dreams will continue to elude you. If the wind of life is strong you will get beat up and blown or knocked over. It will express as illness, disease, negative thinking, unhappiness, low energy, judgments, poverty complex, fear of the future, the list goes on and on. It's a disconnection from the powerful, omnipotent and masterful being that you truly are. You will not be the person you know you could become and you won't achieve the results that you desire in your outer world. You must remember that your inner world dictates what shows up in your outer world. End of story!

Now look again at the infinity symbol in Diagram 7. In the center of the sign there is another state that transcends the pain and pleasure cycle. That is power. When you can see the challenge and opportunity simultaneously you synthesize and integrate both sides of the equation, and the pendulum stops swinging. You are able to see yourself, your piece of art, fully because you see the full contrast of all your shades. You see that every challenge, obstacle, and painful experience as well as every pleasure and joyous or uplifting experience were all gifts from the universe so you could own your disowned parts. So you could see all of yourself, so you could see all of the shades of your rainbow and become grateful, loving, inspired and enthusiastic about life again. This is when your pendulum (life) stops swinging from side to side because you see it all as a gift and can stop playing the role of the victim. You step back into your source and become poised, purposeful and powerful. This is your true essence: power.

This is what I call the horizontal journey of life. These are the steps:

1. Avoid pain: lowest state of awareness
2. Seek pleasure: moderate state of awareness
3. Integrate pain and pleasure for power: highest state of awareness

Okay, fantastic! So all you have to do is see the blessings and gifts of both sides of the equation and you're done, right? I wish life were that easy. Once you dance on one rung of life and integrate that level, you are in a complete state of power for that level of consciousness. You will have fun there and enjoy it, but over time you may get a little bored and crave more out of life. So what's the next step? We are all conscious spiritual beings having a physical, mental and emotional experience. The richness of these experiences is completely dependent on your level of awareness. The more aware you are of the powerful, omnipotent, omnipresent being that you are, the richer and fuller your life becomes. This requires constant growth, progress and evolution. The same way that a child falls in love with one puzzle, completes it and then becomes bored with it because they are ready for a more complex one, we must also seek the next growth opportunity.

Innately you are constantly seeking the next opportunity for growth and evolution. So just like walking up a set of stairs, once you achieve your highest state of awareness at that rung or level you take a vertical step upwards to the next stair or level of consciousness. At this new level you will again do the three-step horizontal journey. So know that you are a masterful, purposeful and powerful being beyond anything you could imagine and your life is the unfolding of this awareness and experience. This is the ultimate journey of life.

THE JOURNEY OF LIFE

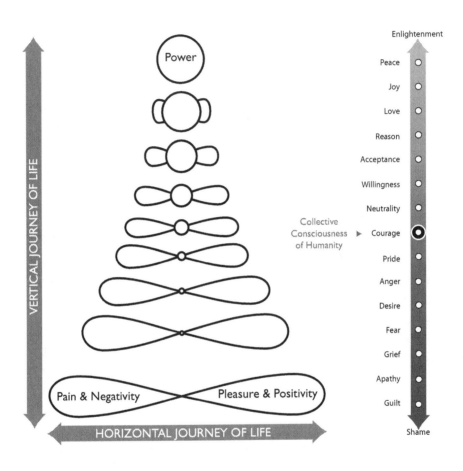

Diagram 8

If you look at Diagram 8 you will see that every infinity sign is getting smaller as you move up to higher states of consciousness. That is because the journey of life and accessing your full power, potential and master within is both a horizontal and vertical journey. Each time you master one level you transcend vertically to the next rung. Again, eventually you integrate that level of awareness by becoming grateful for every experience, no matter how good or bad. You will notice that as your pendulum swings at this new level the highs and lows are less extreme. You will also notice that the circle in the middle, *power*, gets larger as you evolve. The more you're in your power, the less the winds of life will affect your internal compass. You will observe the positive and negative, the pain and pleasure simultaneously, and gratitude will become your natural state. You will integrate that level of awareness or consciousness and shift your internal thermostat to a greater resonance.

The scale on the right of Diagram 8 was written by Dr. David Hawkins in his book *Power vs. Force*. He calibrated and mapped out every level and state of human consciousness. Check out his book if you haven't already: it's truly awesome. Notice how at the lowest level of awareness, a person will predominantly be in a place of shame and guilt. Several levels higher it is the place of fear and desire. This is where so many people still live today—talk about a great reality check. The majority of human consciousness is now resonating at the first level of empowerment, courage. We still have so much more potential for human evolution; we haven't even scratched the surface. So it's time for you and I to step it up, because the universe is waiting! We have a great assignment and a lot of work to do, my friend. As you continue to integrate and evolve several states you will predominantly be in a place of willingness and acceptance. Several more levels up you will be in a consciousness of love, joy and peace. As you continue to grow and connect deeper within, you will embark on the highest state known: pure consciousness and living in the light.

Once again, take notice of how the pendulum swings less and less with the highs and lows of life as you grow vertically. Life is the process of mastering our present state: this is the horizontal process. Once we master that, we evolve to the next vertical rung and begin the horizontal process again (the roller coaster of emotional ups and downs). As you continue to integrate different rungs of consciousness or awareness by becoming grateful, you will start to own all your disowned parts. You will become more whole and more empowered. The most powerful people on earth are those who have journeyed vertically where the highs and lows of life no longer affect them. The most disempowered people are stuck at the bottom in the pain and pleasure cycle of a very large infinity rung below the consciousness of courage. This is the ultimate journey of life, which in itself is the destination. The further you and I can evolve, the further we can facilitate and inspire the process in others. The generations that follow will also be grateful, as they may begin their journey from where we left off.

The Next Level

"What could you not accept, if you but knew that everything
that happens, all events, past, present, and to come, are gently
planned by one whose only purpose is your good."
—A Course In Miracles

The key to this vertical journey to move beyond the limitations of your finite body and mind into your infinite abundant self is to take accountability for everything you have done and have not done. Become accountable for every person, place or thing you have hurt and taken advantage of. You must see how that has served you and them. You must see the perfection of the pain and pleasure cycle, feel both sides simultaneously and become grateful from the depths of your being.

This is the complete synthesis and integration of one state of awareness and the ascension to a new state. When you do this, you are dropping from your head to your heart, which is full of love, gratitude and compassion. When in doubt, ask yourself, "What would love do in this situation?" This is the evolution of your soul and being.

Remember these five steps when you want to make a change in your life:

Step 1: Get clear on what you desire

Step 2: Create leverage from the inside-out

Step 3: Break the old pattern and way of processing

Step 4: Replace the old pattern with inspiration

Step 5: Integrate pain and pleasure for power

PART III

As we move into the next strategies, it's important to note that a fundamental change is taking place. The first five strategies focus on a person at an individual level—creating change within one's self. Shifting paradigms from the inside, taking inspired and progressive action, using your whole mind and managing your life all have to do with creating autonomy. It allows you to build your house with a solid foundation. Continually readdressing, visiting, processing and changing as a result of these strategies will add more support to that foundation. Let it become more and more solid so nothing can shake you.

When I studied in school, the process was highly systematic. General biology came before cell biology and microbiology. Physics came before quantum mechanics. Algebra came before calculus. The same holds true for personal growth, mastery and your evolution.

Self-mastery is the foundation from which all other relationships will grow. We must have dominion over ourselves in order to grow bigger than ourselves. Independence, autonomy and self-mastery are the natural by-products of consistently applying the first five strategies.

Once we achieve this, we begin to move beyond ourselves and build natural associations with everything around us. In doing so, we create a person who is interconnected with other people, places and things. It is not what we say or do in our relationships, but it is whom we are that creates strong and trusting bonds. Applying the first five strategies allows our words and actions to come from our core.

As we move through the next four strategies we are entering a new dimension. We begin to connect and express ourselves "out there" in the world. We open up the potential for deep, meaningful relationships and associations. New opportunities for learning, productivity, growth, evolution, service and contributions will arise. However, this is also the realm that people associate with failure, human pain, suffering and dis-ease.

Virtually all adults live in this spectrum of the outer world. The fragmented clarity of what people know about themselves is what contributes to pain, suffering and contraction in the outer world. Most people have not worked through the first five strategies in a healthy and balanced way. They tend to define themselves based on their material assets and what they have accomplished or accumulated. Now, there is nothing wrong with accomplishing and accumulating wealth. In fact, some of the most autonomous and actualized people I know have extraordinary affluence. Yet they do not let their "things" define them. They know there is something far greater in this world. They are in tune with themselves and are able to fully express everything they are into the people, places and things in their world. People who have complete awareness and autonomy over who they are become the people who create and integrate this spectrum of life with the most success.

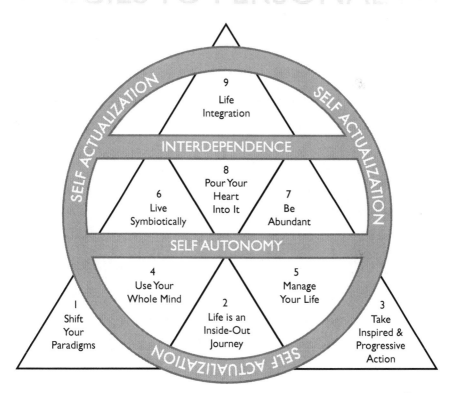

9 STRATEGIES TO PERSONAL POWER

SELF ACTUALIZATION

INTERDEPENDENCE

9
Life
Integration

8
Pour Your
Heart
Into It

6
Live
Symbiotically

7
Be
Abundant

SELF AUTONOMY

4
Use Your
Whole Mind

2
Life is an
Inside-Out
Journey

5
Manage
Your Life

1
Shift
Your
Paradigms

3
Take
Inspired &
Progressive
Action

Diagram 9

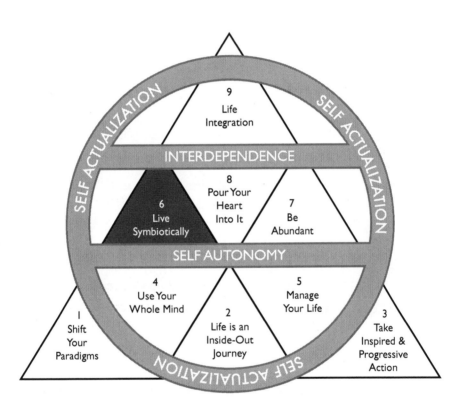

CHAPTER 8

STRATEGY 6 — LIVE SYMBIOTICALLY

"The most important human endeavor is the striving for morality in our actions. Our inner balance and even our very existence depend on it. Only morality in our actions can give beauty and dignity to life."
—Albert Einstein

Within the human body, an entire network of processes occurs without our cognitive awareness. We can examine many of these innate processes and apply them to our outer world to create more balance and harmony.

The human gastrointestinal system (GI or gut) has more than 100 trillion bacteria—each of which is a permanent lifetime resident. Some of these microbes are harmful and responsible for many of the infectious and acute diseases that people experience. However, the smarter microbes have evolved and grown with the changes of our inner ecology. These bacteria have been evolving over millions of years in synch with the human digestive and immune systems. These microbes have taken the evolutionary journey of continually reshaping what they are to be fully adaptable to their new environments. This environment is the gastrointestinal (GI) and immune system of our inner ecology.

These microbes help us by working with us to kill foreign invaders and pathogens, and we help them by giving them a beautiful home, our inner ecology. The perfect balance of these microbes prevents diseases and illnesses within our gastrointestinal and immune systems. By intelligently deciding to be adaptable they have created a symbiotic bacterial utopia. A symbiotic relationship is one in which all participants benefit.

Other microbes have decided not to change with their environment, and they actually fight our gastrointestinal or immune systems. In turn our immune system wages a war against them. These microbes usually have short life spans, as their relationship with us creates a competitive environment in which only one party can benefit.

We can learn a lot from the microbes deep inside us. If we want to get the most out of our lives and provide a path for generations to come, we must learn to live symbiotically with other people, the earth, places and things. This simply means that all parties involved will benefit from the experience and relationship.

When You Win, I Win

"Happiness is not a matter of intensity but of balance,
order, rhythm and harmony."
—Thomas Merton

If we want to live symbiotically, we must create a new paradigm. This is essential in creating long-term, established relationships as we move beyond ourselves into the world "out there." This paradigm creates an environment in which all our human interactions benefit every person and thing involved. Similar to our microbes, we shift from a place of competition to a place of collaboration and cooperation. We begin to see the veils of duality crumble when we establish symbiosis. The consciousness of win/lose, right/wrong, strong/weak loses potency. We shift to a place of greater awareness and balance. Rather than seeking outer power, we express our inner power in everything that we do and create. All people, places and things can experience success, happiness and joy.

This may sound like an idealistic and impractical way to live your life. But every successful relationship you've had has been symbiotic—all parties benefited. This holds true for you, your partners, your children, your family, your friends, your colleagues, your work, your business, your finances, the environment, the earth—absolutely everything.

Know When to Say "No"

"Every issue, belief, attitude or assumption is precisely the issue that stands between you and your relationship to another human being; and between you and yourself."
—Unknown

Several years ago I moved back to Vancouver after being gone for eleven years. I was starting my new professional life in a fresh environment. I had family in Vancouver and lots of old friends, yet I had no desire to rekindle old flames with everyone. I knew that there were only a select few people with whom I could create symbiotic relationships.

Last year I was walking down Robson Street in downtown Vancouver on a sunny Saturday afternoon. The sidewalk was crowded, full of people walking comfortably, carrying shopping bags, drinking iced coffees. As I was walking somebody passing me shouldered me extremely hard. It stopped me in my tracks. I looked up and saw a muscular, intimidating man who was covered in tattoos staring at me as if he wanted to pick a fight. I looked deeper and recognized him. I realized he was an old good friend whom I had not seen in almost 17 years. As I recognized him we both smiled and gave each other a massive hug.

"What's up?" he said. "How long has it been? I saw you interviewed on TV and told everyone, 'That's one of my old boys.'"

We both had some time so I asked if he wanted to get a coffee. I don't believe in accidents—I knew there was some reason I was meant to connect with him. I spent the next half-hour hearing about his journey. He had just spent the past four years in jail, had children and was living the only life he knew. I felt as if I were looking in a mirror that reflected how things could have unfolded for me. He hadn't changed a bit and I clearly had changed immensely. He spoke the entire time and I simply listened. I actually learned a lot about who I used to be from hearing his perspectives. He told me that a lot fell apart when I left my circle of friends. He said that I was the glue that held so much together, and that after I left, all our friends started stabbing each other in the back. I was surprised—I didn't know any of that. He told me that I did things right, and that people were always happy working with and being around me.

I had an epiphany. Was it possible that I created symbiotic relationships back then? Perhaps! The more important lesson for me was with how this interaction ended. He wanted to become friends again and start hanging out. However, it was clear that he had no desire to change his life. If he had, my intentions would have changed.

An important lesson in living symbiotically is to know what will serve you and what will not. Having the ability to say "yes" is easy when opportunities exist. Saying "no" is much more challenging.

I have an incredibly busy schedule—I work seven days a week along with leisure and play. My Centre for Optimal Living is nonexistent without me, I'm a professional speaker and author, I'm an ultra-endurance athlete, I spend quality time with Kate, I work on my mind, body and spirit every day, I spend time with family and friends, and I travel. My days start at 5:00 a.m. and end at 11:00 p.m. I will rearrange my schedule to make time for anything important, as I'm flexible and embrace change—but it was clear that there was nothing I could get out of this relationship. I knew it could never be symbiotic.

Investing time and energy into something that was destined to be out of balance would be a waste of time for both of us. Integrity is the great equalizer in life, so I came straight out and told him we lived in different worlds and I had no interest in being a part of his world. I got up, hugged him tightly as if I would never see him again and said, "You're the master of your life and you can always be who you dreamed of. Be well."

You have many circles outside your principled life. Refer back to the drawing you made and see where you can say "no" to non-symbiotic endeavors so you have more time and energy for the symbiotic ones. This simple change will allow you, as well as everyone and everything around you, to manifest into more of what you intend.

Integrity Breeds Symbiosis

"The measure of your life will not be in what
you accumulate, but in what you give away."
—Wayne Dyer

There may be situations or endeavors you're involved in that appeared symbiotic initially, but over time you realized they were not. This is another time to step up with integrity and say "no."

At my Centre for Optimal Living I have seen thousands of amazing and beautiful people and families. I keep my door open to all people, yet when I work with people we create a partnership. In this relationship I facilitate optimal living, health and wellness from within and they must create a more health-promoting lifestyle. I am a part of the picture, but they must play a large role in the process. They must adopt the five pillars of Optimal Living; Optimal Nerve Flow, Optimal Mindset, Optimal Minerals & Nutrients, Optimal Biomechanics and Movement, and Optimal Stress & Toxin Reduction. If one of us does not live up to our initial agreement, we lose the symbiotic relationship. If they don't hold up their end of the agreement and don't change, they won't be happy with their progress and I won't be happy with their ability to integrate and experience more. Symbiosis is lost. I only want to be a part of win/win situations. I end these relationships and refer them to a doctor who may better serve them given their circumstances. It allows me to create more space for the people who want to work with me symbiotically.

When you have the ability to say "no" you feel liberated, as there is no need to change anything outside of yourself, manipulate others or put your ideas onto them. You can remain in integrity, since you haven't wavered from your fundamental principles. You can say, "I choose only symbiotic relationships and I feel great about it."

To live symbiotically, you must be in integrity. Integrity is being, saying and doing the things that adhere to ethical and moral principles within you. It is a state of being whole. My old friend, the one I had coffee with, also told me that he always knew deep down inside that I was good. I asked him why he felt that way. From his lenses he felt I always did the "good or right thing" even when nobody was looking. He told me he knew about my random acts of service. Every month I would spend hundreds of dollars on diapers, food and toys and drive to the worst part of town, giving them to families who couldn't afford them. At the time, I told friends about it and they made fun of me, so I just did it myself in secrecy. Although at the time I had no idea why I did it, today I fully understand.

Whenever I performed those anonymous acts I would have an amazing night's sleep—in fact, those were the nights that I slept best. The joy and gratitude these families would have was immense. They would always ask: Why? I told them it was because I enjoyed seeing the look in their eyes, especially the children. Another symbiotic endeavor!

Living symbiotically demands thinking abundantly in addition to living in integrity. There is enough of everything out there for everybody. Integrity and abundance are states of consciousness. This applies to your health, wealth, relationships, career and nature. When you know in your heart and mind that there is so much available, you know that every person and thing involved can grow and benefit. With integrity and abundance you can pour your inner joy, passions and fulfillment into all that you become and do. Living symbiotically is the natural by-product.

Step 1: First Listen ... then Respond

"Listen a hundred times. Ponder a thousand times. Speak once."
—Unknown

To efficiently and effectively respond to our environments and create symbiotic dynamics, we must also learn how to truly listen. Listening is the foundation from which we can create outstanding communication with ourselves and then with other people.

There's an immense difference between hearing and listening. Hearing is the act of receiving communication. Listening requires thoughtful attention to fully understand a complete message and more importantly its underlying meaning.

Once, when I was 13, I was in a really bad place within myself and I truly didn't want to share how I was feeling. But my father insisted on talking to me. He said, "Nobody cares about you more than us. We want you to be happy. Why are you so upset and mad?" I hesitated and said, "Oh, I'll be fine." He said, "If you can't trust me, who can you trust?" I replied, "Okay, here goes. Well, actually . . . I hate school."

Instead of trying to fully listen and derive the underlying issue related to my problem, he cut me off. "What? How come you don't like school? You're acting like a child. Do you know what I sacrificed for you? You're spoiled; you're ungrateful."

In Indian culture, education is considered extremely important and is very high on the cultural value list. To tell a man who embodied the lenses of being Indian that I hated school was unacceptable.

"You need to apply yourself," he told me. "You're too busy screwing around. Education is your future. Without education you are nothing. You want to be a beggar on the street?"

The picture was solidified again as a 13-year-old. He didn't understand me, he didn't get it, I couldn't talk to him, I couldn't trust him and I would just have to figure things out on my own: this was the paradigm I had created.

For some reason we feel that we always need to rush in and save the day with our own paradigms, lenses and opinions. The challenging part is that most of us never even fully try to understand the underlying concern.

I believe that communication is the most important skill in life. I also feel that our education system doesn't fully recognize the importance of communication. Most of our formal education teaches us how to respond, not listen.

I think about what the Greek philosopher Epictetus said: "We have two ears and one mouth so we can listen twice as much as we speak." My father gave me the greatest gift by not listening to me. As a result, I have never repeated that pattern again because I never want anyone to feel the way I did. This gift has enabled me to become an extraordinary listener and be completely in tune with the deeper underlying messages beyond the words. This has even allowed me to change my messaging to match people's value systems so I can touch the lives of even more people. When you see the challenges of your life as blessings in disguise you open the doorway for something greater to materialize. Thanks for the gifts, Dad!

As you are working through this book, you are reading. You may take a few notes, writing. You may share something about this book to a family member or friend, speaking. Then finally you may listen to others. Communication is an art and science. We must use our whole mind to be effective communicators. Reading, writing and speaking are left-brain functions. Listening is a right-brain function.

As I mentioned earlier, more than 90% of our educational system focuses on left-brain functions, so that by the time most children are adults they are utilizing only 2% of their right brain. That means that we are hardly even trained to actually listen to what others are saying. In some magical way we are supposed to just figure it out on our own. We are responding before we actually understand what is being expressed.

To master the art of understanding we must first listen to ourselves. The human body and mind is a self-healing and self-regulating organism. It does nothing by accident. If you have an ache, pain, symptom, sickness, broken heart or disease, the first thing you must do is listen. What is my body trying to tell me; why is it behaving this way? What can I change in my life to improve my health or well-being? What should I do to kick start the healing process within me? Who should I ask for help? Simply asking yourself and listening for an inner answer would yield the fastest results.

Yet we've been domesticated to live in a paradigm that says our minds and bodies are weak and flawed, and that they need something from the outside to fix them. These symptoms, sicknesses or diseases of the mind or body are simply the effects of other causes. To find the causes, we have to listen so we can understand. If you're in a state of symptoms, sickness or disease, it's due to a lack of balance or dynamic homeostasis—and these effects are communication messengers telling you to get back into balance. Turning off the effect is turning off the messenger—it's not addressing the underlying problem. I once spent months in a bed listening to myself, hearing that inner voice. I had a lot to make up for, as I had treated my mind and body so harshly. Remember, life is an inside-out process.

Once you begin to listen to yourself, you can listen to the environment. For example, if you have a plant and it appears dry, the simple act of observing and listening to what it's communicating may be that it requires more water, minerals or nutrients. We can actually transform our entire relationship with the earth if we focus on communicating with our environment and creating more symbiotic dynamics through fully understanding.

The same is true of our relationships with people. When I had the conversation with my father about school he heard me, but he did not listen to me. Listening flows from our character. When we are deeply connected to our own principles and character we can listen for the sake of serving the person speaking. A self-actualized person provides a safe, nurturing environment for one to speak and one to listen.

When I work with people at my Centre for Optimal Living I spend more than an hour with them during my initial consultation. I spend most of that time listening. I want to know who they are and what is going on within them. Once I start listening, I listen more. Then when I feel I'm getting a clearer picture, I listen even more. Finally, once I have fully connected to them, I then listen more. It's the foundation from which I build relationships with people. From there, I can begin to understand them. It allows us to embark on a process of creating a symbiotic dynamic. Then finally I will respond, only after I have completely listened and understand them. My response always comes from my whole mind and inner character, my heart.

I've observed that when most people interact, they are "half listening." They are actually hearing to reply, not listening for the sake of understanding. They're listening through their own paradigms and filters and projecting their opinions. This is left-brain listening. They don't comprehend the big picture of what is being said. The left-brain can't do it—it's concerned only with the details. This is the source of all failed relationships in business, work, marriage, family, friendships, or even with yourself. Half-listeners are simply projecting their own story onto other people. Conversations end with a lack of clarity and understanding.

When you listen, listen, and listen, you begin to develop the character to become fully empathetic. It allows you to experience another person's outlook or emotions and what it's like to be inside their mind and body with their story. Many times throughout my life I have disagreed with many people. Yet unless I was asked for my opinion I wouldn't state it. I have phenomenal relationships with people who I strongly disagree with simply because we can empathize and live symbiotically. It allows us to fully and deeply understand each other emotionally and intellectually.

As a healer I have developed an ability to listen to people without having them even say a word. That's because 60% of listening is actually based on posture and body language and 30% is based on mannerisms and sounds. Only 10% is based on the actual words people speak.

So how do you become a true listener? It's a process of utilizing your entire interpretation and perception system, your nerve system. Here's what I do:

- **I listen with my ears.** What are the words they are speaking, how do they sound, do they sound their age, what is their story, where are they within themselves, what is their present state of consciousness?

- **I listen with my eyes** to observe their posture, body positions, gestures, mannerisms, how they walk and move. The structure of their body dictates its function.

- **I listen with touch.** Yes, I actually touch people. This may be a handshake, a touch to the shoulder or elbow, or even a hug. You can listen and understand a lot about a person by very respectfully and politely touching them. How did their handshake feel, did they fully engage in hugging you, or was it a distant tap? In my Centre I get the opportunity to touch people's bodies during an assessment to determine where they create patterns or unintegrated experiences.

- **I listen with my right mind's intuition.** It allows me to listen and more fully understand with my heart, which gives meaning to everything I've heard.

Develop Trust

"Listening is a magnetic and strange thing, a creative force.
When we really listen to people there is an alternating current,
and this recharges us so that we never get tired of each other.
We are constantly being re-created."
—Brenda Ueland

Listening with your whole mind is extremely powerful, as it will give you much more information to help you better understand a person.

You will actually be able to get right inside another person's mind, body and soul. You will understand them, and equally as important, they will feel understood. This environment is deeply rewarding, therapeutic and beneficial for everyone involved. It's symbiotic.

There are many ways to fully listen to and understand people. You can observe their family dynamics. If you are in their home you can look at their bookshelves. (You can learn so much about a person by simply knowing about the books they've read.) You can also learn a lot and more fully understand people by observing the behavior of their children. Children are extremely sensitive to the subatomic climate of their home and will behave accordingly. Adults usually dictate the climate of their home. Please keep in mind this is not about judging people—it is about listening and understanding them so you can serve them best.

When I work with people, in order to fully serve them I must understand them. They will also feel understood, which creates a climate of trust. It is impossible to create symbiosis and change if the people involved do not trust each other.

When I told my father that I hated school he did his best at that time to serve his son. He was concerned and felt that he needed to dictate the importance of education and the repercussion of leaving school. He evaluated what I said by disagreeing, he advised based on his experience, and he interpreted based on his paradigm, motives and behavior. He did not try to fully understand me.

Like my father, I now believe that education is fundamentally important. I actually do my best to learn one thing new every day and am a major advocate of higher education. Last year a teen came to my Centre—he was not enjoying his high-school experience. He was sharing and I was listening. He said, "It's not relevant, it's boring, and I hate it." I sat there and did not respond. Silence is a powerful tool to allow people to fully express what's really occurring. It was silent for more than a minute and during this time I tuned into his system, vibrationally and posturally. Remember, 60% of listening is anatomical and physiological.

I reflected on what he said. "Sounds like you feel it's a waste of time."

I also reflected on his feelings. "You don't feel very happy about school."

The dialogue had begun.

He replied, "No, it sucks!"

"Well, what is it exactly about school that sucks?"

"Everything."

"Well, is it the campus, students, teachers, courses, curriculum?"

He never replied.

"Is there anything about school you enjoy?"

"Maybe."

"Like what?"

"Hanging out with friends."

"Cool, anything else?"

"Nope."

"Do you like any teachers?"

"A few."

"Do you like the school facilities?"

"Yeah."

"What's your favorite subject?"

"P.E."

"Okay, now I'm a little confused. You said school sucks and you hate it. You're also saying you enjoy hanging out with friends, you like some teachers and enjoy P.E. All these things are a part of school and you enjoy them. There's a lot more to school than just going to class, right?"

"Right."

"So what part of school actually sucks, then?"

"The math part."

"Okay, so you don't like math."

"Yeah, it sucks."

"Well, why does it suck?"

"I just don't get it."

"Sounds like you're having a hard time with it. What grade are you getting?"

"D."

"How does that make you feel?"

"Stupid."

"Do you think you're stupid?"

"No."

"Okay, let's pretend, say, you got a B on your next math exam. How would that make you feel?"

His entire physiology and posture changed and he opened right up with a big smile and said, "Pretty damn good."

"Would you still hate math?"

"Probably not."

"What if I could introduce you to somebody who could help you understand math better? It might even make it easier and fun."

"I don't know."

"Do you know that I used to hate school? I got really bad grades and I thought teachers didn't like me."

"Really? But you're a doctor."

"I know, go figure!" I said. "Have you tried your best to do well in math?"

"Yes."

"Well, what if that person I know could help you understand math more?"

He was silent.

"Why don't we make a deal: I'll talk to your parents and ask them to call this person and you decide then if you want to work with this person?"

"Okay."

"Do you still think you hate all of school?"

"No, just the math part."

"Do you think you hate the math part or just the doing-poorly part?"

"Well, if I understood it, I might like it."

"Exactly!"

As we journeyed through this conversation we both learned that school was not the problem and source of his unhappiness. It was his ability to do well in a certain subject that revealed the source. He wanted to avoid this challenge, not overcome it. The source of this matter was his fragile sense of self-worth and confidence disguised as an issue in school. His parents and I addressed it and developed a strategy to support him.

By creating a climate of trust through observing, asking and listening, he was able to fully express himself. I was able to understand and serve him by addressing the source through a symbiotic dynamic.

Once we have fully listened, we begin to understand. Then we can respond—effectively and appropriately. When we understand other people, we're being considerate. When we respond to them we're asking them to understand us in the trusting environment that we've created. And when you listen to someone, you have an awareness of their paradigms, perspective, intelligence and consciousness. You have a greater appreciation of who they are and may even feel reverent toward them. With the same understanding and respect for yourself you can respond from your heart and mind. Any need to make others wrong and lose a symbiotic relationship will diminish. You will feel less compelled to project your view onto them.

If there's someone in your life you have difficulty with, meet with them and create an opportunity to listen to and understand them. Look at your work, your home, your leisure or your school relationships, or any challenge or problem you're experiencing. See them through the lens that will bring greater clarity and understanding.

Create regular one-on-one opportunities with any person that is important in your life. Kate and I love to go out for dinner every week. This is our time to enjoy and connect with each other on deeper levels. We listen to each other and seek to understand each other. We try to see life through the lenses of each other's consciousness. The human element cannot be underestimated: it is through this deep understanding that we will stop reacting and begin responding with our hearts. The door to creative ideas and solutions will be wide open.

Step 2: Schedule Heart Chats

"Most communication resembles a Ping-Pong game in which
people are merely preparing to slam their next point across; but
pausing to understand differing points of view and associated feelings
can turn apparent opponents into true members of the same team."
—Cliff Durfree

In most relationships in business, education or even at home, opportunities to express our true feelings are rare. These emotions get so built up within us that our physiology is inundated with feelings from the past, making it impossible to be in the present. The built-up emotional tension makes it hard to focus on whatever task is in front of us. It's like trying to pour more water into a glass that is already full.

Emotions or feelings that aren't expressed create obstacles to teamwork, creativity, synergy, collaboration and intuition, all of which are vital to the success of any venture.

The key to creating symbiotic relationships is to have structured communication processes in which everyone may speak without the fear of being ridiculed, judged, interrupted or condemned. In a heart chat, unintegrated emotions can be processed and released. This technique may be used in all situations: at home, in a work meeting, in a sports team's locker room and during times of deep healing.

These chats can be done on a regular basis, during times of conflict or renegotiation, during major transitions or any time when you want more authentic, open communication.

Heart chats have simple guidelines:

- One person will be given an object and only they have the right to talk when holding the object.

- Nobody else can talk until the object is placed in their hands.

- Nobody is ridiculed or judged for anything they say.

- Once a person is done talking, the person next to them, clockwise, will be given the object and they may begin to express themselves.

- Everyone should talk about how they feel and strict confidentiality should be maintained—nothing should be repeated to anyone outside the heart chat.

- Once everyone has spoken there must be a unanimous agreement that the heart chat is complete. If not, continue around the circle until time has run out or nobody has anything left to say.

It is important to have the guidelines written down for everyone. This technique was created by author and personal-development consultant Cliff Durfree, and it's intended to get to the heart of any matter at hand. I have conducted thousands of these heart chats and have noticed many transformations: enhanced listening skills, a constructive expression of feelings, better conflict resolution, release of resentment, integration of old issues, greater mutual respect and understanding, and greater connection, unity and bonding.

My wife and I use a customized form of a heart chat whenever we have a difference. We follow all the above guidelines, except we hold hands. Sounds strange, but the amazing thing about this is that it's impossible for us to argue with each other when holding hands. We lose our emotional charge in seconds and get to the crux of the issue in minutes. It is truly the most constructive way to handle change, differences or conflict. I encourage you to try it next time you are in a difficult or trying situation with your partner.

Step 3: Be Honest

"Our lives improve only when we take chances – and the first and most difficult risk we can take is to be honest with ourselves."
—Walter Anderson

When many people journey through life they tend to create a specific lens of other people, places and things. Most of these points of view are based on assumptions that have not been validated, so many people don't tell the truth because it's uncomfortable. We might make others feel uncomfortable or hurt their feelings, so we bend the truth.

Life is complicated enough as it is. If we cannot be honest with others, they will not be honest with us, and we both cannot objectively deal with a situation because reality has been distorted. When we tell the truth we free our energy to deal with the experiences of our life in the way that they actually are, not in how we think they should be or imagine them with our lies. Every time you water down the truth or distort it, you give away your power, vitality and create a new unintegrated story that holds you back. You lose the balance of living symbiotically.

At my live training events and advanced seminars I often get people to engage in a process called Truth Bombs Revealed. It's a powerful yet simple process. I get people to partner with a complete stranger and tell them to share a secret they've been holding on to. Each person goes back and forth. It's amazing to hear everything that so many of us keep bottled up within because we fear other people will judge us or disapprove.

There are no comments, suggestions or feedback; there is just openhearted listening and sharing. People start out slowly and test the waters with simple white lies. Eventually people really start opening up, as they can see that there is no judgment or reprimand from anyone. I eventually get everyone to sit back down and ask people to stand up and share their lies with the group, while holding a compassionate space. This is when people truly start opening up and talking about deeper, more painful issues. Finally, I get the group to start yelling out their lies and secrets in unison at the top of their lungs for the entire world to hear.

After I have taken them through this experiential process, which completely shifts their internal states, I ask if any person feels any less loving or accepting of anyone. Every single time, the exact opposite has actually occurred. People feel so much lighter, open and connected to everyone else. There are so many things we've all been hiding that aren't so horrible and are usually shared by other people. We are not alone with any of these secrets or lies; we are part of a community of humanity.

I have spent the majority of my adult life holding back the truth of the environment I was raised in, who I was as a teenager and what I had been through. I was ashamed and afraid of what people would think of me. I was worried I would be judged. Over the past several years it has been rewarding and enlightening to retrace the journey of my life. Today, I am completely transparent to anyone who would like to hear the truth of my life.

Ultimately, my purpose is to inspire and transform the consciousness of humanity so we can move beyond limitations of our finite minds and bodies and access our infinite, abundant and powerful self from within.

Telling the truth has brought me so much closer to my mission and the people who will be a part of it. My life's story is even being written into a screenplay and being considered for a movie. It never would have been possible if I hadn't abandoned my fear and simply told the truth.

When we free ourselves from the burdens of our past by telling the truth, we completely change our vibrational resonance and internal ecology. I have seen people living with illnesses, diseases, depression, anxiety, aches and pains that have completely disappeared over time after they revealed their truth bombs. People begin to look younger, lose weight and feel more vitalized. Truly we are releasing a lot more than just some withheld information.

It takes an immense amount of vital energy and life force to hold back our truths. When we release and integrate this vibration we will have more resources to master and create success in all areas of our lives. We will become more adventurous, spontaneous and willing to be our natural selves.

Step 4: Follow Your Agreements

"Unless your heart, your soul, and your whole being are
behind every decision you make, the words from your mouth
will be empty, and each action will be meaningless.
Truth and confidence are the roots of happiness."
—Unknown

The final step in living symbiotically was inspired by Don Miguel Ruiz, the author of *The Four Agreements*. This book was one of the pillars of my life's transformation. At all of my advanced seminar programs,

I begin by sharing the agreements and ask everyone to adhere to them for the duration of the program.

Agreement 1: Be Impeccable with Your Word

"Small minds talk about other people, average minds talk about events, extraordinary minds talk about ideas and possibilities"
—Unknown

This agreement is the most important, yet the most difficult to honor. By simply choosing words you have the power to destroy or empower the lives of millions. It's vitally important to say only what you mean and avoid using words to speak against yourself or gossip about others.

Successful people are the masters of their words because they know that they will create a ripple effect in the world. We must be conscious of our thoughts and words so we can create meaningful relationships, develop self-confidence and build dreams. Focus on words that foster encouragement, appreciation, love, acceptance, possibility and visions.

To quote Don Miguel Ruiz, "Impeccability of the word can lead you to personal freedom, to huge success and abundance; it can take away all fear and transform it into joy and love."

Agreement 2: Don't Take Anything Personally

"When science finally locates the center of the universe, some people will be surprised to learn they're not it."
—Bernard Bailey

The next two agreements are born of the first. So often in life we take personal dominion over what others say and do. We are trapped in this conscious state of personal self-importance. If somebody says you're stupid, looks at you a certain way or ignores you, you agree with what's being said or expressed. You take it personally.

Today I have come to a place in which I care a lot less about what people say, think and feel about me and I care a lot more about what they say, think and feel about themselves. Consider this for a moment. I am a person living in a house, that's on a street in a specific community. That community is in a city, which is in a province of the country called Canada. Canada is on the continent of North America, which is in a certain hemisphere on planet Earth. Earth is one of nine planets in a galaxy called the Milky Way. In the Milky Way there are many other dwarf planets, asteroids, stars, comets and meteors. This is one galaxy. In the entire universe there are literally billions of galaxies. In the grand scheme of this intelligent universe, how big is each of us? It is clear to me that none of us are the center of the universe, so let's stop acting like we are. (How's your self-importance treating you now?)

Given the vastness of the system we live in, it is crystal clear to me that we are incredibly small. My self-importance has gone completely out the window and I invite you to join me. What others say and do is simply a projection of their own reality and has absolutely nothing to do with you. When you completely integrate this you will be immune to the opinions and actions of others. You will live your life being the master of your own ship. You will be free!

Agreement 3: Don't Make Any Assumptions

"The harder you fight to hold on to specific assumptions, the more likely there's gold in letting go of them."
—John Seely Brown

We often assume that we understand and appreciate what is going on in other people's minds and lives. We make these assumptions based on a set of false perspectives and lenses. We may even take it further by putting these false assumptions on everything around us.

Her life is so easy.

If they only knew how tough it is for me.

He has more support than I do.

The assumptions we make go on and on—and they deeply disempower us.

The problem with making assumptions is that we believe they are true. We draw conclusions about other people, places and things: what they're doing, why they're doing it, what they're thinking. Then, instead of taking responsibility for something, we take it personally and blame the other person (or people). Making assumptions leads to a life based on a completely false set of beliefs.

We waste valuable time and resources wondering what other people are thinking, doing and intending. Fortunately, the remedy is simple: find the courage to just ask for clarification or express what you truly want. People who are on the journey of life mastery do not waste any time assuming or wondering. They communicate as clearly as they can to avoid misunderstandings, sadness and drama. They are not afraid of being rejected, so they simply ask.

When people do not have the facts, they imagine the worst. They assume facts that do not exist and form prejudices around these assumptions. So much of the heartache that people experience every day could be remedied if we all stopped making assumptions.

Consider what your life would be like if you knew all the facts behind people's behaviors, actions, and words. In working with people I've learned that there is a reason for every person's way of being, situations, problems and even opportunities. By simply asking, life becomes crystal clear.

Remember, the quality of your life is directly related to the quality of the questions you ask. The more we can get out of the way of ourselves, the easier it is to ask other people and ourselves the right questions. If you are ever in doubt about a situation or have an emotional charge from another person's words or actions, all you have to do is ask for more clarification. And when it comes to your own beliefs or opinions, I strongly encourage you to ask yourself, "Do I truly believe that? Why have I drawn that conclusion? Is this belief moving me closer to or farther from mastering my life?" The more you ask, the more answers you will receive and the more impeccable and empowered you will become. With just this single agreement you can begin transforming your life immediately.

Exercises to Live Symbiotically

Step 1 — First Listen . . . then Respond
Step 2 — Schedule Heart Chats
Step 3 — Be Honest
Step 4 — Follow Your Agreements

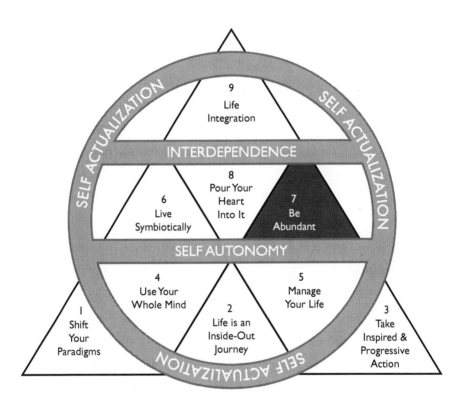

CHAPTER 9

STRATEGY 7 — BE ABUNDANT

"There is a science of getting rich, and it is an exact science, like algebra or arithmetic. There are certain laws which govern the process of acquiring riches, and once these laws are learned and obeyed by anyone, that person will get rich with mathematical certainty."
—Wallace D. Wattles

One of the largest sources of stress in people's lives is their ability to attract abundance. I am not a financial expert, nor do I claim to be one. However, I do understand universal laws that, when applied properly, will allow anyone to create the mindset, strategies, persistence and patience to be abundant with mathematical certainty. In fact, creating financial independence has little to do with balancing your checkbook and has everything to do with your mindset, beliefs and resonance. If you want to attract abundance into your life, you must first *Be Abundant.*

When I was a child, my family lived in an attic and I would think about how poor we were. I remember asking my father why we didn't have much money and telling him that I was unhappy. I told him that when I grew up I was going to be rich and drive a big truck and have a big house to play in. He laughed at me and told me that too much money was bad and the people who have a lot of money are crooks and do bad things to others to obtain that money. (My father was raised in India; a country that he felt was corrupt.) Many people I have worked with and met who have a hard time attracting abundance into their lives developed limiting beliefs consciously and subconsciously as children, just as I did.

These are the limiting programs and paradigms that play through our minds and physiology every day. Holding on to these ideas will hold you back from expressing your full potential in every area of your life. When I was a student at university I was told by economists and sociologists that you can predict, with 95% probability, the outcome of a child's life by simply looking at their parents—the types of jobs they have, where and how they live, the transportation they use, the people they spend time with, the conversations they have. Absolutely everything can be predicted. When I heard that, I was 20 years old and amazed that only 5% of people will not live out their predetermined family destiny.

Being Abundant is an Inside Job

> *"There is a secret psychology to money. Most people*
> *don't know about it. That's why most people never*
> *become financially successful. A lack of money is not the problem;*
> *it is merely a symptom of what's going on inside you."*
> —T. Harv Ecker

So many people say to me, "Sukhi, money is my greatest challenge!" Or "If I had more money, then everything else would fall into place." It has always amazed me that no matter how much money people have, whether it's hundreds or millions of dollars, many of them are singing the same song: "If I only had more!" Being abundant will change what you can create in every area of your life—physically, mentally, emotionally, spiritually, vocationally, socially, financially, with your family, with your inner character and with your quality of life. You can see how important it is to be abundant if you are to truly master your life.

If you feel you are a deeply spiritual person, or mentally and emotionally grounded, or extraordinarily healthy, but that you don't have the money for extraordinary experiences, you have a hole in your being and are not fulfilling your ultimate destiny.

On the flip side, maybe you were raised in a very affluent family and community. Your internal resonance for financial abundance was set very high the day you were born. You have the finances and resources to experience and have whatever you desire. Yet there is something missing in your life. There is emptiness, or perhaps your health is compromised, your spiritual life is nonexistent, you have no relationship with your family or lack an authentic social life, you have emotional swings or your quality of life is just lacking. You are abundant in some areas of your life yet bankrupt in others.

Whatever your scenario, know that to take your life to the next level you must be bigger and more abundant. You will have to think bigger, take bigger risks, take bigger action, and most importantly develop a greater grasp on how the universe and its laws work. You must become abundant to the deepest parts of your being.

Back to Physics 101

"Your most important asset is the conscious control of your own life."
—Eric Butterworth

This strategy of being abundant has transformed every area of my life. I knew when I was sitting in that classroom learning the probability of my life's outcome that I was going to do whatever it took to fall in the five percent of the population. I was going to live bigger. I wanted a better life for my unborn children. I wanted them to be raised with unlimited possibilities and potential. I wanted not only a relationship with my wife that facilitated this dream, but a home and community that resonated it, as well.

Today, I live in a custom home worth millions of dollars that my wife and I designed. We have breathtaking views of the ocean and mountains, as it's located in the most affluent and abundant community in my country. Another gift is that I can spend time with people who have created mastery in some, if not all, areas of their lives. I am surrounded by abundance. I have the opportunity to learn from these people and teach them, too. I recently had the opportunity to have dinner with a gentleman whose companies earned more than $60 billion in the past year. This guy plays very big. We spoke about finances, health, family, what inspired us—and most importantly we spoke about spirituality and the nutty world of quantum physics.

I believe that quantum physicists and biologists are some of the greatest thought leaders; they're modern-day mystics. What they have taught us is that there are two worlds occurring simultaneously. The world of Newtonian physics is what most of us have been taught in school. It involves direct cause and effect, linear thoughts and a mechanistic worldview that is embedded in a three-dimensional world. The other world is embedded in quantum physics, and has been explored since the 1950s, pioneered by the work of Heisenberg and Einstein. This realm is nonlinear and operates with subtle energies that are often intuitive because they are beyond our five senses.

To access your inner power and fulfill your dreams, you must master the art of operating in the two realms simultaneously. Spending too much time in the linear leads to smallness and a cynicism. Spending too much time in the nonlinear leads to a lack of grounding and poor results. I met a person once who told me that when I race I should change my molecules into a bird and fly to the finish, then transform back into my physical body before crossing the finish line. My reply was, "Sure, buddy, and how's that crack you've been smoking?" This is an example of blowing a principle so far out of proportion that it becomes absurd. For mastery, we must respect the linear Newtonian results that we can see with our eyes while acknowledging what's happening on a nonlinear quantum level in the realm of spirit. We must strive for balance between the two.

This may be the most challenging strategy for you to implement into your life. I've been practicing it for over 20 years and only in the past several years have I felt that I'm finally getting it right. That is because it's so easy to sway to one extreme or the other. Most people have a tendency to lean too far into the linear Newtonian direction and believe that they have no direct effect on the world around them, which is simply a crippling lie. Living in this mechanistic paradigm, they are caught in a world of linear cause and effect, pushing hard to try to make things happen. This is the perfect way to fry your adrenals and deplete your vitality and health, causing disease in your mind and body. In the end this will actually inhibit the flow of abundance that comes to you from the universe.

To become bigger we must practice (and master) the laws of the quantum world while still accomplishing in the Newtonian world of action. Mastery of both is when your greatest potential and extraordinary infinite self emerges.

It's All About Energy!

"If one advances confidently in the direction of his dreams, and endeavors to live the life which he has imagined, he will meet with success unexpected in common hours. He will put some things behind, will pass an invisible boundary; new, universal, and more liberal laws will begin to establish themselves around and within him; or old laws will be expanded and interpreted in his favor in a more liberal sense, and he will live with license of a higher order of beings."
—Henry David Thoreau

Everything within the universe is made of atoms, and all atoms vibrate, resulting in energy. The entire universe and everything in it (including you and me) is made up of energy. The relationship you desire, the new car, the dream house, the money, the vacations, the health, all come from the space that we see. This space is filled with energy and is known as the zero point field. Understanding that anything and everything comes from this field is the key to being abundant. Every single idea, thought, or possibility emerges from this field and lives in the quantum realm. To bring anything from this quantum realm into the linear physical realm is very simple. But please do not confuse simple with easy. It takes an immense amount of focus, impeccability and congruence to achieve this.

The field of space contains waves. Once those waves become particles, they've leapt from the world of possibility to the world of physical form. So how do we pop these waves into particles so we can experience them? Everything in the zero point field has a subatomic frequency, or resonance. You are also a physical being, made of atoms, that has a specific resonance. In short, you are a field of energy (physical being) that operates in a larger field of energy (the universe). The reason 95% of people's destinies are predetermined is because they will not shift their frequencies. If you're living in a mind and body that is of a lower resonance it is impossible for you to attract higher energy vibrations—known as "bigger results" in the physical realm—and vice-versa. Now you know why the rich get richer, the healthy get healthier, the happy get happier and the poor get poorer. It has everything to do with your internal vibration and resonance. Just like tuning into a different radio station requires changing the receiver's frequency, to create a different level of abundance requires changing your internal frequency.

Several years ago I attended a seminar in California. One of the economists who was presenting said that the world we live in is so abundant that nobody should be living in poverty. He said that if we took all the wealth in the entire world and put it into a big pot and then evenly distributed this wealth to every person in the world, everybody would be living well above the poverty level.

But then he went on to explain the problem: within five years, every single person would go back to living the same standard of life they had before the redistribution. How does that make any sense? The people who were homeless would be homeless again. The people who lived paycheck to paycheck would be back in that cycle. The people who were in debt would be in debt again. The people who were millionaires or billionaires would be wealthy again within five years. It is because being abundant has nothing to do with the cards life gives you—it has to do with your internal thermostat, your resonance.

This zero point field of space connects everything from the finite to the infinite like an enormous web. The world around you may appear to be lacking something, but it is actually filled with unlimited potential and possibility. This is where you and I have come from and it is where the gift of creation lives. When you fully embody this universal truth, your life will transform in extraordinary ways. (Can you see the importance of "e-motions" and the power they have to transform your life?) Every strategy and tool I share with you will begin to shift your internal thermostat to higher vibrations so you too can be more abundant.

Live Beyond Your Genes

> *"These genes are for risk, not for destiny."*
> —*National Press*

I've worked with many people who have told me that they cannot help their present situation because it is in their genes and therefore is their destiny. In the 1980s geneticists believed that genes controlled our lives and destinies. Therefore, they focused all their efforts to better understand the complete set of genes that define all the heritable traits of a human being—the Human Genome Project was born. They believed that this code would be the key to preventing poor health, thoughts, choices, behaviors and lives.

Along their journey, these scientists learned a surprising lesson. They uncovered a revolutionary understanding of life and how it truly works. They called this new science "epigenetics." This new scientific field has shattered the foundations of biology and medicine, along with our understanding of how we actually create our lives.

To better understand this new science and its powerful implications let's look at this word *epigenetics.* "Epi" in Greek actually means "above or over." Today, our children are still being taught the prehistoric understanding of life in that genes control the traits of life; however, epigenetic science has proven that life is controlled by something above the gene. That something above the gene is the gateway to accessing the zero point field and understanding our true role as co-creators of our reality.

It was previously believed that genes turned themselves on and off. What we now know is that signals from the environment select gene blueprints and control the manufacturing of specific proteins. In other words, genes do not control their own activity, the environment does. Genes are molecular blueprints, similar to a blueprint for the construction of a house. Genes are not the contractors that actually construct the house. When we were building our new home, my wife and I made so many changes with different contractors that the final piece was quite different from the original blueprint. We were controlling what parts of the blueprint would be expressed and what parts would be changed. Genes do not read themselves, which means they are incapable of activating their own expression and are therefore not self-emergent or self-actualizing.

Similar to this creative process, epigenetic mechanisms can modify the read-out of a single gene so it can create more than 30,000 variations from the exact same gene blueprint. (And I thought having one or two variations from our home's blueprints was a lot.) To compound this, there are an estimated 20,000 to 150,000 genes within a human being. There is controversy over the exact number, so let's be ultra-conservative and say there are only 20,000 genes. This means that a human being's genes can be expressed in at least 600,000,000 different ways physically, mentally, emotionally and spiritually. Clearly science has shown us that genes do not equal destiny.

So what controls how a gene is expressed and turned on and off? Drum-roll, please . . . YOU! Yes, that's right: you control your genes. Epigenetics has taught us that as organisms interacting with the environment, our focus, thoughts, state and perceptions control epigenetic mechanisms that act as the contractor selecting and expressing the genes that will be expressed and in what forms.

The evolution of you and your life is not about getting easier, it's about becoming more accountable. Here's the news flash: everything in your life, from your health to your wealth and everything in between, has been created by you and your interaction with the environment (zero point field). To move beyond your finite body and mind, you must learn to access the infinite potential and abundance within you and your environment.

You're the Driver of Your Life

"We fail to realize that mastery is not about perfection. It's about a process, a journey. The master is the one who stays on the path day after day, year after year. The master is the one who is willing to try and fail, and try again for as long as he or she lives."
—George Leonard

In spite of this new understanding of genes and life, the basic science textbooks, the media and especially the pharmaceutical industry continue to resist movement toward this clearer, more empowering scientific truth of life. These outlets still perpetuate the dogma that genes control our life. News articles are constantly promoting that a gene has been found to detect this or that trait, illness or behavior or that a new drug or technology will save us from our predetermined destined life. All of this is simply not true.

Behind every gene is a genius controlling it. The problem is not the gene; it's the driver who's in control of it. According to cell biologist Dr. Bruce Lipton, this is how our modern system handles problems: Let's say you just sold your vehicle, which has a standard transmission. The new owner apparently cannot drive a stick shift, and as they drive away the car jerks back and forth as you hear loud grinding sounds. A week later they call you and say, "That car you sold me, the clutch is bad!" So you tell him to take it to the mechanic, the "car doctor." The mechanic "doctor" diagnoses the problem and says, "Yup, the clutch is bad, we need to fix it." In other words, "perform surgery and prescribe some drugs." The clutch transplant operation and new fluids are a success. The new owner is very excited and happy. They drive away bucking, jerking and grinding the gears same as before. Before you know it, that driver's back to the repair shop stating that the new clutch does not work anymore. The mechanic diagnoses the problem again and says the car appears to have Chronic Clutch Disease. So he gives the owner a prescription for a new clutch surgery every two months. The doctor—I mean mechanic—ignores the role that the driver has played in creating a diseased clutch and attributes the problem to the vehicle's genes or defectiveness.

This is how allopathic medicine perceives and treats human disease. This is how our educational systems educate and disempower our children. This is how you and I have been taught how our lives will unfold. This mechanic's diagnosis ignores the role of the driver, which is the cause of all causes.

Become the Deserving Driver

"You are searching for the magic key that will unlock the door to the source of power; and yet you have the key in your own hands, and you may use it the moment you learn to control your mind and thoughts."
—Napoleon Hill

As you interact with the environment or zero point field, you are literally turning your life on and off. Your ability to attract and be abundant is in your complete control. Let's say that you want to make $250,000. You are on purpose by constantly thinking it, feeling it and acting upon it. This intention and action with the universe will turn on certain genes and regulate their expression within you, and you begin to become the person that deserves $250,000. Conversely, if you're putting out the intention of $250,000, but then getting stressed out over your bills, telling people how broke you are and being pessimistic, you will turn on other genes and regulate their expression with you, and you will become or continue to be the person of this resonance and vibration. This resonance will not be in tune with that of the person deserving $250,000. Either way the universe says, "Your wish is my command," and you are a prophet and conscious creator both ways.

Whenever your emotions, thoughts and actions send out consistent signals to the universe, your prayers are always answered by helping you *be* the person that deserves that resonance and vibration. When you send out an abundant intention of what you want for any area of your life, such as health, wealth, family, or relationships, that is your future intention. That wave interacts with the zero point field for the future. Yet, if you are being less abundant with your daily thoughts, emotions and actions, that present state will interact with the previous higher self-intention (for the future) and they will cancel each other out. The future self will not harmonize with the present self, and the abundant intention will not be manifested within you and take physical form in the world. You see it's all about energy—and those vibrations are simply not in sync.

As a healing doctor I have witnessed how powerful we are as human beings. The amount of potential energy within one meter of the zero point field has the capacity to boil the water of every ocean on the planet. Do you still think this universe is not abundant? It is the most abundant source of energy available to us; all we need to do is access it.

The only way for healing to occur within any person is for them to elevate their consciousness. When a person shifts to a new vantage point of awareness, they can see who they have been with their thoughts, emotions and behaviors. Their thoughts, emotions and behaviors have created a specific internal resonance and gene expression. Once there is an internal shift, a new possibility and internal ecology will be created. Personally, I do this by accessing people's systems through the nerve system. I harness everything within me to facilitate this process. It is so important to know that nobody can heal you from anything—only you can heal yourself. When I am successful in facilitating the healing process, it is because my certainty is greater than their uncertainty. As a result, the driver has been changed. The new driver cannot stand to be in that old body, and as a result the genes facilitate cellular reorganization to a higher state of resonance. Cells and tissues regenerate to a higher state of organization. Remember, there are no limitations of matter, only consciousness.

Confirming States

"When we shift our awareness or "frequency" from self-consciousness; where fear, impossibility or feelings of separation reside, to cosmic consciousness; which is in total harmony with the universe and where none of those feelings exist, then anything is possible."
—Rhonda Byrne

Most people tend to think that if they take a specific action they will get a specific result, but this is not entirely accurate. Whenever we send out an intention to the universe, our actions are nothing more than a confirmation of this future pull. Your actions don't create your results; they confirm to the universe that you're ready and willing to participate with the intention you put out by keeping your resonance in a place of allowance. Your deepest desires will come from your human will or spirit. Love, inspiration, enthusiasm and gratitude are the highest and most powerful human emotional states. Your desires will come to you only when you are in these states. Your job is to simply act and be in accordance with your deepest desires. In this state of resonance all you have to do is wait for it to unfold in the physical realm. This is the key to being abundant.

Exercises to Be Abundant

Step 1: Develop an Abundant Mindset

"Man's mind once stretched by a new idea, never regains its original dimension."
—O.W. Holmes

To access your inner power and create unwavering certainty, you must master your mind. To attract abundance you must figure out what you actually want. Once you break through that barricade and decide on your desires you must hold the mindset of believing they're possible and that you truly deserve them. Then, with unwavering intent, you must focus on them and visualize the desires as if they have already arrived. Finally, you must be willing to work persistently and patiently, taking action with disciplined effort and perseverance.

Most people will never even get to the first stage of developing their abundance. They have underlying false and limiting beliefs about what is possible for their wealth, health and every other area of their lives.

The key to developing an abundant mindset is to eradicate your mind and body of all limiting ideas and beliefs. I was raised in an environment where the theme was that money was the root of all evil, you couldn't be kind and attract abundance, and that you must have money in order to make money. Most of the world also believes the crippling lie that your genes determine your destiny. Most of these limiting beliefs developed during our childhood and they act as blind spots, preventing us from seeing our true potential. The reality is that your life is not determined by your genes or luck, but by your ability to access the infinite abundant potential that lies dormant within you.

Follow the exercises below to shine light on your blind spots and develop an abundant mindset.

1. To release your blind spots, you must first become aware of what they are. Make a long list of all the beliefs that are preventing you from accessing your full potential. For example: *I'm not smart enough, I'm not strong enough, it's too hard, I'll never*

be happy, I can't be a millionaire, I can't have more than my parents, etc.

2. You must now interrupt these patterns by making a list of new ideas and beliefs that directly challenge the old limiting blind-spot beliefs. Argue with them, ridicule them and have fun with this process. This is the start to shifting your consciousness to a higher state.

   Some of the interruptions I have used in that past are: *I am a high school drop-out and genius, I am the strongest man alive, this is freakin' easy, if that guy's a millionaire I should be a billionaire, the more I give the more I receive, if running 100 miles is insane . . . I'm insane*, etc.

3. Create a statement that is directly opposite to the limiting beliefs. For example, if you listed a belief that said you need money to make money, create a statement that says, "I don't need any money to make tons of money." If you believe your destiny is cancer, say that your destiny is a mind and body that expresses radiant vitality, extraordinary health and well-being.

Once you develop the statements, the words must send shivers down your spine if they are to shift your resonance. You must repeat them daily and believe you are abundant and deserve all the abundance the universe has to offer you. You must keep thinking these thoughts of prosperity and images of outrageous health, wealth and everything in between. You must flood your mind with these abundant thoughts, ideas and beliefs. Doing so will eventually push out the limiting blind spots and the lower resonance that dominate your essence. These intentions create a new tension from within your nervous system and will plant within your subconscious mind ideas of prosperity and abundance.

Like tuning an old guitar, your new resonance will harmonize to higher, more harmonious sounds and vibrations.

Consider this wisdom from personal development coach and business consultant Bob Proctor:

You must begin to understand, therefore, that the present state of your bank account, your sales, your health, your social life, your position, at work, etc., is nothing more than the physical manifestation of previous thinking. If you sincerely wish to change or improve your results in the physical world, you must change your thoughts, and you must change them IMMEDIATELY.

Step 2: Shift Your Focus

> *"If you don't put a value on money and seek wealth, you most prob-*
> *ably won't receive it. You must seek wealth for it to seek you.*
> *If no burning desire for wealth arises within you, no wealth*
> *will arise around you. Having definiteness of purpose for*
> *acquiring wealth is essential for its acquisition."*
> —Dr. John Demartini

Do you know that if you wanted to feel depressed right now that you probably could? All you would have to do is focus on something horrible that has happened in your life. We've all had bad experiences. If you spend enough time just focusing on the devastation of the experience, the challenges, the low emotional state, the heartache, gruesome pictures, sounds and smells, you'll begin to feel a little sad or even depressed. (The easier it is for you to get into this depressed state reveals the lack of integration you have with those experiences—more on this later.)

This same logic can be used to experience something completely different, too. In life, you get what you focus on. This applies to your relationships, family, health, wealth, recreation, quality of life, and having an extraordinary life. If you focus on the lack of each area of your life, that lack will expand. But if you focus on the potential and abundance of each area of your life, the potential and abundance will expand. Whatever you focus on expands. We cannot afford to focus on a crappy, limiting self-image or outcome. We must value and focus on what we desire to experience its creation in our world.

Follow the exercises below to shift your focus and expand your abundance.

1. *If you want to improve your financial abundance, you must first decide to value your wealth and make a conscious decision to become wealthy.*

Several years ago I was slowly growing my financial house, but my heart and focus was not completely engaged. I still had old programs running through my head like a record player that kept skipping and playing the same verse: money is bad, you can't be a spiritual person and be a millionaire, deciding to acquire wealth is not a noble act—the list went on and on. With this negative focus, all of a sudden I started to lose money. This was such a great blessing. It was a kick in the butt to wake up and to be more accountable to this area of my life.

I found myself with a net worth of -$175,000. Yes, it was that bad. Although I knew the laws and principles, I wasn't correctly applying them because I was letting the circumstances around me ("I'm broke") dictate the circumstances within me (my focus). I was doing well in most of the other areas of my life, but this was one of the last to catch up. But when I applied these steps, I went from being in a $175,000

244

hole to having a net worth of more than $1 million in less than 16 months during the worst economic downturn of my life. In less than two years this more than doubled to well over $2 million, and it continues to grow today. Clearly, with the right focus and creativity you can create whatever you desire once you make it a priority.

2. *Make a conscious decision to define what being wealthy means to you.*

I know some people who would like to have hundreds of thousands of dollars for retirement. I know others who want several million. I also know others who want a billion dollars. There is no right or wrong: what is important is that you decide and become crystal clear on what you want, not on how you're going to get it. Decide on what this will bring you—whether it's more vacations, more experiences, early retirement, philanthropy, a new house, a new car, and so on.

Now that you know what it means to you, figure out what your dream life would cost. The life you are living right now is the accumulation of the thoughts, ideas and resonance of the past five years. The life you will live tomorrow is the accumulation of what you are focusing on today. Personally, it took me years of focusing on my ideal life in every possible way before I actually began to fully live it. I had a lot of work to do to shift my internal resonance and awareness. The key was that I never gave up. Too many people begin a process like this and after several weeks or months they give up. People stop because they are not seeing the changes in their life. Do not fall into this trap. Your life is in your control. It is your choice. As my meditation teacher taught me, you must be patient and persistent.

Think about your dream life and the lifestyle you would like to have in the next two to five years. Think about the home you would like to live in, the clothes you want to wear, the vehicle you want drive, your vacations, savings, investments, net worth, experiences, etc. For every area, figure out how much money you would need to spend to get them. Now look at every area and begin to feel the emotions of actually living your dream life. Any thoughts or ideas that tell you that these things are impossible for you must be cast aside. The key is to bring your state to a place of deserving and expecting. You must feel deep within you how important it is that you achieve this life and you must hold laser-sharp focus.

3.   Know your financial house.

People who are not financially literate get controlled by their finances and will eventually end up stressed out, unhealthy and unhappy. I have seen this with thousands of people. Make the choice to increase your financial intelligence by shifting your focus around money. Remember, the more money you have the more choices you can make and the bigger difference you can make in this world by having the resources to express your gifts. If this resonates with you and you want more wealth, you must decide from the deepest parts of your being, the depth of your heart, to be wealthy and not focus on any worry or doubt.

The first step is to calculate your net worth. Anything that you own and puts money in your pocket is an asset, and anything that takes money out of your pocket is a liability. **Assets – liabilities = net worth!** You may need to hire a professional or use some software to accurately determine your net worth. Having a snapshot of where you are today will enable you to shift your focus to creating a more abundant future.

Now determine what you *want* for tomorrow and retirement. Having financial independence will free you up to pursue your passions, experience life, be philanthropic, and serve the projects that are close to your heart. Lastly, shift your focus and become financially literate. I am not a financial expert, but I have studied the mindset and strategies that create wealth by learning from some of the greatest wealth experts and integrating their teachings into my life. My wish is for everyone to become financially independent by becoming a student of financial mastery.

Step 3: Spend Consciously

"Too many people spend money they haven't earned,
to buy things they don't want, to impress people they don't like."
—Will Rogers

Most of us have been raised to spend way too much and to live beyond our means. This mindset will always keep you in debt, prevent you from saving as much as you should and shift your focus to consuming versus creating more wealth and abundance. It applies whether you make $50,000 or $500,000.

I once worked with a man who was making what most would feel is plenty. He was a very successful businessman who was raised in an affluent family, and he'd made close to $750,000 each year for the past ten years. The problem was that he was unfulfilled, unhealthy and in debt. Yes, in debt. The problem was that he was accustomed to increasing his lifestyle beyond the income he actually made. At a core level, he was looking for things outside of him to create a better feeling inside himself. He spent way too much money on trips, cars, and partying. Every year he kept sinking more and more into debt. He was unconsciously spending more money on liabilities, hoping they would lead to more inner fulfillment. The mindset and strategies I used to transform him began with doing the inner work that enabled him to revamp his awareness around money and his lifestyle.

You too can become a conscious spender, especially once you understand the difference between emotional purchases and objective ones. I learned from Warren Buffett and he taught me that if you cannot separate your emotions from spending and investing, your financial life will be a roller coaster ride filled with turmoil.

Follow the exercises below to become a conscious spender.

1. *Take an inventory of all the things in your home that you rarely or never use.*

Look for clothes, jewelry, kitchen ware, bathroom ware, blankets, sporting equipment, CDs, toys, vehicle accessories, tools, etc. Anything that you haven't used in the past several months should fall into this category. The reality is that most of these items were purchased emotionally in an attempt to fill some void deep within you. Since you haven't used them, it's safe to say that you likely never needed them in the first place. Now calculate the total cost of all these items. The cost may be similar to your credit-card debt.

Now make a conscious choice over the next 30 days to ask yourself every single time you purchase something whether you truly *need* the item. If you don't need it, put it back on the shelf and walk away. At the end of the month look at how much money you saved. This should motivate you to make some new long-term habits.

2. *Get out of debt.*

It's time to create a plan to pay off all your debts. Look at how much money you make every month and put at least 10% of that money toward paying off your debts. Start by paying off your smallest debts first. This creates momentum and allows you to be successful. Over time you should also begin to increase your debt payments. As a result of living within your means you will begin to have more and more money even if your income does not increase. Over time, as your momentum picks up even more, start to pay off your credit cards and mortgage early. By simply making biweekly payments instead of monthly payments you can shave several years off your mortgage as you reduce the principal and therefore pay less interest. When a debt gets paid off, that amount should be added to the "paying yourself first" account.

3. Pay yourself first.

This is known as the Babylon Law of Financial Success. The vast majority of people will pay their rent/mortgages, bills, and taxes first and they say that there's nothing left for themselves. A small minority of people will actually pay themselves first. A part of what you earn should always go to you. This is what I want you to do: think of a number that you feel you can pay yourself every month. Now stretch that number by 10%. For example, if you feel you can pay yourself $100 every month, start with $110. Every single month this amount should go directly into a forced savings account. Kate and I have several forced savings accounts and we give them abundant names such as: Dream House Account, Extraordinary Experiences Account, Wellness Account, etc. Then, every three months (quarterly) increase the amount you are putting into this forced savings account by 10%. In the example above, after three months it would be $121, in the third quarter it would be $133, and in the fourth quarter it'd be $146. This continues monthly with quarterly increases year after year. You can see how quickly your forced savings will begin to grow.

To compound this, once you have paid off a debt or loan, that payment should now be put every month into this abundance account. Remember, there is no risk to saving. You are simply putting money into an account and saving it. Once it has accumulated to a significant amount you can then seek out an investment opportunity to allow that money to grow.

I began this when I was in college, starting with only $10 every month. Over the past decade it has grown enormously, but most importantly it has made me accountable for every single dollar I earn, spend and invest. Ultimately, this process and education is an investment in my family's choices and what we experience.

To spend more you must earn more. If you would like to purchase a new vehicle, new home or take an extravagant trip, you must earn it. For example, if you would like to purchase a new vehicle, don't go out and purchase that vehicle blindly from an emotionally-driven place. First find out what that vehicle will cost you every month; payments, fees, interest, taxes, insurance, gas, maintenance, etc. Once you know the exact amount, you must save that amount for the next twelve months. For example, if the total cost is $1,000/month, you must create a new bank account in the bank, label it "New Car Account," and every month without hesitation or question deposit $1,000. The money cannot come from your forced savings account. After twelve months, if you have $12,000 in the account, you have earned the right to purchase that new car. Do this for all major purchases. It may sound intimidating or even silly, but it makes you live within your means and keeps you honest and stress-free.

If you want more money you either have to spend less or make more— either way you will have earned it. I personally know that if we're not growing, we're dying. If I'm not becoming more abundant every year of my life, I'm moving against the flow of life and you would be, too. So set your conscious thermostat to continually rise and make it your goal to earn more.

When you make more money you can invest more and spend more, and you can create an extraordinary lifestyle through multiple sources of abundance. Increasing your financial literacy helps you become more accountable in the choices you are making.

Step 4: Create a Legacy

"A person can make himself happy, or miserable, regardless of what is actually happening 'outside,' just by changing the contents of consciousness. We all know individuals who can transform hopeless situations into challenges to be overcome, just through the force of their personalities. This ability to persevere despite obstacles and setbacks is the quality people most admire in others, and justly so; it is probably the most important trait not only for succeeding in life, but for enjoying it as well. To develop this trait, one must find ways to order consciousness so as to be in control of feelings and thoughts. It is best not to expect shortcuts will do the trick."
—Mihaly Csikszentmihalyi

What is the ultimate purpose of my life? This is a question I have been asking myself for more than two decades. The answer to this question was the catalyst that forced me to change my focus and direction to end up where I am today. Ultimately, my purpose is simple: to make an extraordinary difference in the lives of other people and to be a catalyst and enzyme for human transformation and consciousness.

Sure, this started out very small. The first week I left my parents' home after spending months in isolation in a catatonic state, I began to simply cut the lawn of my elderly neighbor. She would always try to pay me, but I would refuse. Sometimes she would even sneak money into my sweatshirt while I was busy working. When she did, I would go to the flower shop and buy her fresh flowers with it. I was only interested in making a difference in her life; I wasn't looking for a job.

Today, I have the gift to transform the lives of millions. What first began as random acts of kindness have evolved into creating a legacy for myself that I believe is extraordinary. This never would have been possible if I'd never asked myself this one question. Today, I continue to ask myself such questions.

I urge you to sit in quiet contemplation and ask yourself, "What is the ultimate purpose of my life?" Your legacy can be anything you want it to be. Perhaps you would like to become a successful entrepreneur, fill a need in the world, raise healthy, happy and conscious children, or be an extraordinary athlete. Whatever it is, find your tune and sing it to the world.

Follow the exercises below to begin creating your legacy:

1. *There are ten distinct areas you must address in your life:* Intellectual Life, Emotional Life, Physical Life, Spiritual Life, Financial Life, Vocational Life, Family Life, Social Life, Inner Character and Quality of Life. To keep track of where you've been in your life, how far you still need to go or how far you've already come is a powerful exercise.

   • Look at how you did in each area five years ago and give yourself a score from 0 to 10 for each area. Zero means you achieved nothing in the area and 10 means you were absolutely living your life's purpose and desires.

   • Just like you saw in diagram 4, draw a large circle on a separate piece of paper and divide that circle into ten pieces of pie. Each piece of pie represents an area of your life wheel.

- Again, make an even scale for each pie with zero being the center and ten being the outer edge.

- Fill in the area within each pie corresponding to the number for that life area. For example, if your number was a zero you wouldn't shade anything, if it was a five you would shade half the piece of pie, starting from the center, and if it's a ten you would shade it completely. Go through this for all ten areas.

Once you are finished you will have completed your Life Mastery Wheel from five years ago. Now take a long, hard look at the shaded areas of this wheel. Is it smooth and symmetrical? Or do you have some areas at 8, 9, or 10 and some at 2, 4 or 5? How well would this wheel roll down the street? Its stability, smoothness, and speed is equal to that of your life for the past five years. How enlightening has this exercise been for you?

Now do the exact same process for the Life Mastery Wheel for today. Assess all ten areas for today and look at this wheel. How has it changed in five years? What has improved, what has digressed, and what has stayed the same? Remember, all living organisms are either growing or dying. If the wheel is the same or worse than it was five years ago, you are dying. Take a few moments to write a paragraph on what you have learned about yourself from this comparison.

2. *Be like a kid and let your imagination run wild.*

Are you ready to grab hold of your life and squeeze all the inspiration, power and potential that you know can be yours? This is your opportunity to completely let go of the "how" and dream at the highest possible level, to create images of your wildest possibilities and ultimately let your life transcend to its greatest level. I go through this process at least once a year and read and review it daily. If you go through this process actively by doing the exercise and taking action, it will reward you immensely with a vision for your future that is so compelling you'll be pulled like a magnet through the tough, dark and challenging times of life.

- Again, write down all ten areas that are required for you to Master Your Life.

- Next to each area write down what it would take for that area to become a ten.

- Write a paragraph for each area that is your perfect ten. For example, in the past when I did this for my physical life I said that I wanted to run a sub-three hour marathon. Then it evolved to a 30-mile race, then a 50-mile race, then a 100-km race, a 100-mile race—and it continues to grow today. Financially I wanted to be out of debt, and then I wanted to be a millionaire. And again it continues to grow today. Remember, whatever your mind can believe, you can conceive.

3. *Now that you know what you want and have a vision and legacy for your life, you must start becoming the person who is worthy of all this abundance.*

You must turn these waves of possibility into particles of reality. The fastest way to do this is to take these ideas from your head and drop them into your heart. Your heart has fifteen times the vibrational frequency of your mind. This means that the magnet in your heart is far more powerful. To drop these ideas into your heart you must hold the images in your mind's eye and feel the four most powerful emotions related to every area of your life. These four emotions are gratitude, love, inspiration and enthusiasm.

254

Every single day when you wake up and before going to bed hold these emotions within your heart and cells and imagine all this abundance as if it has already arrived in your life. I have done this every day for more than ten years. In an ideal world you will do it for 30 minutes in the morning and 30 minutes in the evening.

4. Take action!

Next to each of the ten areas of life write down at least 20 action steps that you can take that will begin moving you toward the realization of this new, abundant you. You must start today or else you will never start. You must take action on one of these steps right now, once this exercise is complete. Your life and your legacy depend on it. Every single day you must perform at least one action step that will move you one step closer to living your dream and legacy.

5. Live the dream every day.

Remember your emotions of love, gratitude, inspiration and enthusiasm. So many people go through life putting off their joy and happiness. This is meant to be fun. You fulfilling your life's purpose, your dreams, there's nothing as great as this. Deciding to express these emotions everyday and seeing the opportunity within every challenge will enable you to enjoy the ride. It is also very important to remember that the direction you are moving is far more important than the individual results you are achieving. My life is living proof that if you continue to move in the right direction, you will not only achieve the life you are pursuing, you will transcend to levels you may not even be able to imagine today.

Step 5: Give Abundantly

"Nature gives all, without reservation, and loses nothing;
man or woman, grasping all, loses everything"
—James Allen

Many years ago, when I was still a student in my early twenties and still going through intense counseling and healing, I had many days of extreme low. Some mornings it was an extreme challenge to simply get out of bed and go to class. Every day was different in its severity, but I would still choose to get up, get dressed and do my best.

One morning when I was having a very challenging day I was riding my bike across campus with tears streaming down my face. I rode onto the football field jumped off my bike and threw it against the fence several times. I began to punch and kick the fence as hard as I could until blood started pouring out of my fists. I was trying to release a deep pain within me. As I collapsed to the ground in exhaustion I looked up and saw the serenity in the blue sky and felt the sun warm my face. As I felt the polar duality, my emotions went from anger and fear to a deep calmness and peace. In this state I smiled and asked myself, "What else do I need to be doing to turn my life around?" The moment I said that, a girl from my physiology class that I had never spoken to picked up my bike, straightened out the wheel and walked it over to me. She helped me up and noticed my beat-up, bloody hands. She looked in my eyes, smiled at me, patted me on the shoulder and said, "It's gonna be all right, just hang in there."

This was the first time I had been touched by a complete stranger. It was the first time that I had experienced somebody giving for the sake of giving, and I felt a deep sense of gratitude and hope for her and the world. She was like an angel that came and answered my question.

I needed to start giving for the sake of giving. When you give for its own sake, you will feel a rich emotion deep within yourself and know that something you've said or done is making this world a better place because it has added more value for everyone involved. The stories that move me most are the ones of people who have given unconditionally, with no attachment, by following the highest spiritual act.

As Tony Robbins once said: "The secret to living is giving." One of the greatest feelings in life can be derived from the spiritual act of giving. Not only will you experience states of pure inner joy and inspiration, you will be practicing a universal law that states you cannot serve others without it coming back to you in multiplied forms.

Yet you must not fall into the trap of giving to others for your own elevation or gain. You will lose the essence and vibration of this act. If you begin to give to others and this world consistently on a measurable scale you will know that your life matters and is infinitely abundant. I have spent years giving of myself and today it's a large part of what I do. I spent years at a crisis line, talking people through their devastation or trauma. I took elderly people out for afternoon tea so they could have somebody to talk to and hug in their day. Over the past several years I've spent many days at homeless shelters and even Christmas day helping people getting back on track. Kate and I have spent Christmas mornings handing out blankets, socks, hats, gloves and treats to homeless people so they could feel loved and special on a day they have nobody to celebrate with. The list of how you can give is endless.

You must own this to your core. Many people I know give ten, fifteen, even twenty percent of their income and say that they give for the sake of giving. Then they look for their name in the paper, a newsletter or on a plaque for their contribution. Any giving is great, but if you're looking for acknowledgement or personal reward, you are missing the boat of this spiritual concept of abundance.

You must give to test your faith. If you have more money than you know what to do with, giving money will not test your faith. You must give that which you lack most. If you lack time, it is time you must give. If you lack money, it is money you must give. This will liberate you to a new state of consciousness and raise your thermostat for abundance. Am I pushing your buttons yet? If so, I apologize; my intention is to simply see you grow in abundance beyond anything you've ever experienced.

Kate and I have a friend who recently shared she was going through a challenging time financially during last year's Christmas season. Every so often she would have a woman come over to help her clean whenever she could afford it, as she was a single mother with two teens. During this time she had told the cleaning woman that she had no money so she couldn't afford her services. A few days later an anonymous card showed up with an abundance of money in it. This friend of ours was so grateful, but had no idea who it was from. A year later her financial situation improved and she was able to re-hire her cleaning woman for occasional help. During this last Christmas she received a card from her cleaning woman, and she realized her handwriting was the same as the handwriting in the card she'd received the last year.

I know that this cleaning woman understands at her core that the universe is abundant and that she is part of that abundance. She is choosing to express that abundance in her unique way. I know that she does not have a ton of expendable income. Yet she gave for the sake of giving, expecting nothing in return.

We live in a world that has very strong attachments to money. You may be asking why we need to give money. If you have resistance to giving money, then money is what you must give for your ultimate growth in abundance. If it is time, love, energy, or whatever you are most charged or resistant to, that is what you must give most.

Personally, for most of my life I have been afraid to give love because I spent the first half of my life feeling unloved. If you have ever met me you will see that what I have given most over the past 20 years is love—and it has freed me to love more.

Steps to Be Abundant

Step 1 — Develop an Abundant Mindset
Step 2 — Shift Your Focus
Step 3 — Spend Consciously
Step 4 — Create a Legacy
Step 5 — Give Abundantly

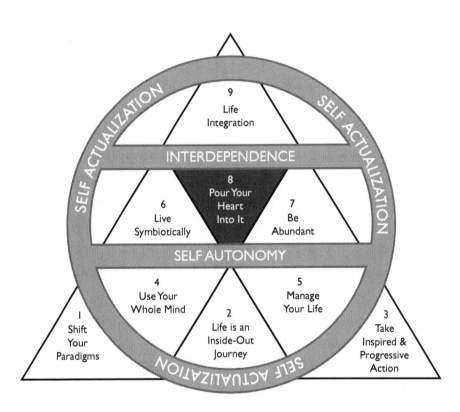

CHAPTER 10

STRATEGY 8 — POUR YOUR HEART INTO IT

"Many people die with their music still in them. Why is this so?
Too often it's because they are always getting ready to live.
Before they know it, time runs out."
—O.W. Holmes

Regardless of where you are on your life journey, inner peace, inspiration and happiness come from loving what you do and doing what you love. All great accomplishments have occurred when people gave everything they had within them to bring their dreams to fruition. When we pour our hearts into what we're doing, something magical happens to everyone.

Years ago during Ironman Canada, I spent several hours at the finish line watching athletes from all walks of life complete this ultimate challenge of mind, body and soul. Ironman is an ultra-endurance event that consists of a 2.4-mile swim, 112-mile bike ride and a full marathon run of 26.2 miles. A race of this magnitude requires enormous amounts of hard work, dedication and commitment. Athletes generally start training for it 12 months in advance. Many of the professional athletes will complete the race in 8 to 9 hours—and the title of "Ironman" is given to people who complete the race in less than 17 hours.

The race began at 7 a.m. In the evening, Kate and I went to the finish line and watched as the 17-hour cutoff drew closer—the deadline was midnight. It was pouring rain, yet thousands of people stood outside cheering as each athlete made his or her way to becoming an "Ironman." The energy was truly indescribable. I found myself in tears as people ran across the finish line as everyone cheered. To see young children look up at mommy or daddy and appreciate the dedication, commitment and accomplishment of a goal was priceless. To these children, their parents were now "Ironman" and anything in life was possible. To embark on an endeavor and pour your heart into it is to fully express the essence of being alive.

As the cutoff approached, many of us were waiting for 78-year-old Sister Madonna Buder. She began Ironman at the age of 61 and had been participating for more than 17 years. We knew she was very close as the countdown was on. Unfortunately, when the 17-hour cutoff passed, Sister Buder was not in sight. The announcer informed us she was less than half a mile from the finish line. It was past midnight, pouring rain, and many people had been awake since 5 a.m. However, thousands of us at the finish line were cheering as loud as we could. As an endurance athlete, I knew how much of a difference this could make on that final stretch. She could hear us, and our cheers fueled her. After several minutes a very tired, almost drunken-looking Sister Madonna Buder came shuffling down the final stretch. She would not be crowned "Ironman" today, but she possibly got the loudest cheer and ovation of the entire evening. I was in tears and speechless. She did not look well, yet she managed to finish and even crack a tiny smile. She says she sees the finish line as if it's the pearly gates of Heaven. She gave it her best and poured her heart into it. She was my hero that day.

What we get out of life is directly related to what we put into it: this is the secret to living an extraordinary life. The only way to find the limits of what's possible is to go beyond them into the impossible.

A few years ago I decided to remove the title "work" from my schedule—simply because in Western culture the word "work" has a negative connotation vibrationally; it's seen as a task that we must endure yet not fully enjoy. I truly love my work but I refer to it as simply "serving people at my centre," "writing," "speaking," "transforming consciousness," or "inspiring the world." I was finding that when I called it "work" it was becoming challenging to pour my heart into it. And for the past two decades I've made it a priority to pour my heart into everything I do.

Whether I am serving at my centre, writing, speaking, training, spending time with family, going out for dinner, watching a movie, or reading a book, I pour my heart into it. When I'm training for an ultra-marathon I generally run three to four marathons every week. If it's Ironman I log up to 30 hours each week swimming, cycling, running and resistance training. I usually complete these training sessions early in the morning before most people have even had their morning coffee. After my exercise I meditate, visualize and journal. This is my daily routine so I can show up and be as big as possible in life. Once I'm fueled and cleaned up, I get ready to serve in one of my modalities. Before I begin serving people with my innovative healing approach at my centre, I isolate myself in my private room and find my zone. This activity heightens my ability to perceive the patterning throughout people's systems so I can serve them to the best of my ability.

It's important to know that we are new and different every day. What we call our "best" one day may be different from our "best" other days. I always recognize and honor this natural principle of life. Each day my goal is to be fully present and do my best by pouring my heart into everything I do. When we live this way we leave no room for judgment. After all, we can never do any better than our best.

Connect With Your Values

"I believe that a life of integrity is the most fundamental source of personal worth. I do not agree with the popular success literature that says that self-esteem is primarily a matter of mindset, of attitude – that you can psych yourself into peace of mind. Peace of mind comes when your life is in harmony with true principles and values and in no other way."
—Stephen Covey

When we live from our whole mind, in the perfect balance between left and right brains, we open the channels to our heart. If you are finding this challenging to understand, you're locked in your left brain—I ask that you work on becoming more in tune with your right mind. On the other hand, if you are an overly emotional or sensitive person and feel overwhelmed at times, you are locked in your right brain. I ask that you work on connecting with your analytical left brain.

Life is about balancing and finding dynamic homeostasis. We need to express all of ourselves. When we find this "sweet spot" we get into a state of "flow" and the gateways to our hearts fully open. As a result, we can pour it into everything that we do. Life becomes more purposeful and meaningful. Our ability to connect with others increases. We begin to understand others from a place of gratitude and respect. We begin to look at the world from new vantage points and perspectives. We create new paradigms and shift our internal programs. We're inspired to take action. We integrate and become more conscious.

We begin to live more from our values and less from our needs. When we live from our needs we are not following the natural momentum of life; instead of living from the inside-out, we are living from the outside-in. We're seeking approval from others. We need to feel accepted, recognized and appreciated. We seek control and the need to be right, perfect or important. The desire to stand out, be busy and dictate to others our beliefs becomes our way of personal expression. When we live from our needs, we begin to lose the spark and light within us, as we're constricted and living life from the outside-in. We are living against the grain of life.

When you begin to live from your values, the lens of your life will change. These are the conditions and characteristics of yourself and your life that matter most. This is living from deep inherent principles of life. This is living from the inside out. It is pouring your heart into everything you do. Living from your values, you'll seek adventure, freedom of expression, integrity, optimal health, authenticity, curiosity, nature, creation, connection and discovery.

Trust vs. Fear

*"Don't ask yourself what the world needs, ask what
makes you come alive and go do it. Because what the
world needs is people who have come alive."*
—Howard Thurman

Physics has taught us that these deep inherent principles of life are the values that lie deep within us at a subatomic level. This same subatomic tone is actually inherent within the fabric of life, as well. Remember, atoms make up the fabric of life. We enter this state of consciousness through dynamic internal homeostasis. It is a state of purity and wholeness. This state allows us to connect with our hearts and express everything that it represents to the world outside of us. This is the essence of pouring your heart into it.

As you know, in physics the world outside of us is known as the unified or zero point field. According to modern physics it is the deepest, most powerful level of nature's functioning. Every single second of every day of our lives we interact with this field.

Our ability to create more of what we desire is based on our state of subatomic resonance. The unified field is made up of waves and particles. When an atom takes on its particle formation, it is a physical thing that we can see and touch. A car, a road, and a tree are all particle-formed atoms. The wave formation of an atom cannot be seen or touched. The waves of the zero point field act as pure potential and possibilities waiting to be accessed. The higher frequencies of this field can only be accessed when our hearts are aligned with our minds. Right-brain people do this more easily; left-brain people cannot perceive it. When we pour our hearts into what we do, our inner and outer worlds shift. We can focus our attention and intention on what we desire and shift the wave formation to a particle existence. When we pour our hearts into what we do, we begin to live a life we love and love the life we live.

Furthermore, our inner ecology completely changes from a place of fear to a place of trust. The physiology, chemistry, anatomy and pharmacology of the body and mind are completely different in these states. In a place of fear, our endocrine system releases more cortisol, adrenaline and epinephrine. We move out of our balancing act and lose dynamic homeostasis. Our cells and tissues begin the process of becoming disorganized, decayed and diseased in this survival state. We have less luster and thirst for life. Mentally and emotionally we begin to shut down and our paradigms contract. Our outer world is always a reflection and representation of our inner world. They are deeply connected atomically and physiologically. We begin to become cynical and less optimistic, and we stop fulfilling our life's purpose.

When we shift to a place of trust, we increase our ability to integrate and increase our state of balance within. We heal, as cells and tissues go through protein synthesis. Our paradigms, worldviews and consciousness grow exponentially. We take smart risks and look at things more clearly. The people, places and things we look at will also begin to change. We become leaders, pouring all that we are into everything we do. We develop a deeper reverence and thirst for life and pursuing our passions. Pouring our hearts into all that we do creates a principled, centered life of inner peace, power, authenticity and fulfillment.

The Power of Your Heart

"Here's to the crazy ones. The misfits. The rebels. The troublemakers. The round pegs in the square holes. The ones who see things differently. They're not fond of rules, and they have no respect for the status quo. You can quote them, disagree with them, glorify, or vilify them. But the only thing you can't do is ignore them. Because they change things. They push the human race forward. And while some may see them as the crazy ones, we see genius. Because the people who are crazy enough to think they can change the world, are the ones who do."
—Apple

There is something extraordinary about the vibrational resonance of our hearts. When you begin to utilize your whole mind, a door opens to allow you to connect with the highest human emotional states. These states are feelings of Love, Gratitude, Inspiration and Enthusiasm. In order to pour your heart into what you are doing and who you are being, you must be resonating at the frequency of these emotional states. When you begin to do so, your most extraordinary life will begin.

Your heart has 15 times the vibrational frequency of your mind. When you move a thought from your head to your heart and get into these emotional states, the universe will conspire, and the people, places and things in your life will begin to shift. All the areas of your life you desire to master will begin to line up with great synchronicity.

The vibrational frequency sent from your heart is similar to a radio broadcast signal sending its waves to the universe for everyone to hear. Once the universe hears and feels it, it begins to reshape itself from the dominating waves of your heart. Just like the waves sent out from the dial of different radio stations, you determine what you're listening to.

This universal law is always occurring and always in effect. Once you learn to master this art of pouring your heart into all that you do, your life will change and reshape to your deepest ideals and dreams with mathematical certainty.

The only journey in life is the journey from within.

Pouring Your Heart into Your Dreams

"A journey of a thousand miles must begin with a single step."
—*Lau Tzu*

Steven Spielberg dreamed of becoming a film director since he was a child. In fact, he began making amateur movies when he was very young.

Spielberg's legendary journey to the top exemplifies the strategy of pouring your heart into your dreams. He dreamed of working at a major studio, but had no direct contacts or connections to get his foot in the door. So he created an opportunity. At Universal Studios in California, there is a tram that takes people on studio tours for a behind-the-scenes glimpse into the industry. Spielberg devised a plan to get into Universal Studios by simply purchasing a ticket for the tram tour. He learned he could easily step off the train without anyone noticing.

One day he boarded the morning tour wearing a suit and carrying a brief-case. He sneaked off the train and hid between sound stages until the tour ended. He walked around Universal Studios that day as if he were already working there, smiling at people and saying hello. Eventually he made his way to an exit, but first he went out of his way to wave at the security guard—every time he did it, the guard waved back.

Spielberg did this everyday for three months. Talk about pouring your heart into it. During this time everyone thought that he was already an employee of the studio. Each day he went out of his way to speak with and befriend different directors, writers and editors. After some time he actually found a vacant office and took it over as his own. He even listed his name in the building directory. If he'd been stuck in his head, logic would have talked him out of all of this.

During this time he made it a priority to get to know Sid Sheinberg, who was the head of production for TV at the time. He brought some of his college film projects to Sheinberg one day, and Sheinberg was so impressed that he gave Spielberg a contract with Universal Studios.

Steven's first full-length film, *The Sugarland Express*, won a screenplay award and received critical acclaim at the 1974 Cannes Film Festival. Unfortunately, it tanked at the box office. But he didn't let this minor setback slow down his stride.

A year later he discovered and fell in love with a book titled *Jaws*. The studio was already planning to adapt the book and had already chosen a well-known director to film it. Spielberg desperately wanted to direct *Jaws*, but he had a lot against him. His first movie was a financial disaster and the director for *Jaws* had a proven track record. But he was determined to direct it and did everything he could to persuade the producers to dismiss the chosen director and give the film to him. Again he poured his heart into it and the universe conspired on his behalf. *Jaws* was his.

This film was a tough assignment. Right from the start he faced major challenges with technical problems, and it went way over budget. Spielberg still did everything he could to make it a masterpiece. *Jaws* was released in 1975 and the critics loved it. It also broke box-office records and within a month of its release it had brought in $60 million.

Of course, we're all familiar with the rest of Spielberg's career—he went on to direct such films as *E.T., Schindler's List, The Color Purple,* and *Saving Private Ryan,* not to mention franchises like *Indiana Jones* and *Jurassic Park.* (And "director" is just one hat he wears.)

Spielberg embodies the art of pouring your heart into your dream and becoming one of the best in the business. Spielberg continues to pursue his dreams; he even created a production company with two other Hollywood moguls—they call it "Dreamworks."

Dreams do work: they begin in our minds, and only when we pour our hearts into them does the universe conspire to bring them to fruition. And when your dreams begin to manifest in physical form, they will continue to appear so quickly that you may even begin to wonder where they'd been hiding during the more challenging years. Knowing the power of your heart allows you to stay in a state of acceptance and allowance so the universe may deliver your masterpiece life.

Your Heart Performs Miracles

"The best and most beautiful things in the world cannot be seen or even touched, they must be felt with the heart."
—*Helen Keller*

When I began my journey of self-exploration I would always hear authors and personal-growth speakers say that the heart performs miracles. I would sit back and think, "What on earth are they talking about? I thought the heart pumps blood to the rest of the body." My understanding of universal laws and subatomic particles was very elementary at the time.

Over the past two decades I have grown and evolved enormously. I've had the gift of experiencing states of well-being and consciousness that I never even knew were available to us. Essentially, my ability to tune into and feel the energy and vibrations of other people has become palpable. So much of what I've studied and learned I've been able to apply to life.

One of the greatest gifts I've received has been to participate in the healing process—both personally, with myself, and professionally, in the service of others. I have an innovative approach to facilitating the healing process within people, and as a result I've been able to work with people suffering from many ailments. I have worked with people living with terminal illnesses, cancers, cardiovascular diseases, autoimmune diseases, chronic syndromes, anxiety, depression, aches, pains, and the list goes on. I've worked with newborns, people who are almost centurions and many ages in between. I've worked with people who drove hours to seek my services and people who flew in from other cities and countries. In working with people from all walks of life, I've been able to witness the enormous healing capacity of the human mind, body and spirit.

Small Choices Lead to Big Outcomes

"All healing is first a healing of the heart."
—Carl Townsend

Years ago, when Kate and I got married, we decided to celebrate the rest of our lives together by spending a month on the sacred lands of Peru. It had always been a dream of ours to go there to experience the ancient Andean culture and visit sacred sites. We have a dear friend there who is a traditional shaman healer of that region. His name is Jhaimy Alvarez and he is like a brother to me. We first met in Vancouver years before this trip, when he was sharing his teachings on a global tour. At the time he worked with an interpreter, as his English was very poor. It was fascinating that we connected on such a deep level yet we could not even communicate with words, as I couldn't speak a word of Spanish at the time. We had a deep heart connection.

In Peru, he worked as a healer and guide. We had Jhaimy as our guide during our trip and he delivered an extraordinary experience. We spent weeks seeing ancient sites, learning ancient wisdom in sacred ceremonies, and experiencing a deeper and deeper connection to each other and our hearts. We even did the seven-day trek through the Salcantay Glacier to Machu Picchu, which was another amazing, heart-opening experience. It was safe to say that Kate and I were essentially cracked wide open, basking in a state of love and compassion.

On our way to Lake Titicaca we stopped in a small town called Racchi, which has ruins dating back to the time of the Inca. We arrived early in the morning and toured the site. Jhaimy asked if we might take a short time to help the people of this tiny community. I said, "How can I be of service?" We found an old, run-down building and Jhaimy announced to all the people at the center of town that a special healing doctor from Canada was here and was going to heal them from their illnesses and ailments.

A few people strolled into the building and I began my magic, literally. I just dropped into my heart put my hands on their systems and after a few minutes told them how to continue to facilitate the healing process. As time passed the line got longer and longer. Kate was outside getting people ready, and my healing brother Jhaimy was working his magic on the other side of the room. The amazing thing about this experience was that I was so connected to my heart I could feel the transformations occurring before my eyes. Similar to the way I work at my Optimal Living Centre at home, I was working in complete silence.

Several hours later the line did not get any shorter as people kept flocking to the building. Jhaimy asked me if I wanted to go, since we were so far behind schedule, but I declined and said, "More lives need saving." We both kept working away, pouring our hearts into it. We were two people from different cultures, different training, different languages, and different worlds doing virtually the same thing with our hands, clearing and healing these people's systems using our hearts.

Once the sun set, I could feel my energy and vitality coming down after a day of pouring everything I had into the healing. Toward the end of the day, a woman walked into the room with her five-year-old son in her arms. He looked nearly dead. He was completely limp, with pale skin and underdeveloped muscles. His eyes were rolled back into his skull and he could not walk, talk or respond. I actually checked his pulse to see if he was alive. He had a very faint pulse and was in the worst condition I have ever seen. He was standing at the doorstep of death. His mother told me that over the past two years, for no discernible reason, her son had simply begun to die. The doctors could not diagnose him and were helpless as to what to do. At first I jumped right back into my head and thought about all the possible illnesses and diseases that could cause his deterioration. I then told myself that there was nothing I could do; all my Western education and my logical left mind said that he was going to die in the next few days.

The woman looked at me and began to cry and say things to me in Spanish. Her tears touched my heart and tears began to roll down my face, too. I turned my mind off, dropped back into my heart and took her boy from her arms. I looked over at Kate and she looked at me with certainty and nodded her head. At that moment I prayed and asked God for support. I poured everything I had into this little wilted body to kick-start his nervous system with my tonal healing work. After several minutes I picked the boy back up and handed him to his mother. I said some words to her that came straight from my heart. Tears rolled down our faces. I was done for the day and would spend the next 24 hours violently ill, purging all the energy my body had soaked up.

Your Power and Potential is Unlimited

"When you see it and feel it right in the wholeness of your being, you then have created the condition that makes the result inevitable."
—Unknown

When this trip was over and I returned home, I often thought about this boy and wondered how his story would unfold. I had been in contact with Jhaimy but he had never returned to the town of Racchi since that day. Several months had passed. Then, through a series of synchronous events, a few friends of mine decided to visit Peru. They were also on tour with Jhaimy as their guide and they passed by the town of Racchi to visit the ancient Inca ruins. While Jhaimy was standing in the town square, a frantic woman approached him, screaming at him and asking if the special healing doctor from Canada was with him. He said no. She then pointed to a field close by and said that was her son. He was out there running around, playing soccer, laughing and smiling as a typical boy his age should be. Jhaimy was speechless. She told him that after that day I worked with him, he began to come back to life and he was still improving. She told him to thank me from the bottom of her heart and said I saved her shining light.

The word "health" is related to the word "holy." This means that healing is the return to wholeness. That is what this boy experienced; I was simply the catalyst that removed the barriers to his wholeness. I would go even further to say that all healing is a spiritual experience because

275

that is the essence of wholeness. We are all on a journey toward greater wholeness.

I share this story because it exemplifies the power we all possess deep within ourselves. The intelligence that created this entire universe lives deep within your heart and is the gateway to that omnipotent, pure and powerful potential. When we pour our hearts into life, we transform ordinary to extraordinary and miracles occur. In fact, most of our daily lives are filled with small miracles—we just need to see through the lenses of our conscious hearts.

Your Heart is the Key to Transform Your World

"Our business in life is not to get ahead of others, but to get ahead of ourselves— to break our own records, to outstrip our yesterday by our today."
—Stewart Johnson

We all face issues and deal with concerns as individuals, communities, countries and on a global scale. You may struggle with your physical health, mental or emotional well-being, relationships, career or even finances. You may struggle at the community level with homelessness, crime, or violence. Or the challenges may be more global, with issues related to our ecosystem or conflict between nations. Whatever it is for you, every issue we face as humanity was put in motion by a set of human choices and behaviors. Therefore, everything in life is the result of actions that people have chosen to take or not take. Once we realize that we are the conscious creators of our worlds, we can begin to create our lives from a more connected, powerful and authentic place.

We all have complete control of our internal worlds. As a result of our decisions from within, we take action in the outside world to create specific results. When you connect with your powerful conscious heart, you are in tune with your highest, infinite self. The actions you take from this place have the capacity to transform your home, business, community and world. The only limit to the impact you have in your life is the limit you place upon yourself. So why not dream big? When you pour your heart into your life you will utilize your imagination and have unwavering commitment. Ordinary people like you and I have the capacity to do extraordinary things with this level of commitment. You will persist until you find a way to make things work. You will never give up. You will even have the capacity to become somebody's hero.

I believe that every person on earth has the inborn desire and capacity to make the world a better place. I do not believe people are inherently bad. I believe people get disconnected and do bad things. I believe this disconnection is the source of unhappiness, disease, poverty and war. The solution is a reconnection, a connection to self, connection to your heart, and connection to a higher state of being.

Most people do not tap into this higher state of consciousness and life until a major challenge or life-threatening situation arises. Your challenges give you the opportunity to go within and to connect to a source of power that you were previously unaware of. Your heart has that much power. There are no obstacles too great or challenges that cannot be overcome. This is all of our natural states.

Exercises to Pour Your Heart Into It

Step 1: Begin Every Day with Exercise, Meditation, Visualization & Journaling

Exercise

I get up at five a.m. almost every day so I have three hours with which to begin my day on purpose. I train with the seasons, and I recommend you do the same. When it's sunny and warm, I'll ride my bike, run on seawalls or trails, and swim in the ocean. In the winter I'll train indoors or go snowshoeing or snowboarding. Wherever you live, there are activities you can do to push yourself.

I also recommend that every person go anaerobic every day. This essentially means pushing yourself for as hard as you can for as long as you can. This is an all-out sprint (pushing yourself to the limit whether you're running, climbing, cycling, rowing, or whatever you're doing). Going anaerobic is exercise with little oxygen and training aerobically is exercise with oxygen and can be sustained for hours. This anaerobic set should last for one to two minutes and is an-all out effort.

Even if you are doing aerobic training I recommend still going anaerobic daily. There is an 81-year-old Ironman triathlete named Lew Hollander who has been competing in the world championships in Kona for 20 years. He is a motivational speaker and has been going anaerobic every day for many years. He says that if you want to be living an extraordinary life at 81 you'd better be paying close attention to what you are doing in your thirties, forties and fifties!

The benefits of exercise are endless. Going anaerobic requires that you pour your heart into it for that all-out effort. And how you do anything is how you do everything in life. Start your days with it.

Meditation

After I finish physically training I meditate. My meditations may last for five minutes or two hours, depending on my schedule for the day. There are so many meditations for you to choose from; find one that works for you. Once you have pushed your physical body there is no better way to get connected on a deeper level than meditation. Your nervous system is also primed to be in a state of theta wavelengths after exercise, so it makes the meditation that much more powerful.

Meditation is simply the art of becoming more aware of your mind (and its chatter) and your physical body. It offers the chance to connect with your essence and zest. Simply put, it's awesome. Meditation has transformed my life, as I've been practicing it daily for more than 20 years.

Visualization

Once you are so connected and hooked up to your core it's best to then visualize yourself living your life in your ideals. Think of every area of your life in the Life Mastery Wheel: Physical, Mental, Emotional, Spiritual, Financial, Career, Family, Social, Character and Quality of Life. Stretch your mind—there is no limit to what you can visualize. The universe is abundant. You just need to access it; to see it, feel it and believe it. You know you are mastering this practice when you are embodying one or all of the states of Love, Gratitude, Inspiration and Enthusiasm.

This is a powerful way to begin seeing your life and creating it in your ideals, ultimately fulfilling your mission and purpose in life. You can become, do and have anything you desire in your life. You first must see it in your mind's eye and then drop that vision into your high-frequency manifesting heart.

Journaling

Once you have completed the above three morning rituals, start writing things down in your journal. Write down anything that comes to you. Writing something down makes it a physical proclamation to the world. I always write down "I am…." statements. Again there are no rules, no right or wrong. At this point in the process most of what you write will be coming straight from your heart, so do not filter it with your mind.

Over time you will begin to see trends in what you are writing—those trends will ultimately be your life's inspired desires asking you to go out and fulfill them.

Many people have told me that they cannot get up close to five a.m. My answer to them is this: Can you afford to not get up early to start your day with an investment in yourself? Even if you only have 30 minutes in the morning to invest, you can still begin your day with these morning rituals.

My personal experience and the feedback I've gotten from thousands of others is that it is virtually impossible to have a "bad day" when you start it this way. This is so much better than reaching for your morning coffee just so you can keep your eyes open on your commute to work. Instead, you will go into the world from a connected, whole and empowered place and you will pour your heart into all that you are, do and have.

Step 2: Practice Gratitude

Every morning when I get up, I roll over to the edge of my bed, put my feet on the ground and thank the universe for giving me another day to fully experience life. For me, every day above ground is something to be grateful for. As I go through my day I always sit back and think about or write down all the things in my life for which I'm grateful.

I want you to always carry a journal with you and be grateful for anything and everything in your life. It doesn't have to be complicated. You can be grateful for having food in the fridge, a bed to sleep on, your family, friends, career, a sunny day—the list is endless. Practicing gratitude is one of the best ways to drop into your heart and pour it into everything you do.

Whatever you focus on in life expands. Practicing gratitude keeps you connected to your power and source. Be grateful for the challenges, obstacles and roadblocks, too: the universe will never give you anything you cannot handle. They are simply gifts disguised as obstacles put in place to further your evolution and growth. I always take them as a compliment. In fact, I get at least one "knee-capping" every week and I do my best to be grateful for it. As I process and integrate it I know that it will only strengthen me on my journey. Maintain a daily attitude of gratitude. The key is to practice gratitude from moment, to moment, to moment, to moment. . . .

Steps to Pour Your Heart into It

Step 1 — Begin every day with exercise, meditation, visualization & journaling
Step 2 — Practice gratitude

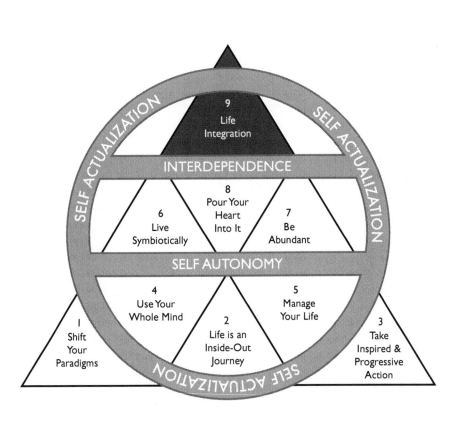

CHAPTER 11

STRATEGY 9 — LIFE INTEGRATION

"Somebody should tell us, right at the start of our lives,
that we are dying. Then we might live life to the limit,
every minute of every day. Do it! I say. Whatever you want to do,
do it now! There are only so many tomorrows."
—Michael Landon

Life integration is the process of combining every aspect of yourself into an integrated whole. It means being in complete harmony within yourself and everything in the environment. When fully realized, integration is the foundation from which all the other strategies are built, as well as the ultimate practice and manifestation of your life brought together as a synchronous orchestra.

Earlier, we explored the physics and biology of the process of integration. If you need to refresh your memory, I encourage you to reread that section, because this is the most important strategy to practice. In this final strategy I am going to build on that section and share how your whole self becomes so much more than the sum of the individual parts once integrated.

Your Eternal Team

*"The strength of the team is each individual member . . .
the strength of each member is the team."*
—Phil Jackson

Think of every cell within your body as being an individual person—a person with his or her own ideas, beliefs, and perspectives. They even have their own blend of the 4600 human personality traits, such as being optimistic, sad, fearful or trusting. Your body is made up of literally 50 trillion cells. That's a lot of different people trying to live their own life in their own unique way.

Now think of all your cells as being members of your team. (Yes, that's a huge team.) Imagine if every single member of your team was working toward the same goal, intention, dream and life. You literally have an entire army within you that can handle any challenge, roadblock, curve ball or obstacle that life has to offer. You actually don't even have to *imagine* it—because it's the essence of life integration. You have that much power. Life integration means getting every member of your team focused on the same outcome by listening to and following through on the advice from their head coach: YOU.

At the lowest level of human existence, we're in a state of survival. To transcend this state of survival our basic human needs must be met. These needs include water, food, shelter and some kind of nurturance or human interaction. This is a low state of consciousness; if a person is constantly trying to achieve these basic needs, they cannot handle the complexities of modern society. People living at this level of awareness tend to live on the fringe of society, or might display unusual antisocial behaviors or attitudes. They simply exist. They don't actually live life fully. These people cannot see the bigger picture of life.

Once these basic necessities of life are met, a person is prepared to begin building the foundation of their life. This can only begin once one has decided to actually open the floodgates of change. It facilitates the process of nurturing and cultivating integration, and it'll perpetuate change, growth and evolution within every facet of one's life.

The first five strategies of this book aim to help you understand more about yourself and become more self-aware. The net effect is an increase in your self-worth, self-esteem and confidence. Once you achieve this powerful state, you are ready to address the world with more clarity, certainty, purpose and power.

Your house will now be built with a rock-solid foundation that no person, place or thing can disrupt. You will get to know yourself in a much deeper and more meaningful way. Your ability to make a difference, be of service and express your deepest values will emerge. You will begin to live life from an inner-guided principle-based direction. Integrity and a sense of principle will emanate from you, and a deep sense of clarity, purpose, power and peace will emerge from within.

Integration of everything you've experienced will begin to shift your paradigms to grander states of awareness. You will become much more open to new progressive ideas, and old controlling ways will begin to break down. You will begin to follow the natural progression of living life from the inside-out and not the reverse. The need to procrastinate and keep yourself busy with trivial pursuits will diminish, and an inner drive and inspiration to act progressively will emerge.

Integration Leads to Continuous Growth

"If you can see your path laid out in front of you step by step, you know it's not your path. Your own path you make with every step you take. That's why it's your path."
—Joseph Campbell

Most people are locked in a pattern of left-brained thinking. Now, this analytical and logical mind is extremely important and must be nurtured. There is no possible way I would understand the matrix of people and the world if I did not have such a strong foundation in the left-brain sciences of math, physics, chemistry and biology. However, I had to evolve beyond strict left-mind thinking and fully realize the potential of my right brain. When you actively focus on pursuits that facilitate integration and utilize your whole mind, the way you see your life and world will be transformed. With this foundation in place, you can begin to manage your life based on these inner principles and allocate the appropriate time, energy and commitment to everything in your life.

When you use integration to harness the teachings of the first five strategies, you'll achieve a state of self-actualization and independence for the level of consciousness that you're expressing, and it will be built on the strongest foundation of principles. From this foundation, you'll be able to fully engage in creating your ideal outside world.

As you begin to live symbiotically, you'll transcend the consciousness of scarcity, control and competition. An inner desire and inner resources to heal and rebuild yourself and your relationships will emerge. That is especially true of things that may have deteriorated or been less functional in the past. Magic begins to unfold.

Your relationships with people, places and things will become deeper, more solid and adventuresome. Everything around you will benefit from your higher state of intention and awareness. Relationships and interactions with others will also transform as the need to place your beliefs and lenses on others diminishes. You'll interact differently—with clarity and the ability to listen to and understand people authentically. As integration further continues, higher states of consciousness will yield an inner passion and drive to pour your heart into absolutely everything that you do. Your world will continue to evolve as you see it through different lenses.

Fooling Yourself into Integration May Cost You Your Life

*"One of the greatest moments in anybody's developing experience
is when he or she no longer tries to hide from themselves,
but determines to get acquainted with themselves as they really are."*
—Norman V. Peale

For years I didn't understand why I was in such a dark place when I was young—but now I get it. I stepped out into the world and furnished my house before the foundation had even been poured. I was innately aware of certain principles by simply observing and integrating the actions and behaviors of people I deemed successful. Unfortunately, my lens of what success and happiness entailed was completely distorted. I embraced the ideas of thinking big, but I only marginally expanded my paradigms. However, I also lived life from the outside-in. I did not have a compass of deep moral principles and I didn't use my whole mind. I was caught in the paradigm of "What you see is what you get," and I ignored the intangibles of life. I was stuck in my left-brain, fighting so hard to change the circumstances of my life that I took immense action, got things done and I did a decent job of managing this twisted life I created utilizing force, not power. As a result, I failed to create an image of myself that was strong, connected, powerful and enduring.

I did not harness the first five strategies well. My house was built from straw and deep inside I had extremely low self-worth and self-esteem that I covered up with a tough outer shell. While I tried to look like I had it all together, I was bankrupt and dying from within. Many people live in this place and feel that it's simply their destiny—a life that they must learn to endure. This is not the case. My house could've been easily blown over if the wind was strong enough—and once the wind of life picked up I was crushed and destroyed. My intention for you is that you do not wait for the storms of life to pick up and shatter your house before you embark on the journey to access your infinite self and create an extraordinary life fulfilling your dreams.

Challenges are Blessings in Disguise

"I am not what happened to me, I am what I chose to become."
—Carl Jung

The reason I was able to flourish in the distorted life I created was that I expressed Strategy Six: *Living Symbiotically*; Strategy Seven: *Being Abundant*; and Strategy Eight: *Pour Your Heart Into It* relatively well. However, I was expressing those strategies with distorted lenses because the first five strategies were being expressed in unhealthy and imbalanced ways. As a result, I had no integration at a core vibrational and physiological level. There was absolutely no self-awareness.

I believe the only reason I didn't die was that, as a result of my expressing those three strategies, some intangible divine intervention saw some potential in me and decided to protect and support me. Purely from an objective standpoint and using my education in biology, anatomy and physiology, I know I never should have survived those treacherous years. My mind and body experienced a living hell.

In a warped way, people in that underworld did benefit as a result of being associated, building a relationship and working with me. On some innate level I must have understood how the human mind operated and worked. I listened to others deeply. I fully understood where they were coming from. I was committed to undersell and over-deliver.

I also understood how to keep my ego in check and maintain a low profile. Everything I did was kept on a need-to-know basis. In fact, most of the people who were closest to me didn't know the details of what I was up to. I was paranoid and had a hard time trusting people, so I figured I could never be incriminated if they had nothing to share.

I did what I did the absolute best I could, given the circumstances of my life. Most of the interactions I had were with people almost twice my age. Things moved fast for me. Before I could sit back and reflect on the life I had created, I had gotten so deeply involved that I didn't know how to slow down. In the last couple years, the only way I could cope was to completely numb myself and disconnect from truth with copious amounts of drugs, entertainment and other distractions. This downward spiral eventually became far too strong to cope with. If things hadn't changed I would not be here today. My darkest days have been my greatest blessings and you would not be reading the words and messages on these pages without those gifts.

Power vs. Force

"Love is misunderstood to be an emotion, actually, it is a state of awareness, a way of being in the world, a way of seeing oneself and others."
—Dr. David R. Hawkins

Dr David Hawkins wrote an extraordinary book titled *Power vs. Force*. Essentially what he did was calibrate people's emotions based on their level of consciousness and numbered them from 20 to 1,000. Shame was the lowest level at 20 and is associated with death, illness, poverty and helplessness. At the extreme other end are the highly conscious states of living in pure power and light, calibrated from 700 to 1,000.

Everything below the consciousness of 200 drains your energy and slowly kills you and this world. These emotional states are known as guilt (30), apathy (50), grief (75), fear (100), desire (125), anger (150) and pride (175). You may feel as if pride is a high conscious state, but it only feels good in comparison to the states below it. Even pride drains your life force and power and leads to unfulfilled dreams. People living in these states of consciousness are pushing through life using force, and life constantly pushes back, creating an immense amount of resistance. In the mid 1980's, for the first time in humanity, global consciousness just began to transcend the level of 200. Thanks to people like you.

This first state of powerful consciousness is courage (200). People at this level of awareness create pure symbiotic relationships as they extract out of this world the same amount as they invest into it. We are seeing a global shift as business and economics is just beginning to move into this unchartered territory. As we continue to work through the 9 Strategies of Personal Power, you will transcend the dualistic nature of that rung of consciousness and step into personal power. This is the horizontal journey of life. Once a solid foundation of personal power has been built at this level of awareness, your being will take a vertical leap to the next level of consciousness and begin doing the dualistic dance again from this new level of awareness.

These higher states of consciousness are neutrality (250), willingness (310), acceptance (350) and love (500). This is when true, authentic and pure happiness begins. Life's dualistic nature is far smaller and one's state of internal power is far greater. Dr. Hawkins stated that one person at the conscious level of 300 counterbalances 90,000 people below the level of 200. He also said that one person at the conscious state of peace (600) would counterbalance 10 million people below the level of 200. This means that all these people counterbalanced at a lower level of consciousness would instantly move away from the forceful dualistic roller coaster of the their lower states of awareness and move into personal power. They would begin making vertical leaps to a higher rung of consciousness.

If you truly want to live your best life and make an extraordinary difference in the world, you must do the inner work. It's an assignment. Not only will it transform your life, but you will have have the capacity to transform the entire world. This is why I'm on this journey and that is why I have written this book for extraordinary people like you.

Life Integration is the final strategy to personal power at a specific level of consciousness. Once you transcend to a new awareness the landscape of your life will look completely different—because you are resonating at an entirely different frequency. At this new level of consciousness you will again be able to utilize the 9 strategies to master this new level of awareness.

Dark Night of the Soul

"We change the world not by what we say or do,
but as a consequence of what we have become."
—Dr. David R. Hawkins

Life is constantly feeding you opportunities, possibilities and challenges. They come in the form of people, places and things. All of them are gifts for your evolution and growth, moving you beyond the finite limitations of life and enabling you to live from your infinite self. Life is constantly showing us a mirror of our inner world so we can learn, grow and integrate. Every time we judge or persecute others, we are simply reflecting that tone and vibration back onto ourselves. This way of being is going against the grain of life, which is truly grounded in progress, growth and evolution. If we continue to ignore these deep inherent messages and the universe knows that you have an immense amount of potential to contribute to the world, which we all do in some shape or form, you may experience something quite extraordinary.

When I was 18 I experienced the "Dark Night of the Soul," an ancient concept depicted in the Dead Sea Scrolls. It's a process that many spiritual seekers may go through at some point in their lives. This concept is not mentioned extensively in personal growth and spiritual texts, but because I have experienced it firsthand and supported so many people through the process I wanted to shed some light on it, as it is life integration magnified.

The only way to truly evolve and grow is to look upon the dualistic nature of yourself and life. At times it will be light and happy; other times it will be more challenging. The dark night of the soul, once understood, is one of the most transformational experiences one may ever encounter. It's an overall beautiful experience in which a much higher conscious state within you is trying to emerge. It sees the limitations of your finite mind and body. As a result, your false ego begins "dying" and your entire system surrenders to a higher state of consciousness, such as acceptance or love. The finite self or false ego is going through a process of being called out and you are essentially attending its funeral. The experience is packed with so much potential energy that one will literally make massive vertical quantum leaps in their levels of consciousness once they are on the other side of it.

Although this is profoundly such a beautiful and sacred experience it is commonly misunderstood and manipulated. I experienced my dark night for years, but it climaxed in three very intense months. Until I fully understood what it was, I always wondered why I only sought support in the form of love from my family. During those three months I was so deep in the dark fog I wanted to end my life almost every day. I have never experienced more physical, mental and emotional pain in my entire life. The dark night may be triggered in the physical world as a disease, illness, anxiety or significant loss. It ultimately leads to feelings of deep depression, guilt, shame, frustration, helplessness, anger, self-pity or loneliness. When you are in it, it's impossible to see the light of day. It's almost as if you're feeling the collective pain of humanity. If this happens to you or a loved one, my invitation for you is to provide support so they can fully integrate the experience. See it as a rite of passage or even a spiritual detox. The pain is nothing more than the unintegrated and suppressed challenges (gifts) of yesterday finally refusing to be ignored and bubbling to the surface.

You can synthesize and transcend multiple levels of consciousness in a fraction of the time during the dark night of the soul. You can jump from a level of fear (100) to willingness (310). Something that would normally take lifetimes can happen in months or years with life integration.

You will know if you're in the dark night if you've tried everything conventional to get out of it, yet it continues to persist or gets even darker. During this time it's the most alone that you may possibly ever feel. I couldn't leave my bed for three months. That's because my ego self knew that I'd found it and it couldn't hide from me anymore. Therefore it could no longer control me: I was going to control it. It's a fear of losing this finite control of life, which we truly never had to begin with.

The only way to truly process and integrate this experience is to surrender to it. Your finite mind and body cannot control this infinite rite of passage of the ages. You must let the experiences of life work through. The reason you might experience this dark night is because a spiritual yearning for the higher rungs of consciousness and quantum leaps are being put into place. This process is a fight between your finite ego and infinite self. And you get to decide who wins.

When you can shift to surrender and move to the states of forgiveness and love, the integration process begins. The bigger your ego, the longer this process may take. For me it was years. But know that right after the shift comes a calm, peaceful, loving and tranquil state. It's a state of authentic pure power, not an ego force. Not everyone will have this experience, but if you do, know that it's a gift and the rewards for integrating the dark night of the soul are so far beyond what you can possibly imagine.

Close Your Integrity Gap

"Twenty years from now you will be more disappointed
by the things you didn't do than by the ones you did.
So throw off the bowlines. Sail away from the safe harbor.
Catch the trade winds in your sails. Explore, dream, discover."
—Mark Twain

The most important strategy in this book is life integration. The ability to integrate is to learn, adapt and grow from everything that life offers us. In the first 18 years of my life I would give myself an "F" in this department—I failed miserably. Yet those years gave me the opportunity to completely destroy one life and create another. I share this with you simply because you may be that person who knows deep down inside that you are out of integrity.

Imagine your life in your greatest ideals. Where are you living? What are you doing? Who are your friends? What vacations are you taking? Dream as big as you can possibly dream with absolutely no filters. Now think about your present life—where and how you are living. The distance between your present life and the perfect vision of your dream life is how far out of integrity you are. Plain and simple, you owe it to yourself and the universe to step up and start living your authentic dream life and sharing your gifts with the world. Over the past two decades, all I've been doing is closing my integrity gap. I invite you to do the same.

If your integrity gap is large, it's because you're only processing part of life's experiences. Like a broken computer, your master control nerve system is beginning to break down. And if you have a significant integrity gap, you're using some kind of coping mechanism and allowing yourself to be distracted by addictions. Whatever those coping mechanisms or addictions are, they're likely things your culture has brainwashed you into thinking are normal and average: television, computer games, alcohol, coffee, food, cigarettes, sex, relationships, drugs, shopping, shiny new trinkets, the Internet, and so on. We keep ourselves busy enough to disconnect, and we stop living life guided by the powerful compass within.

I know many people who appear to have it all from the outside, yet they are rotting away on the inside. They smile and laugh and go on as if everything is wonderful, but their disconnect and pain are palpable. They are stuck in the masculine left-brain energy of force. My heart goes out to each and every one of you who are in this place. I have been there and I know how challenging it is to live your life this way. In truth, it's no way to live.

The greatest gift we have as human beings is free will. The free will to change the choices we make. When you are not integrating the experiences in your life it is as if you have placed these heavy anchors on your past experiences, allowing them to arrest your nerve system and physiology. As a result, you inhibit your growth and evolution.

Stepping Out of Your Comfort Zones

"Destiny is not a matter of chance, it is a matter of choice."
—William J. Bryan

One of my favorite sayings is "Life begins at the edge of your comfort zones." If you want to continue to grow, evolve and experience more life, you must constantly seek experiences that are outside the range of your comfort zones. You must do this in all ten areas of your life. At the edge of our comfort zones are the experiences that are the greatest catalysts for transformation.

A great example of somebody following their heart by stepping out of their comfort zones to integrate and express their full potential is a man named Howard Schultz. It takes a person with a vision, unwavering certainty and persistence to step out of their comfort zones to see an idea come to fruition.

Schultz and his wife lived in New York City and decided to take a chance by moving to Seattle to work for a small coffee distributor. The distributor also had a few local retail outlets, but its primary business was distribution. Schultz was 29 years old and had just gotten married.

After a year of working in Seattle he had the opportunity to visit Italy on a purchasing trip. While in Milan, he noticed that coffee was an important part of the Italian culture a typical day for locals began with a rich cup of coffee at a café with friends or family. And again after work, friends and family would convene at these local coffee bars to reconnect before heading home. It was the hub of the Italian social life. Schultz began to have grand visions that were so far out of his comfort zone that he didn't know what to do with them. His idea creating coffee bars as the hub of social life in North America had never been attempted. He had no idea how to execute such a grand vision. Yet the very thought of it inspired him and he became enthusiastic about his vision.

When Schultz returned home he became so consumed with the idea that he could no longer ignore it. It became his mission. The only problem he had was that he had no idea how to fulfill his mission of creating a national chain of cafés based on the Italian social coffee bar. He was a small-time employee of a tiny coffee distributor. He decided to approach his employers with the idea and asked them if they were interested in expanding their local coffee shops. His employers were reluctant because they were primarily coffee wholesalers, so they wouldn't give him their full support.

Schultz was going to have to do it on his own and it scared the hell out of him. But despite his fear, in 1986 he opened his first coffee bar in Seattle and it was an immediate success. Shortly thereafter, he opened another coffee bar in Seattle and a third in my hometown, Vancouver. The following year, he bought the company he once worked for—his vision had gotten that much bigger. Schultz believed to his core that his coffee and cafes would completely alter the way North Americans conducted their lives. Now *that's* a huge vision.

Implementing his grand idea was so far out of his comfort zone that he failed miserably. For three straight years he lost money, and in 1989 alone he lost more than $1 million. But Schultz never gave up. He had a firm conviction, and he kept putting his heart into his vision to make it a reality. He knew his losses would eventually turn into profits—he just had to be persistent and patient.

Schultz was right. Not much later, his dream became a reality. His little café called Starbucks Coffee has revolutionized the coffee experience in North America. He first expanded into Vancouver, Portland, LA, Denver and Chicago, and later to the East Coast cities and then overseas. Starbucks sales have increased nine-fold every year since the late eighties. Schultz envisioned business people stopping in before and after work. He pictured people being social with Starbucks in hand. He envisioned young people having dates over coffee rather than cocktails. He envisioned families coming in for refreshments before or after seeing a movie. The ideas and potential in his heart and mind were endless.

Starbucks has become a household name all over the world and an amazing example of one man stepping way out of his comfort zone to fulfill a dream. For stepping so far out of his comfort zone the universe has rewarded Howard Schultz immensely by making him one of the world's wealthiest people.

Increase Your Bandwidth

"Your vision will become clear only when you look into your heart. Who looks outside, dreams. Who looks inside, awakens. . . ."
—Carl Jung

Like many people, cafes have special significance for me. I've spent a lot of time in cafés and have had phenomenal conversations and experiences in them. The years before I met Kate I had a series of unfulfilling relationships and decided I was going to be single and not date anyone for at least a year. This in itself was getting me way out of my comfort zone. Every Friday and Saturday evening I would go to a café, order a beverage, and read a book. After a few weeks I would look forward to my 'dates' with some great literary mind.

Eventually, that which had been outside my comfort zone moved within it. I essentially increased my bandwidth. When I finally did meet Kate, for the first time, it was at a Starbucks. And so many pages of this book were written in Starbucks. When we follow the voice within us we are serving our highest purpose and we make this world a better place. I commend everyone who has followed her or his heart because it truly is the path less traveled.

The reason why this path is seldom traveled is because the ideas and visions of this vibration tend to be so outstanding that we let the chatter within our heads keep us small. As a result, we disconnect and revert to the status quo. There is an anatomical and physiological basis for understanding how we integrate and process information—and in turn create extraordinary lives. To be extraordinary it's important to fully understand it.

Keys to Integration

All the ideas, visions and experiences that lie at the edges of your comfort zones are beyond the vibrational limit of what your internal processor, your nerve system, can handle. In other words, you have a specific processing capacity and you can easily handle and integrate any experience within it. All the experiences, ideas and visions beyond it may challenge you until you grow beyond that limit. What you are actually growing and expanding is your nerve system. Your nerve system has a specific bandwidth, and the experiences that are just outside your bandwidth or processing capacity have the greatest potential to be catalysts for your evolution and growth.

STORED POTENTIAL

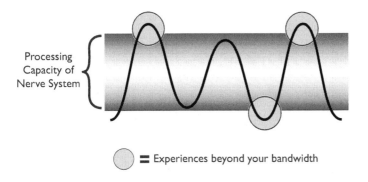

Processing
Capacity of
Nerve System

⬤ ≡ Experiences beyond your bandwidth

Diagram 10

The circles in diagram 10 are the experiences that have the potential to increase the flexibility and adaptability of your nerve system once they've been integrated. What's amazing is that your bandwidth can continue to grow throughout your life, expanding your perceptive abilities and states of consciousness. This is the essence of evolution: a biological system integrating ideas, events and experiences over lifetimes. The question is: Are you growing and evolving? Growing and evolving fulfills your innate purpose for being here and results in a profound and extraordinary life.

NEURAL BANDWIDTH EXPANDING

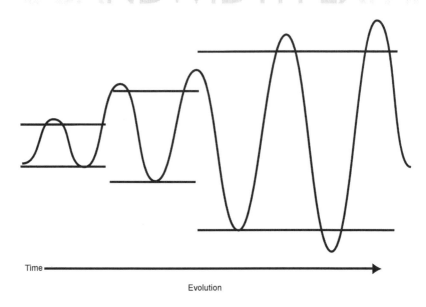

Time ⟶

Evolution

Diagram 11

As you begin to integrate your life, you, the whole, begin to become far greater than the sum of your parts. Your disparate parts become more unified, forming a single entity. This is the most powerful, empowering and whole part of what it means to be an open, dynamic biological system. This process in itself is "The Journey." It is not an event or episode. This is life. And it is the most rewarding journey available to us. To fully experience life, learn from life and perpetuate the cycle of more self-expression and learning from everything you experience—no matter how far in or out of your comfort zone it is. Your heart and mind will begin to express new possibilities, new ideas and new alternatives. Life integration is about moving from ordinary to extraordinary. Integration gets you into the ultimate state of authentic power, which is self-actualization for your level of awareness.

It's Simple, But Not Always Easy

"The future depends on what we do on the present."
–Mohandas K. Gandhi

This journey may be one of the most terrifying and challenging processes that you embark on. It certainly was for me. When I began it, I was going through withdrawal and I was depressed, suicidal and dangerous. Yet I stuck to it. Those were the darkest days of my life. But I knew that if I could get through it there would not be anything in life that I would fear or could not accomplish. I was right!

Each hour became slightly easier. Then hours turned to days, days turned to weeks, weeks to months and months to years. Sometimes I can effortlessly work through the nine universal strategies of personal power and life. Yet there are also times when experiences are extremely challenging, and I feel stuck and get flashbacks of my darkest days. Yet, I stay on purpose! I simply say to myself, "At this moment I do not have the awareness or perspective to see the gift, opportunity, and learning that could come from this experience or idea. So let's not judge it, let it simply sit with me and in time I will process, integrate and overcome this challenge and grow." If somebody would have told me two decades ago, when I was looking down the muzzle of a sawed-off shotgun, that I would have the life I have today, I never would have believed them. My life today is so far out of the comfort zone I had two decades ago—and the only reason I experience this life today is because I have grown into it.

This journey has brought me more life, experiences, joy, abundance, love and adventures than I could've possibly imagined. The life I live today is my wildest dream. I have traveled the world and made deep and meaningful connections with so many extraordinary people and places. I am able to completely embrace and feel the intangibles of life. What is essential to life is invisible to the eye and can only be felt with the heart.

You will never know what life has to offer if you never leave the safe shore. Integrating through the first five strategies will continually build the internal security and strength to discover, create new adventures, and grow. There is no question that in order to facilitate this integrative process we must grow beyond our comfort zones. In life you will never be able to steal second base with your foot stuck on first.

Life is a Journey and You Make It Worthwhile

"Death is not the greatest loss in life. The greatest loss is what dies inside us while we live."
—Norman Cousins

I have risked more than others have thought was reasonable. I have dreamed more than what others believed was possible. And I continually serve and give all that I am. Integration occurs everywhere. Conception is taking two parts to create a greater whole. Integration is creating a new life. You have that much power!

Life integration is a process that gets disrupted when something from outside of you begins to control the things within you. Your internal thoughts, ideas, physiology and biochemistry will all get disrupted. We must be aware of the dualities and differences in life. The essence of integration is to embrace and respect these differences based on your level of consciousness. Where things are strong they may be solidified deeper to your core. Where they are weak they may be improved. It is within these differences that the seeds of change are planted. New lives, new ways of doing things and new sources of creation are implemented through life integration. It facilitates a new cultivating climate and environment. Within this environment, facilitation is the key.

In my programs, seminars, online services and Centre for Optimal Living I simply facilitate the life integration process. As a healer I do it with my hands-on tonal adjusting, an art that I continually grow and develop. I cannot express the power and potential of this integration process. I personally have utilized the services of so many extraordinary people over the past two decades to help me integrate, grow and evolve. And I continue to do it today.

Work with an Expert

"When I let go of what I am, I become what I might be."
—Lao Tzu

Last year I began serving a woman who had lost a loved one in a tragic accident. It had been several years since the accident, but she was still in a grieving state. She was also plagued with disease to her liver, kidneys and intestines. She was severely underweight, depressed and had lost her zest for life. She had seen many doctors, specialists and healers trying to treat every symptom, ailment and disease she had. This is the paradigm and consciousness of our present healthcare system, which is truly a disease-management fear-based system. It treats the parts and ignores the whole.

After our initial consultation, I explained to her how her system was stuck in a holding pattern. She still had not integrated the loss of her loved one. Her system was like a record player that kept skipping, playing the same verse over and over for the past several years. In this subatomic and cellular environment of fear and grief it was only natural that all her cells were decaying, degenerating, and becoming disorganized. I told her the only thing I could do was to help her integrate this deep loss so her record would stop skipping and the environment within her could move back to dynamic homeostasis.

Every four years our body is completely brand new because every cell goes through a process of reorganization and regeneration. The better our brain communicates with every cell, the greater the levels of regeneration and reorganization will be. After working with her and helping her integrate, she has an entirely new life today. She has a greater sense of purpose and clarity. Her cells and tissues are becoming healthier. She has completely grieved the loss of her loved one. She has a relationship with her family again. She has more energy and vitality, and she experiences joy. It is important to know that I did not do this. I simply facilitated the process of integration so she could begin to heal herself from the inside out.

Similar to this woman, I would not be where I am in my life today if I did not have the love, support and facilitation of family, friends, mentors and healers. We all may benefit from them. Utilize them and incorporate them into your life. People who specialize in the integration process may have many titles. They may be a chiropractor, osteopath, physiotherapist, massage therapist, coach, or counselor. It has less to do with their title and more to do with their understanding of the whole mind, body, soul, nerve system and integration. There must also be a connection and sense of trust between you and them. Who they are as a person must precede what they do as a healer. This is paramount, because their state of consciousness is fundamental. If you feel you would like my support, you can visit me at www.drsukhi.com.

If you work with an integration specialist when you feel you need it, along with continually readdressing the nine universal life strategies of personal power and working through the steps to fully achieve them, you'll be greatly facilitating the integration process toward self-growth and renewal. Treat this book as a guide and a workbook that can be reread and reused over and over as you reach new heights of awareness. As you grow, evolve and integrate you'll be reading and learning with new lenses, and more insights will jump out between the lines of what I have written. You should practice the steps and exercises after each strategy to reach your highest state of authentic power for your present consciousness. Nurturing yourself toward higher and higher levels of autonomy and then gradually processing into higher states of self-actualized interdependence will yield vertical leaps of consciousness and ultimately enable you to build a profoundly fortunate, connected and extraordinary life.

Having crystal-clear intentions to facilitate new levels of consciousness through self-integration is what changes the world. I have seen it with hundreds of thousands of people over the past years. It is writing the script for future generations, generations that will know true peace because we'll be in a consciousness of love and above. Selfish and adversarial veils will begin to break down. We will begin to focus more on service and contribution. We will begin to observe more and judge less. We will become more loving and less possessive.

This process of integration to higher states of awareness of life is occurring as you are reading this book. Whether you are aware of it or not, life is evolving and growing. I am simply providing a framework from which people can do this with greater ease, efficiency, intention and purpose. The natural ebb and flow of life perpetuates this profound cycle.

Where are you on your journey of life? Are you happy with your life? Are you fulfilled by your circumstances? Do you feel on purpose? Are your health and well-being amazing or are you experiencing states of symptoms, sickness, or disease? Do you have a reverence and deep sense of joy and inner peace for who you have become? Do you love how you spend your days and the relationships you've created personally and professionally? If you truly love your life, I commend you and thank you for contributing to making this world an extraordinary place. I trust you will continue your amazing journey. If there is room for improvement or even radical change, I invite you to embark on the most extraordinary and rewarding journey that life has to offer: the journey to Master Your Life!

"When you are ultimately truthful with yourself, you will eventually realize and confess that 'I am Buddha, I am Spirit.' Anything short of that is a lie, the lie of the ego, the lie of the separate-self sense, the contradiction in the face of infinity. The deepest recesses of your consciousness directly intersect Spirit itself, in the supreme identity. This is not a state you are bringing into existence for the first time, but simply a timeless state that you are recognizing and confessing—you are being ultimately truthful when you state, 'I am Buddha, the ultimate Beauty.'"
—Ken Wilber

Breathe deeply, stop comparing, do your best, practice the first eight strategies and bring it all together with Strategy Nine: Life Integration.

Exercises for Life Integration

Step 1: Experience life beyond your comfort zone

It's impossible to grow beyond your present state of health, wealth or quality of life if you do not seek experiences that force you to grow. *Every single day, practice at least one thing that makes you a little nervous or scared.* It can be absolutely anything. It might be smiling at your neighbor, speaking with a stranger, exercising, having a conversation with somebody about a heated topic, going on a roller coaster, whatever. Once you have practiced this every day for several weeks you will have gained the momentum to progress to Step Two.

Step 2: Begin to expand your life mastery wheel

There are ten areas of your life that must command your constant attention if you want to transform from ordinary to extraordinary. This is your Master Your Life Wheel. You must address the following areas: Physical, Emotional, Intellectual, Spiritual, Vocational, Financial, Family, Social, Character and Quality of Life.

For every area, list several things that you dream of experiencing. For example, you may have a goal to run a marathon one day in the area of your physical life. You may also want to run a million-dollar company in the area of vocation and finances. You might want to open a yoga or meditation studio to help people better connect within. If you can think it, you can have it. This is your opportunity to dream as big as you like and begin living your most extraordinary life.

After you have written the lists for all ten areas of your life, ***write down action steps that you could do today to begin becoming that person***. These action steps will be outside your neural bandwidth and comfort zones, so they should intimidate you. That is good: it means you're playing BIG.

Once you've written down your action steps, you must begin to actually take action on these steps to begin expanding yourself.

Every single day, practice at least one action step that is beyond your comfort zone so your wheel of life begins to expand.

Step 3: Be grateful for every person and experience that has helped you grow

In life we tend to judge other people. We judge what they have done or said to us (or what they've *not* done or said), and we make assumptions. What we hold on to will only hold us back in life. If you think about a past experience or person that hurt or crossed you in some way, and the memory still brings up an emotional charge, you have not integrated the experience. Not only is it lying dormant within you, it's acting like an anchor, keeping you from moving forward and expressing and being the vibrant person and all that you are.

Many people have a hard time forgiving other people. To fully integrate life you must not only forgive, but you must transcend forgiveness to actually become fully grateful for the gift they have bestowed upon you.

You might be thinking, how is that horrible experience a gift for me? Remember, the universe will never give you anything you cannot handle.

Every experience has the opportunity for massive growth and evolution for you. Not integrating these experiences will cause you even more pain and angst in the form of illness, disease, poor relationships, small and cynical perspectives of the world, a lack of abundance, and so on.

It is our duty to integrate these experiences. You know you have fully integrated an experience when you think about it and feel a deep sense of peace and reverence for the people and places involved in it. After all, they facilitated your growth and evolution as a human being.

I have experienced many hardships and very challenging events in my life. I have experienced betrayal, injustice, humiliation, abandonment, and rejection, the five universal gifts disguised as wounds. I have been severely physically and emotionally abused. Through integration, I have also spent the past two decades finding the peace within me for everything I have experienced—and I invite you to do the same.

As challenging as this may be, I am asking you to see how these challenges have helped you become the person you are today. How you have grown? How they have fueled you to be bigger, kinder and more loving? How you are contributing to the world more because of those experiences? I assure you that once you begin this process, your capacity for change, evolution and growth will expand beyond what you've imagined possible.

Step 4: Life integration sessions

I know firsthand that life integration is one of the most powerful ways to grow your life to extraordinary places. Over the past two decades I have been mastering this art to facilitate the process as a healer, coach and strategist. The process is simple: get your nerve system to begin releasing and processing these old events. You will turn to your natural state of health, well-being, vitality and abundance. You were designed for this. The conscious states of love, inspiration, gratitude and enthusiasm are your greatest states of being, and life integration is one the most efficient strategies you can practice to achieve them

To have more people experience this grand state, I have grown beyond my Centre for Optimal Living and have worked with people all over the world. I've had the gift of being the catalyst that's transformed many people's lives. Every month I facilitate live online Life Integration Sessions so people just like you may begin experiencing their most extraordinary lives. The beauty is that all of this will happen in the comfort of your own home. If you want to begin this amazing journey with me, please visit www.drsukhi.com, and you'll take your life to places you never thought possible.

"Integration proceeds by just the opposite route: a deliberate heightening of every organic function; a release of impulses from circumstances that irrationally thwarted them; richer and more complex patterns of activity; an esthetic heightening of anticipated realizations; a steady lengthening of the future; a faith in cosmic perspectives."
—Marva Collins

Exercises for Life Integration

Step 1 — Experience life beyond your comfort zone
Step 2 — Begin to expand your life mastery wheel
Step 3 — Be grateful for every person or experience that has helped you grow
Step 4 — Life integration sessions

Your Health, Wealth & Happiness . . . Your CHOICE!

*"There are two primary choices in life: to accept conditions
as they exist, or accept the responsibility for changing them."*
—Denis Waitley

If somebody had told me when I was a teenager that there was another world and life for me outside of what I knew, I don't know that I would have believed them. Every morning of every day you have the opportunity to be a better person and live life bigger. To be more aligned with your inner values and principles. To take a journey of becoming more whole as you begin to live life from these fundamental truths. *All of this begins with the simple act of a choice.*

This journey for me has been a straightforward process. The strategies outlined in this book are simple. In fact, they can easily be taught to most children. However, do not confuse simple with easy. Applying these strategies into my life, at times, has been some of the most challenging work I've ever experienced. It took a lot less effort for me to live a non-disciplined life, ignoring my deepest morals, values and abandoning integration. Wherever you are in your life, know that there is always room for improvement.

This journey is about choosing to improve your relationship with yourself, other people and nature. Above all else, I lived the way I did because I did not love and accept myself. I had no regard for my life and whether I lived or died. We only have the capacity to love and accept other people, places and things as much as we love and accept ourselves. It all begins with a choice from within.

CHAPTER 12

CONCLUSION: THE FOUR MOTIVATING LEVELS OF LIFE

"We are what we repeatedly do. Excellence therefore is
not a singular act, but a habit."
—Aristotle

Every morning when we get out of bed we have a choice. We see the world based on our state of awareness. Within this consciousness we have a choice to accept all of ourselves or embrace just the smaller fragments. Science and philosophy recognize that there are four major dimensions of our purest nature. We are spiritual beings having a physical, mental and emotional experience called life. These are our primal motivations for how we live our lives. Depending on the science, philosophy or doctrine, these four dimensions can be described in many different ways, as they are present at all levels of life.

The physical component may be seen as the animal, personal, material or economic sector of life. The mental can be referred to as the intellectual, rational, autonomous, or the utilization of resources. The emotional can be described as the social, affective, friendly or way of treating people and things in life. The spiritual can be referred to as the sacred, essence, service or the contribution an organization or person gives to life.

MOTIVATING LEVELS OF LIFE

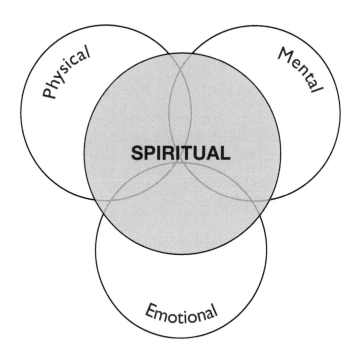

Diagram 12

Life integration allows you to express all four motivations of your nature, allowing them to emerge in an extraordinary, balanced and consistent way. By investing in your greatest asset—yourself—your ability to embrace life and contribute will increase exponentially. The first five strategies allow you to fully penetrate the first two dimensions in a healthy and balanced way. This is the physical and mental plane. Strategies six, seven and eight facilitate the expression of the emotional/social and spiritual planes of your existence. Strategy nine, Life Integration, is what takes these separate planes and allows them to be fully processed into a whole that is entirely greater than the sum of its parts. This is when you completely synthesize the dualistic nature of your level of consciousness and step into authentic power.

Most people spend their entire lives never fully penetrating the physical and mental motivational planes. As a result, they never properly access the emotional and spiritual planes, and their inspired planes will not be expressed in a healthy and balanced way. In this state a person will never express his or her full potential, access their inner power and rock their most extraordinary life.

THE PROCESS OF LIFE

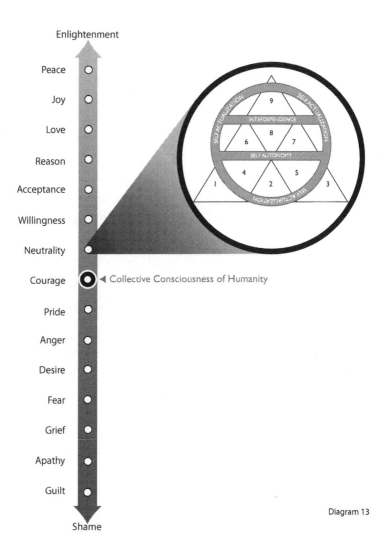

Enlightenment

Peace

Joy

Love

Reason

Acceptance

Willingness

Neutrality

Courage ◄ Collective Consciousness of Humanity

Pride

Anger

Desire

Fear

Grief

Apathy

Guilt

Shame

Diagram 13

As you can see from Diagram 13, life is truly a process. The nine strategies to personal power help you master one level of consciousness. When the foundation for this level of awareness has been solidified, you will then take a vertical step forward in your evolution to a higher state of being. Again the dualistic nature of life will be experienced and with this new level of awareness you will come to new places within yourself, utilizing the nine strategies to personal power again. Know that with each promotion of higher states of consciousness the highs and lows of duality become less extreme and your state of internal authentic power becomes greater and greater. These are the vertical and horizontal journeys of evolution (see Diagram 8).

The physical, mental, spiritual, and emotional or social dimensions of life are present at every level of conscious awareness. At the lower levels of consciousness people have far more density in their physiological make-up and life tends to be dominated by a "what you see is what you get" mindset. At the higher levels of consciousness people begin to move far beyond the limitations of their finite bodies and minds. They can tap into something far more powerful within them and pour it into all they are, all they do, and all they have. This is the infinite self. This is where unwavering certainty and the fulfillment of one's dream live.

Physical Dimension

*"While we are free to choose our actions, we are not
free to choose the consequences of our actions."*
—Stephen Covey

The physical plane primarily involves nurturing our physical body. We must fuel our body with clean and whole foods, consume water, and get plenty of rest and exercise.

Eating a highly organic, plant-based diet with a variety of other natural foods is ideal. Focus on foods that are more alkaline and less acidic. Drinking alkaline water is also recommended. What I tell children at my seminars is to eat foods that are alive. The test to determine whether food is alive or dead is simple. Leave it on the counter and observe it over the next several days. If that food begins to decay and die, it passes the test. It was alive and therefore is a healthy and natural food (of course, it's no longer healthy once it's decayed). On the contrary, if it looks exactly the same it is likely permeated with chemicals and preservatives and therefore is not alive and should not be consumed because it can't give you more life. Foods that are alive have a higher atomic vibration that is essential for our growth and expression of being fully alive.

I believe that over 90% of illness and disease would be eradicated from Western culture if people ate properly and exercised daily. The most common paradigm in life is that we don't have enough time to exercise. I believe that we cannot afford *not* to exercise. Who does not have a spare 20 to 30 minutes in a day? We need to move our bodies every day and combine strength, flexibility and endurance training. Strength involves any form of resistance training, flexibility involves any activities that involve stretching, and endurance involves any activity that gets your heart pumping—such as running, cycling or swimming.

Going anaerobic every day is also important. Choose one of these every day and rotate through them throughout the week. You will begin to become more fit, feel better and have higher energy levels.

Most people are stuck in the physical plane of life. Some are even extremely fit, yet they are not healthy and balanced. Fit may equal healthy, but that's not necessarily the case. When I was a teenager this is where I lived: purely in my physical plane. Because I could not work through this plane I did not utilize the other planes in a healthy and balanced way. My paradigms were small, I was living from the outside-in, and I was primarily using my left brain. I trained two to three hours every day, lifted heavy weights and turned my physical body into a machine as I participated in physical sports with heavy contact such as martial arts, ice hockey, lacrosse, rugby and freestyle wrestling. I created layers of armor through an extremely strong and fit physical body so nobody could see the wounds that lay deep within me. People respected and feared me, and in the culture of that day I was seen as "healthy." This could not have been further from the truth. I was fit, yet I was extremely unhealthy and unbalanced. Internally I was emotionally and spiritually bankrupt.

We must work through our physical plane and nurture and cultivate our body in a healthy and balanced way. As your ability to handle physical stress grows, your daily activities will become more comfortable and pleasant. You will have more energy, increase your paradigm of yourself, and build more self-esteem and confidence. You will be prepared to move into the next plane of your existence in a much more balanced way.

Mental Dimension

*"We must be willing to let go of the life we planned
in order to have the life that is waiting for us."*
—Joseph Campbell

The mental dimension is primarily utilized in our formal education—but that only accesses half of our minds. As you begin to engage Strategy Five and fully manage your life you will begin to engage in activities that harness your whole mind. You will embark on creative pursuits, explore new subjects, read from a variety of sources, and think outside your paradigm while still having the balance of your analytical mind.

Education is the fountain for growth and evolution. I am a huge advocate of lifelong education. When you utilize strategy three and take inspired and progressive action, you can learn from both the formal setting of a classroom and the informal classroom of life. Using both is key. And in all your studies, challenging your mind by learning about diverse subjects is vitally important. Even if you're naturally inclined to study and learn about the arts and humanities, you must challenge your brain with math and science—and vice-versa. That is how you fully utilize your whole mind.

People who are stuck in the mental dimension have an immense amount of mind chatter. They have a very challenging time staying present, as they are constantly thinking about the future with fear or the past with regrets. As a result, they tend to let life pass them by without fully experiencing it. At lower states of consciousness they have very limited paradigms and see things as either black or white, with no shades of gray. This is the stereotypical state of left-brained people. They have a hard time seeing other people's perspectives; they tend to be judgmental and will criticize what they don't understand.

322

Over time, if these people do not evolve and change, they tend to become cynical as they enter older adulthood. They have a very challenging time in Strategies Six and Seven. They do not live symbiotically and create more win/lose relationships and situations. They'll often benefit from another person's loss or harm. They also do not listen to others for the sake of understanding, but merely as an opportunity to impose their values and ideas onto them and state them as "law." They may acquire wealth but will not be abundant from within and remain internally bankrupt. As they age, they tend to develop severe illnesses such as autoimmune disease and cancers.

To integrate and express the mental dimension in a healthy and balanced way, we must use tools that utilize our whole mind. First, any activity that quiets the mind will decrease mind chatter and help us stay present. This can be exercising, yoga, meditation or journaling. Observing one's self is vitally important. We learn and grow though curiosity and observation, and we contract and regress through judgment.

To view your mind is to stand apart from it and watch it run its program, ideas and paradigms. Question what you think and believe. Ask yourself why you think and believe what you do. Discard what is not your truth and own what is. Begin more creative pursuits if you're a left-brain person; pursue more cognitive pursuits if you're a right-brain person. Reading and writing with the weaker of your minds will help it get stronger. As your weaker mind grows stronger, you will be able to work through strategy five, managing your time better and moving into living symbiotically and understanding others more effectively.

As you facilitate integration and step more into your physical and mental planes in a harmonious and balanced way, a strong, independent and autonomous person will emerge. From this foundation, you can create a more balanced, interdependent and self-actualized person for your present level of awareness.

Spiritual Dimension

*"Spiritual relationship is far more precious than physical.
Physical relationship divorced from spiritual is body without soul."*
—Mohandas Gandhi

The spiritual dimension is the essence of who we are. When we break down the walls of judgment, fear and other veils of our culture, we begin to see what really matters in life. This is the full expression of you! Your values, your center, your core. The intelligence that created you from two cells during conception and developed a human being within nine months is the same wisdom that will guide you throughout your entire life. It did not abandon you when you were born. The more it is expressed, the more inspired, uplifted and powerful you will become to sing your song to the world. Living from this place of infinite trust is the highest rung of living symbiotically: understanding and unconditionally loving others, being abundant and pouring your heart into everything you do and stand for.

This source of life powers every atom, cell and tissue in your physical body. It creates a strong and healthy vehicle in which you can drive through your life. Accessing this dimension can be done with the correct intentions through exercise, meditation, isolation, time in nature and Life Integration. Because we are all different, people may access this infinite self in many ways.

The key is to have crystal clear intentions and stay fully present. It has less to do with what you are doing and more to do with your intentions and who you are being. If your intentions are wrong it does not matter what you are doing. This dimension requires an investment of time, yet it yields the greatest rewards, a self-actualized and interdependent student of life: a person living from their core values and principles, connected to their leadership center. This state renews us, refreshes us and allows us to intentionally create our life in our own ideals.

Each morning when I get up and visualize my entire day, I set clear intentions of what I would like to receive, give and accomplish that day. I visualize my inner core values and principles and then look at my Life Mastery Wheel and manage my life. I see each day as a blank canvas and every morning I begin the process of painting the day from my innermost essence, power and values.

Our outer world is in a large part a reflection of our inner world. Becoming in balance and in harmony with your spiritual dimension you will begin to win the battles of inner conflict so they are not expressed as outer conflict in your physical world. You will feel more at peace, vitalized and ultimately know yourself in ways that you may not have known existed.

Emotional and Social Dimension

"Interdependence is and ought to be as much the ideal
of man as self-sufficiency. Man is a social being."
—Mohandas Gandhi

Once you have effectively worked through the previous three dimensions of your existence you will now be able to fully express yourself in the emotional/social dimension in a healthy and balanced way. This dimension primarily deals with how we relate to others. Therefore, practice in this dimension requires us to simply be vigilant of ourselves when relating to others. First we must be living symbiotically. Then we can fully begin to understand other people by completely listening, integrating it all and then responding.

Living a fulfilled and extraordinary life requires that our house be built on the founding strategies from one to five. Only then can we express Strategies Six to Eight in a healthy and balanced way. Strategies Six through Eight do not require a great deal of intellect—they have to do with an ability to appropriately express our emotions. If we do not have self-esteem or self-worth we lose our sense of security. This security can only come from within. If it comes from other people it can be easily taken away from us—it's tantamount to a house built from straw, which provides no real sense of worth or security. When it comes from within it can never be taken from you.

This core power from within you knows the grandest of paradigms and the wisest of principles are deep within our body, mind and soul. It comes from the inside-out, a life lived from integrity where our daily habits and interactions mirror our deepest core values. When we are in integrity with ourselves, we are in integrity with every person and place around us. This is a state of authentic personal power at your present state of consciousness. At this level of awareness you'll become a self-actualized and interdependent person.

A state of happiness, peace of mind and fulfillment will emerge when your life is in harmony with true principles and values. It will not arrive any other way. When you live symbiotically, your inner sense of security will never be threatened. Every person and place involved will benefit.

The highest level of each state of consciousness moves one to a state of service. To serve is to empower and help others in deep and meaningful ways. At first this will come through work and then it will filter into your everyday life: the things you say and do, the way you act and behave, and who you're being. You will touch the lives of others without the need for recognition. It will be done for the sake of simply expressing the whole balanced and healthy being that you are.

As you solidify your present state of awareness through service, your system will begin making the vertical leap to a higher rung of consciousness—a place where you can serve more, dream more and unveil more of your authentic self to the world.

In Gratitude

When I began writing this book, I wanted to paint a picture of who I was as a child, and why and how that led to a series of experiences, actions, behaviors and circumstances. Through my formal and informal education and life experiences I have learned about the matrix that creates the fabric of this thing called life. I've done my best to articulate and express what I've learned and applied into the simplest form possible. I trust I haven't confused you. I have had the great blessing and gift of fully experiencing life from the extreme polar dualities. I know what it is like to be completely disconnected and plagued with a diseased mind and body that emanates the lowest vibrations of fear and helplessness. I also have immersed myself into a lifelong process of learning, healing and evolving.

Today I know what it is like to be connected and live in a mind and body that is limitless, powerful and infinite. I do my best everyday to accept and love myself unconditionally. I am a dedicated student of life learning, evolving and applying everything that I learn to my personal and professional life. In doing so, each day I can serve and more fully accept and love every person that crosses my path. It is my intention that people may learn from my experiences and what I have outlined as a guide for moving beyond the finite limitations of your mind and body and access your infinite and powerful self, being fully alive.

My intention for writing this book and spreading my message is simple. I believe that the strategies and exercises in this book provide a solid framework and catalyst for your constant growth and evolution. My wish is that wherever you are on your journey, you continue to facilitate the process of accessing your inner power and fulfilling your dreams through full Life Integration. Like life itself, this process is not linear and will continuously spiral up and down. There will be times when you are challenged, wading through the deep valley, unable to see the light of day. Yet, there will be many more times when you are moving through life with unbelievable ease and flow, standing at the top of the mountain and mesmerized by breathtaking views.

This book is simply a guide to help you navigate through life's challenges so that the exhilaration of living on the mountaintop becomes the rule, not the exception. The greatest gift we have is our own unique expression of who we are and how we live our lives. I almost left this world with my song buried deep within me. This is my song: to be a catalyst for human transformation, mastery and evolution. To empower people to live fully integrated lives. To help you fulfill your dreams and rock your most extraordinary experiences!

Every Beginning Starts with Another Beginning's End

"Remember today, for it is the beginning of always. Today marks the start of a brave new future filled with all your dreams can hold. Think truly to the future and make those dreams come true."
—Unknown

When we embark on the journey of becoming our infinite self, we completely change this world. We grow, evolve, expand our consciousness and inspire those around us to do the same. We begin to change our scripts and open new doors for generations of tomorrow. We build stronger bonds and relationships to foster this process in everyone around us. This journey is a path that has no end. The further you and I walk down it, the further down our children can begin (and then take it even further).

Life comes from within, and our experiences are the process of becoming more aware of this fundamental principle and truth. This awareness of internal unity or oneness within us and everyone else is the highest state of consciousness anyone can achieve. *Beyond Body Beyond Mind* is simply a guide for that process. Building a mind and body of complete balance and integrity and living a life of trust and service may not always be easy. You may drift and you may waver. You will make mistakes. But know there are no quick fixes, shortcuts or fast tracks.

If we do not embark on the process of creating unity and peace from within, nobody will do it for us. The irony is that we will then pass on our wounds and faults for the next generation and our children to deal with. It is only through inner joy, peace and clarity that we can achieve this in our outer world.

This ever-evolving journey for me has been extremely challenging and difficult at times. There are even times today when I struggle with some of these strategies and concepts. Yet, I persevere. I do my best. I observe, change, adapt, integrate and learn, as this is the journey of life. Today, I care more than others feel is reasonable. I risk more than others feel is safe. I dream more than others feel is probable. And I create more than others feel is possible. This journey is available for anyone who wants to fully experience everything life has to offer. Truly, it is the most worthwhile journey there is.

With all my love, gratitude and respect,

Dr. Sukhi

ACKNOWLEDGEMENTS

There are so many people that have assisted me on my journey in the creation of this book. I want to acknowledge all my teachers, healers and mentors for all your unconditional love and support. I want to thank Katie Karlson for your extraordinary edits and insights. Jon Berridge for the design of the cover and diagrams. Georgia Esporlas for the photography and adventurous photo shoots.

I thank every beautiful person that has stepped into my life for a reason, season or lifetime. Thanks to my mom, dad, brother and family in India for your unconditional love and support.

This book would have never been possible without my extraordinary soul mate and holy love, Kate. You wore so many hats and worked tirelessly to see this dream be fulfilled. I am grateful and blessed to journey through this life with you.

56915987R00207

Made in the USA
Columbia, SC
03 May 2019